What happened to Friday?

by
Tony Ballinger

This book is a collection of my memories from literally being a baby up until my current age of sixty five, although my main focus is up to age forty seven. It is mainly set in Rhodesia although I do briefly include interludes overseas to maintain continuity.

Not every memory is humorous or sad, some of them are darn ugly and cruel but without the ugly memories the reader would never come to know the real me.

The book is also about coming of age and the pursuit of girls so I apologise in advance if you think I am hammering home a particular theme too much but that's how it was for me and I have to be true to the story.

I do know one thing though, you will enjoy the story as an outsider and if you are ex Rhodesian you will love it as every page has a little bit of you in it.

© Tony Ballinger, 2020

Designed and typeset by Mach 3 Solutions Ltd (www.mach3solutions.co.uk)

ISBN 978-1-527274-76-1

All rights reserved. No part of this publication may be reproduced, stored in a retrieval system, or transmitted, in any form, or by any means, electronic, mechanical, photocopying, recording or otherwise, without the express written consent of Tony Ballinger.

Contents

Chapter One:	School to adulthood	5
Chapter Two:	Beyond School	72
Chapter Three:	Africa to Australia via Europe and back again	99
Chapter Four:	From the army to emigrating to South Africa	153
Chapter Five:	Leaving Rhodesia to returning to Zimbabwe	209
Chapter Six:	Leaving Zimbabwe to live in England	238

Chapter One

School to adulthood

My earliest childhood memory is that of me sitting in my nappy on Beira beach with little wavelets washing over my legs. I got annoyed because the water contained a lot of detritus and it was getting caught in my nappy and sticking in my flesh. I turned and looked up towards the sun where my dad stood casting a shadow over me and I started to cry. I will never forget his smiling face and outstretched arms as he bent forward to pick me up and comfort me against his warm, sun-baked chest. He somehow knew what was wrong and brushed the leaves and sticks off and for me the world was put to right and the tears that licked my face could now dry off and fade away.

* * *

I was born on Friday the 13th of May 1955 at Andrew Fleming Hospital. I weighed in at a jaw-wincing 10lbs 6oz and earned the reputation of being a 'lazy bastard' even before I was born, thanks to putting my mother through a day or two of labour. I grew up in a modest home in Eastlea, Salisbury, attending a nursery school down the way and then Admiral Tait junior school followed by Churchill High. They were idyllic days of fun, laughter and sport, all played out beneath azure blue African skies or tumbling cumulus clouds bruising themselves into a catatonic thunderstorm, with the smell of rain advancing before the winds arrived, whipping up leaves and bugs before a massive waterfall of water rushed over us. And the school suitcase would be cast aside while we splashed in childish abandon in the muddy pools that formed all around us, much to our 'houseboy's' chagrin, who would later have to scrub our uniforms clean.

I will never forget the smell of the advancing rain in Africa; something like dust mixed with cut green grass, a unique aroma I have not smelled in any other country. Into this wonderful mix was born my brother, sixteen months older than me. I was the runt and the black sheep of the family. Later, while my brother studied to get his honours degree in civil engineering I chased girls, swam, laughed and got into loads of mischief. Now at the age of 65 I do not regret my choices one bit. I have laughter wrinkles at the corner of my eyes and a cherubic belly filled from good foods and a large heart enriched by amazing memories.

The woman who birthed me, Isabelle Ballinger nee Isabelle Van Os was a gorgeous woman who came high up in several beauty contests in South Africa. She was a bubble of laughter and in later years she succumbed to gravity just as I have and became a shortish, round bubble of joy and mischief. If I picture my mom's face it would always have a smile on it, with a piece of gold flashing against the sun where a dentist had filled one of her teeth.

The Dutch blood that coursed through her veins definitely clashed with the blood of my English father who was a tall, blond-cum dark-haired man of a reserved, gentle nature. He had an excellent sense of humour and his favourite evening trick was to roll various items into the lounge from an unseen part of the passage that led to the bedrooms. It was a childish ritual but we were kids after all and so we would roll over in our pyjamas in peels of laughter and delight trying to intercept each object that rolled towards a corner of the lounge.

Of course, getting into our pyjamas and the bath that went before it was the duty of our 'houseboy' Samson. I make no apologies to the politically correct world of 2020 for how it went down in those sunny days of our youth. My mom and dad both worked and long hours at that so it was Samson's duty to ensure we were fed and bathed by the time they got home. The title of 'houseboy' was not to be patronised or frowned upon, as in many Rhodesian households the 'houseboy' was an integral part of the family, given to authority over the children and the running of the home. They often, but not always, ate the same food we did, prepared by their wise and willing minds and would be given favoured treatment for the schooling of their children and the same medications or doctors used by the 'boss' and 'madam' would apply to them.

Rhodesia was fairly unique I think in that we had male servants, whereas South Africa used mainly female staff. I loved Samson and would often sit in his house or 'Kia', watching him cook in an old tin pot which he used in preference to the enamelled pots we had given him. I will never forget the aroma of slightly burned meat mixed with thick Sadza (corn gruel) and gravy. His generosity of spirit as he ladled out food for me, knowing I still had a meal waiting indoors, was humbling and I would emulate him stretching backwards on his haunches against the plastered wall while dipping a ball of white Sadza into the meat and gravy. He would regale me of stories of his own youth and life in the rural areas, where the pace of a cow dictated life and where time was only in first gear. I love and cherish those golden moments from the bottom of my heart. Although Samson was in his sixties I was still technically his boss even at age six or seven, but I revered his grey hair, wizened eyes, humour and humility. He taught me a lot about grace, for how many adults would take instructions or defer to the whims of a child? His ability to take my mom's tongue-lashings with alacrity was a sight to behold and all the while he held himself tall and proud.

My parents employed Samson for about twelve years, from when I was no more than a toddler to a young teenager and then one day he was gone, his little brown suitcase tucked under his arm, his hat set at a jaunty angle upon his head. A quick smile and a wave goodbye was the last I saw of him and even though I was a 'tough' twelve-something I cried buckets; a family member was leaving us.

*   *   *

One of my favourite past-times was playing with Tinker our little dog when we got home from school. I know not what breed he was but he was short, had longish golden hair with a fixed look of delight on his cute little face. His acceleration from zero to catching the ball was a sight to see, but one day in my zeal I threw the ball too hard and our property, unfenced as it was, let out onto Clyde road and there Tinker died under the front wheels of a passing car. It was my first introduction to death and I shed many tears that made little tracks down my dusty face, especially when his crumpled body, still smiling, was slid into his eternal home.

We never had much success with pets. I remember another dog after Tinker but he disappeared, who knows where and then my brother Brian and I decided we would race pigeons for fun. We built a fantastic coop for them, each with their own little apartment and landing pad, much to my mom's horror as their coo-cooos and poo and flies drove her to distraction. But Brian and I were determined to be world racing champions and followed all the rules to the letter, keeping them caged for just so long before releasing them, which we did with trepidation, only to slap each other in delight when our thirty-plus birds circled around our house, disappeared for a few minutes, did another circle and then landed on each little pad, looking really chuffed with themselves.

About a month later we entered our strongest looking birds, about a dozen of them, into a race from who knows where, I can't remember, it may have been Headlands or thereabouts. We stood there, all twelve or thirteen years old, puffing out our chests in pride as we watched each bird we released circle a few times and then fly off in the general direction of Salisbury a hundred and thirty kilometres away.

We drove home in high spirits with my dad behind the wheel, snacking on Willards Cheese and Onion chips, washed down by copious quantities of Fanta Orange in glass bottles, while we fantasized about collecting the first prize of forty dollars and what we would do with it.

Two something hours later we were home. Brian and I ran to the back of the house to meet my mom who was supposed to record the time the first bird got home, but there was no sign of any of them. Now I'm no expert but I figured the first bird would arrive at the same time we did or shortly thereafter but nothing stirred.

My mom ordered tea from Michael, our new cook and so we sat in a circle looking at the eighteen birds left in their cages while they looked back at us and waited. And waited…and waited… and……waited.

Eventually, just before dark, one lone bird circled the house before nervously setting down on his landing pad. The other birds went apoplectic with excitement, as did Brian and I but the bird itself shuffled its shabby feathers once, waddled inside its cage and dropped dead from a heart attack. We were absolutely mortified! Our star bird, arriving at least six hours after we did, was lying on its back, mouth open, wings twittering away while its feet clawed at an imaginary branch.

"What the hell happened?" I yelled at no-one in particular and when no answer was forthcoming I ran screaming inside, followed closely by my brother. Needless to say no other birds ever arrived, no doubt shot down in their droves by ever-vigilant farmers along their flight-path, all of whom were excellent marksmen.

The following week we sold the remaining birds and lost all hope of being immortalized in bird-racing circles, our bank accounts remaining as depleted as they always had been.

The last pet we ever had was a pretty little cockatiel that appeared to wallow in misery in the corner of the lounge. I felt so sad for that little bird, all alone in a relatively dark corner, that I frequently took it outside and hung it up in a tree, shading it with a cloth against the African sun. I also used to remove the bottom tray and let it scratch and cavort about on the grass, especially when it had just finished raining. I noticed that it liked to eat a bit of grass now and then, probably for digestive reasons, so I added tufts of grass to its feeding trough every night.

Although the bird technically belonged to my mother it was I who fed and watered it, replacing the poo-splattered newspaper at the bottom on a regular basis. Over a period of time I became exasperated by its isolation and loneliness, so I set in motion a cunning plan.

We never got too much pocket money but we did have an Avocado Pear tree in the back garden that produced the most amazing, 'hairless' avocados the size of a person's face. They were enormous! So my brother and I surreptitiously loaded them into a sack when my mother was not around and, placing them on our home-made cart, tugged them up to the Greek greengrocers shop at Clyde shopping centre.

Whenever we arrived at the grocer's door, his eyes lit up and he rubbed his hands together. He could not get our delicious Avos quickly enough as they were very popular with local residents. I can honestly say I have never seen Avos like that anywhere in the world to the current day. We bought a few sweets or an ice-cream and then skipped home with a fist full of dollars.

It was with this rapidly growing pile of banknotes that I set forth to the local pet store in Greendale, where I bought another cockatiel as company for the one at home. I was just about to take it when the store owner asked if I was planning to breed with it. I was nonplussed. I had not thought of the bird's sex. If I bought a male and the one at home was a male, there would be a bloodbath. I listened carefully as the man told me how to sex a bird after which I rushed home on my bicycle to examine birdy num-nums sitting in the corner. After getting my hands thoroughly chewed, I felt I had figured out our bird was a male, which was ideal as the shop-keeper said his bird was a female.

I concluded the transaction and raced home once more to insert our new bird into birdy num-num's cage, just about ten minutes before mom got home from work. I would surprise her and there would be smiles and oohs and ahs all over the place. I gingerly removed the new bird from its cardboard box, opened the cage door and let it hop inside. Meanwhile, birdy num-nums had shrunk into the far corner with its head crest of feathers bolt upright, its beak open and eyes wide in fear. The new 'female' saw this reaction and shuffled rapidly to the far corner before its head crest also shot up.

What happened after that became very confusing because at the precise moment that the two birds took a lunge at each other my mom walked through the door.

"Look mom," I said as the birds flailed against each other, "a friend for birdy num-nums!"

"You fool boy, why on earth did you do this! Num-Num was perfectly happy on his own, Just look at them!"

I turned back to look, feathers were flying everywhere from the midst of blurred movement, of claws, beaks and flapping wings. My mom raised her hands to her mouth in absolute horror as the two birds appeared to dissolve into a bloody, featherless heap on the cage floor. I decided retreat was the best part of valour, making a hasty exit while Michael and Mom, now with oven mitts on their hands, did their darnedest to separate the two bloodied animals, which were obviously two males. It was the last time I ever tried to sex a bird, that's for sure!

* * *

Going back to the beginning, the time arrived when loitering around home as a kiddie had to come to an end. Gone were the days when I would stay at home and lick the mix out of the cake bowl when mom prepared yet another delicious cake. Her fame for a dark fruit cake was not limited to us alone as the bowling club she belonged to cried out for them at their tea-breaks all the time. I remember the frustration of licking endless raw cake mixes off spoons only to discover the cake was destined for the bloody 'club' yet again!

Now I was 'grown' up at the age of five or six or whatever and had to go to kindergarten down the way every day from about eight a.m. until noon. The first day dawned and before I knew it I was alighting from our car into a car park full of wailing, flailing and frightened children. Feeling left out I let the tears rip, accompanied by a huge bawling sound coming out of my wide-open mouth. Progressing through a blur of tears, holding mom's hand and looking at a smiling teacher I became a little less sure this was a concentration camp for miscreants and hiding in the folds of my mom's dress examined the world around me. The first thing I noticed was a sprawling jungle gym in a multitude of colours, ensconced among sandpits, rocking horses, concrete tunnels made to look like a caterpillar and many other childish delights. I noticed that other children had spotted it too from the folds of their mom's dresses and we now looked at each other curiously. This wasn't so bad after all.

After a last shriek of inconsolable terror when all of our mom's drove away in their cars, we set forth bravely into the unknown, which consisted of cool drinks and sandwiches followed by several hours of playing on the jungle gym. The teachers obviously knew that play would settle our nerves and before long we were walloping along on imaginary horses, slapping our sides, playing castle and swinging from swings. And very soon a pecking order developed and we knew who our leaders were. Perhaps, because I was a head taller than all of them with a big-boned body, I took on this mantle very quickly and it has remained with me for the rest of my life. I have never tolerated being led and even now at the age of 65 I don't like taking instructions from anyone.

I quickly developed a following and to my surprise the other kids obeyed me and looked to me to make decisions about who would be the king of the castle, who would be the cowboy, who the Indians were and their little arms would go up and wave around when I was allocating roles. But there was a curious creature in the mix that I had never dealt with before and with whom I felt attracted to and annoyed with at the same time. Girls.

I had never played with girls before and didn't know what got them thinking or excited but I didn't care. I was the leader of my group of boys and it didn't take long for the girls to sidle away to tea parties and doll-dressing sessions (this would drive the gender freaks crazy today). Even in those early days sexual apartheid developed naturally and my opinion to this day is that whatever a child likes playing with then that's up to them. We should never mould them into a junior form of us.

The 'lessons' in those happy sunlit days consisted of colouring in, making plasticine animals, eating food, drinking milk from little glass bottles with either blue or red or green tinfoil tops, which I would peel off and keep by the dozens. I never quite knew why. Endless hours were spent on the jungle gym, which to me taught more about life and relationships than any other time in life.

Arriving at nursery school from day three onwards was so different from day one. Gone were the tear-stained faces hiding in mom's skirt. Now we launched ourselves from the car long before it had come to a halt (wonderful days of no seat belts!), rushing in to greet our pals in a loud raucous clamour of excited immature voices, big smiles everywhere. And the sound of children playing outside at break-time has stayed with me as a fond memory all my life. Even to this day I will park a little way off from a school, open the car window and listen to the peals of laughter, shouting and general noise that comes from the playing field, a sound which is the same the world over and I find comfort in it.

But what I remember most were the smells of the wax crayons, Plasticine (modelling clay), floor polish and the dusty aroma of a government school, which by the way was beautifully adorned inside and out. I remember fondly the depth of colours in the ABCs on the walls or paintings of frogs and animals. The colours were so alive and real, it was a life of colour and as time has passed the thrill over something as exciting as colour has become jaded, with rheumy eyes looking at it all for the millionth time. But back then it was vibrant, alive, exciting and full of mystery. Green was and is my favourite colour, especially emerald green.

I don't have many more memories of that idyllic stage of my life but the one thing I do remember is the Christmas nativity play we put on in which I was Joseph and some little girl I barely knew was Mary. The memory is vague but I do remember leading Mary onto the stage on the back of a real donkey. She looked terrified atop this four-foot animal, which was higher than me by a few inches and unsurprisingly baby Jesus was being held around the neck by the terrified girl. I have never quite figured out why Jesus was already born and being carried around by his neck but at the time it seemed just fine. When the show ended I was really tired and I slumped into mom's ample bosom during the short journey home. Then it was time for a bath by Samson and into my fresh pyjamas before cuddling up to dad on the couch, falling asleep in his warm and comforting arms. No fear, no anxiety, no worries. All was good and safe and warm.

* * *

After nursery school, which was left out our front gate and a one minute drive away, my junior school, Admiral Tait, was right out the gate and about a five minute walk away. Even my senior school, Churchill, which backed off the nursery school, was only a seven minute walk. Without knowing it my dad had bought a property slap bang in the middle of three schools, all within easy walking distance.

My first day at junior school was far less traumatic than my first day at nursery school but nonetheless my tummy growled a bit as mom led me from our old black Vanguard, through the silver-grey fence into the jaws of the nursery school block. This was still referred to as a nursery school as some mothers did not take their children to the fun-group I had been to for the previous year, known colloquially as 'the nursery school' or 'kindergarten'.

I was introduced to a kindly looking woman in her late forties who would be my teacher for the first year in the KG1 block. I took her hand as she led me into a neat, well-provisioned and colourful classroom, turning only once to look back at my mom who was beaming with pride. Of great consolation of course was the fact that my brother was in the same school and at breaktime we would smile and wave at each other, often meeting up but less and less so as we each made our own friends.

I loved my teacher and the year I spent with her. Our introduction to desks, put back to back in little groups where four children sat, made us feel all grown up, especially when we could lift the lid of our desk and put our colouring-in pencils and books away with pride. I loved the open day sessions when mom and dad would appear, along with all other parents and they would fuss over us and go 'ooh and ah' as we proudly showed them our work.

I only remember three friends I met that first year, one was called Dennis who we promptly called Dennis the Menace, along with Raymond Elliott and Lawrence Austin whom I nicknamed Lollipops and to this day when we Facebook each other I still call Lawrence "Lollipops". I think the name stuck as I was at least a head taller than all my mates and Lollipops was "down there" somewhere, but we were great friends and inseparable at the time. We used to play cowboys and Indians at break-time until virtually the last day of junior school, seven years later, although in the latter years we turned more to football or cricket in our breaks and chatting to those strange creatures in skirts which were getting more and more interesting than acting out Tonto on an imaginary horse. It became the norm to try and impress girls as we walked past them, as I did on one occasion only to fall flat on my face, tripping over a loose paving slab!

KG1 was a year where we learned to understand the alphabet and write simple words, using the old A-B-C style of pronunciation versus this awful Ah-Ba-Ca nonsense you get today. Almost all of our teachers, bar a very few, were really good at their craft and took it seriously. They had the ability to dole out discipline themselves and over the years I got my backside warmed more than once. There was none of this lip and swearing that teachers are subjected to these days and even to this day I will defer to and respect the opinion of a teacher.

We also learned how to count, once again using the simple version of just adding and subtracting numbers in an easy, logical way. Not long ago, here in the UK, I watched how multiplication was done at school and it was so confusing that I gave up in horror. No wonder people have to be imported to take over roles in businesses that require these skills, in this green land of ours.

KG2 was just a slightly more advanced version of KG1 and before we knew it I was in Standard 1, the high and lofty status of being in a school and not a Kindergarten anymore. And we would look scornfully at the KG2 kids on their side of the fence as they played cops and robbers while we practiced walking with our hands in our pockets, tie awry around our necks as we sauntered past girls, who were fast becoming our only source of interest at break time.

I mainly remember the rain storms that would lash the school in summer, usually occurring as we left school at 1 pm. School in Africa started at 7 am and ended at 1 pm, mainly due to the heat and a huge thorn tree, positioned between the school blocks and the swimming pool, would become bowed down with various beetles with lovely shiny wings and body armour and we would collect them. They became a hobby of mine where I would barter with other like-minded kids and later on we all got involved in the silkworm craze where we would breed silkworms in cardboard boxes and watch in awe as worms turned into moths, did basically nothing thereafter and died at the bottom of the box after mating, spreading their pin-head sized grey eggs all over the box to start the next generation. We would take the vacated silk cocoons and boil them before unravelling the silk onto empty cotton reels. We never did anything with the silk but it was great fun breeding the worms. Very few mulberry trees that had branches hanging over garden fences ever survived the ravages of us kids pulling off the leaves for the worms, that being their favourite food, while of course we gorged ourselves on the berries, going home to mom with mouths and lips turned purple from the mulberry juice.

Another favourite past-time was playing with our marbles, which turned into mafia-style competitions where the winner would scoop up the loser's best and most coveted glass marble. This is one point where my brother and I came together again and we won bags of marbles. I still clearly remember a black, knitted bag my mother gave us to hold the marbles we won and it soon bulged to the brim with several kilos of glass marbles and metal-ball bearings we called goons (pronounced ghuns in our Rhodesian dialect). I had that bag for years, right up until getting my first job at Barclays bank but who knows what happened to it after that?

* * *

The one thing that really appealed to me at junior school was the theatre opportunities that opened up for us. The arts were promoted in Rhodesia and I used to love auditioning for this part and that. After getting over the initial fear of performing in front of an audience I really came to love it and being the outgoing person that I am to this day, found it a lovely expression of my abilities. To my horror I can't really remember what plays I acted in but I do remember one with a massive boot that was lowered onto the stage and another with my friend David playing a little drum suspended around his neck as we followed his ta-rum-te-tum-tum 'me and my drum, ta-rum-te-tum-tum' (little drummer boy).

I really enjoyed applying the waxy make-up and the smell of those lotions and eye pencils will stay with me for all of my life, something I enjoyed years later with my wife when we did shows together in Johannesburg at Wits University and a few more shows at Reps theatre.

But what sticks out in my memory the most are the girls I mixed with in the changing room (actually our classroom) before the shows started, because, by this time (standard 5) I was profoundly interested in them and a few of them were profoundly interested in boys. It was the latter I took to like a bee to pollen.

It had to happen of course but in the semi-dark classroom with all the costumes hung up on hooks and kit lying everywhere that we explored the physical differences between us. I am sure the girls that took part had no brothers as they were profoundly curious about this thing I pulled out of my pants as were I with the apparent nothingness between their legs! They were entranced by the length of my pubic hair which I cut off in chunks to give to them. I often wonder if any of them still have a neatly tied knot of pubic hair somewhere in a cupboard!

* * *

I don't know what it is with boys, but sadism towards small animals appears universal. Maybe it's a hangover from our hunter-gather years, before the industrial revolution ensconced us in ever sagging chairs in front of a television.

We had no Ipads, computers, tablets, mobile phones and PC's back in those days, thank God! All of our fun, adventure and entertainment happened outside. Whether it was sport, playing cops and robbers with your mates, running through the nearby bush with catapults or whatever, we never sat indoors, at least not until it was too dark to see or it was raining, at which time most of us listened to stories on the radio or read books or listened to mom and dad's old fashioned music from when they were young. They were incredibly wonderful days that left a warm glow in one's heart as dad sipped his beer, mom her brandy and coke and us our one-coke-a-night ration, while Glen Miller played on the radio and the curtains would be drawn against the flashes of lighting and storm outside; flying ants tat-tattering on the Venetian blinds, heading for the nearest light-bulb where they would swirl around, dazzled by its glow. Those that survived our swishing fly-swats ended up in pairs, racing across the floor to look for a place of escape, only to be pegged to the ground by our very accurate pea-shooters that fired needles with cotton wrapped around the shafts. We would pick up their little bodies and look at them without pity as their little legs clawed the air until finally deciding death was their only outlet. Mom could never understand why her needles always disappeared!

Other insects and animals met the same fate but the one that really scared us all to death was the hunting spider that would run across the carpet at a hell of a lick, two front arms stretched out ahead of it. Not a foot remained on the ground and even dad took a few steps away before launching a counter-attack with his shoe to get the ever-shifty insect. They were darn hard to kill! We called them 'Gerrymungels'.

The rains would bring frogs, our favourite victims, even more enjoyable to kill than lizards. We had many ways of killing them, namely using them as cricket balls, to see who could thwack them further than the other (bringing many neighbouring kids in on the contest); we sidled up to river banks, with our faces camouflaged, taking out one frog at a time with our No. 1 pellet guns. We laughed delightedly when one would flick back into the water, swim a few disorientated circles and slowly sink to the bottom. This brought great merriment.

Of course, in those days we could buy fireworks and use them without all the PC bull you get today. All kids and some adults did the most outrageous things with the stuff at our disposal, there were no health and safety inspections or risk assessments at all. Guy fawkes at the community hall one night, with us all in pyjamas, the smell of meat cooking on the braais (barbecues) and moms and dads quaffing beers while Joe Bloggs started to light the fuses of various rockets and cartwheels and others arrayed in front of us. All went well until Joe Bloggs, now eight sheets to the wind, bumped one of the milk bottles that held the stalk of a huge rocket, fuse already lit. The crowd stood mesmerized with mouths aghast as the bottle wobbled and slowly fell over, pointing the enormous rocket accusingly at them! There was massive pandemonium as people went helter-skelter to get away from the missile, knocking each other over, spilling beers and dropping hot-dogs. The fuse hissed and hissed some more before the heavy missile headed into the crowd, splintering off a wall, sending the wooden stalk straight into the thigh of a ten-something year old boy, who bellowed as blood squirted everywhere while his mom shrieked her lungs out and dad turned in circles shouting 'medic….medic!!!' And while this was going on the missile head exploded, sending huge showers of pretty blue, red and green sparks over the rapidly departing crowd, many of whom were swatting glowing embers out of their hair as they ran.

But you know what? There was no board of enquiry, there was no cancellation of the event the following year, even after nearby bush caught fire and almost burned out several vehicles; there was no claim for compensation or finger-pointing and so on. In fact, once the bush fire had been doused more meat went back on the braai, beers snapped open and the party began all over again. The only pause for thought was when the ambulance took the injured boy and his parents away. Those were the days were people were not molly-coddled, like I read in the paper here in the UK the other day that whistles have been banned in schools because they sound too aggressive to children!! What the…? I say fire a few rockets at them, it's good for fun!

I have digressed, what has this to do with killing frogs? Well, I just needed to explain that us kids had access to an amazing array of extremely dangerous squibs with romantic names like 'lady finger' 'Tom thumb' 'fat boy' and the orange and blue-wicked monster 'thunder flashes'.

I am sure that your imagination has raced ahead of the words on this page, yes you guessed it, the coming together of frogs and mini high-powered explosives. Our young minds squirmed with delight as to what we could achieve. The first method was to tie a thunder flash to the back of a frog, wick facing backwards, done this way because just before the thunder flash exploded it would let out a huge jet of white hot embers that made a big hissing sound. The hissing and pain inflicted by the flame would make the frog scuttle forward at an alarming rate, whereby we would take bets on how many steps it would go before it exploded into small chunks of meat, head, legs, intestines and feet. I think the record was about eight paces before disintegration, which resulted in a honorary, ceremonial burial of its remains.

Of course, the thunder flash had the amazing ability to keep burning underwater once the hissing jet of gases had commenced. Now it took great timing to light a thunder flash on the back of a frog and hold it until the pre-explosion hissing started, before dropping it into a bathtub full of water. The frog would race away until it exploded in a red and white gaseous, frothy mess which generated a spectacular spout of water that one would see in war movies when a minesweeper detonated a mine. Needless to say our mom and Michael were not amused at having to clean bits of frog meat off the bathroom wall and surrounds but that was the fun of it, blowing up frogs and annoying mom at the same time.

Lizards came in a close second in terms of our sadistic enjoyment, for their long slim bodies fitted beautifully into a stainless steel pipe, the exact diameter of which suited a massive 'Tom Thumb' or 'Fat Boy' squib, which we would light with glee before positioning over our right shoulder to fire like a bazooka. Bang! and the remains of the lizard would be hurled at least thirty feet away, the one crossing the furthest line getting a big cheer from the gathered boys.

Sadly, birds did not escape our pellet guns and we must have shot hundreds of them in our youth. We even made fires and ate some of them including African Hoopoes (which had no meat on them), doves, pigeons, sparrows and many other types out on farms. I think I lost the appetite for killing birds one day when I shot this tiny little thing sitting on the telephone line about four metres above my head. At first I thought I had missed it, until it wobbled on its little legs, falling over backwards. Its feet must have closed tight on the telephone line in its death-throes because it hung there, upside down with its wings stretched down in an inverted pose of surrender. It hung there for several days until something ate it, but the sight of that pathetic little body hanging there with a half-open eye staring at me has haunted me forever.

* * *

Flying ants (indeed ants in general) fascinated me as a boy. In summer, when the rains came, the flying ants would come out of their nests in their millions and race off to find a mate and build a new nest. It was a race against time as birds, bats and humans ate them as quickly as they emerged from their earthen strongholds. Local tribesmen would put straw over the opening of the nests, to ensnare their flailing wings, which would be pulled off along with their heads, the rich fatty body being deposited in a plastic bag or pot. I used to do the same and would cook them over Samson's fire, in his tin pot, as he added some salt and a tiny bit of cooking oil. Those flying ants were just delicious, tasting a bit like peanut butter, full of fat and protein, an excellent meal indeed.

But what I enjoyed the most was standing under the street-lamp outside the front of our house, sometimes until ten o'clock at night shooting the flying ants with water I sucked up into a huge medical syringe, pushing the plunger hard down to generate a shaft of high-velocity water which I aimed at the fluttering insects that had been attracted to the street lamp. It was an equal contest that gave the insects a fair chance of escape and I may have had to shoot one several times before the weight of water on its wings made it spiral down to the ground where millions of little black ants instantly attacked them, carting them off to their underground grottos. The shooting down of the flying ants was accompanied by me mimicking the sound of roaring aero engines and machine guns tat-tat-tattering away.

And you know what? My parents didn't bother to come and look for me even though I was standing out on a poorly lit public road. There were no fears of paedophiles or child stalkers, just fun and flying ants and perfect safety. Even the Africans that sauntered by would chuckle at me in a good humoured way and ask what I was doing. There was no fear, no animosity, no feeling of racial differences in my heart. The innocence was absolute and I miss it so much.

My other passion for ants, which sadly for them involved them dying in their tens of thousands, was to pit one type against another. The big red nipper termites would face the armour-plated Matabele ants and the smaller termite workers would have to face the tiny little black ants that left their castles to follow the carcasses I left them to do battle on the side of a tree where the termites had built their lofty kingdoms.

After discovering one of these (sometimes massive) vertical nests the termites made, I would break off the main artery where the ants entered the ground. I would watch in fascination as soldier ants with big swishing jaws raced to the breach, followed by worker ants rapidly repairing the damaged clay structure that protected them. But I would not let the repair be effected and instead tempted the small black ants of a nearby castle to venture forth into battle. In a very short while tiny balls of white and black ants, locked in mortal combat, would be falling, rising and swirling around the breach. I was astonished that the worker termites just pressed on trying to mend the breach but I would never let them succeed until at long last, with barely enough light to see by, I would abandon the fight and go inside for supper. The next day the expected result lay before my eyes with a shrivelled piece of termite fort laying empty and hollow with not a termite to be seen anywhere, nor a black ant and no litter of dead bodies. Very efficient killers ants are but they could learn a lot from the human race that seems to delight in murdering itself every forty years or so.

My favourite competitions though, lay in watching Matabele ants taking on the huge red soldier termites, the ones with heads as big as one's small fingernail. These were epic battles, arranged by me so that I could lie on my tummy on the grass looking down at them. My favourite battle of all time was a Matabele ant that killed over twenty redheads, at which point it was exhausted, its antennae hanging in shreds, legs missing but still alive and triumphant. As it stood there a particularly large redhead wandered up and bit its head off! I was so impressed that I put both ants into methylated spirits in a small bottle and kept it in my dresser draw until I was well into my thirties, after which I lost it. The thing that will shock modern youth is that I was a teenager when I did this. No lying on couches becoming an x-box zombie, it was good innocent fun.

The military tactics shown to me by those ants led me to develop a fondness for all things army and for years I collected cuttings from Rhodesian army catalogues and newspaper clippings and I would lie on the carpet and plan attacks, ambushes and so on with my large collection of toy soldiers. Great times indeed.

Friday

It was about this age that I met Friday. He was an African kid that lived near the sports club that my mom and dad played lawn bowls at; the Police club or 'the club' as we called it.

My dad was a very talented (lawn) bowler who actually won the world 'drawing to the kitty' competition, but because of sanctions against Rhodesia he had to compete by himself on the bowling green at the Police club, with independent witnesses doing the measuring for him. He beat, quite handsomely, some Australian I believe. I watched with sadness and frustration as my ever-talented father, who won many Rhodesian championships, remain forever barred from competing internationally, where I am sure he would have won many medals.

I loved going to the swimming pool at that club and developed friendships there that have lasted to this day. Every Saturday at about noon we would bundle into the car, without even locking the house or closing the garage doors and would zoom off to the club for a lovely day out. (When I left Zimbabwe in 2002 I had secured doors, motion detectors, burglar bars, a handgun under my pillow and an alarm system that would bring a rapid reaction force to assist us, but in Rhodesia, with enforced law and order, it was paradise).

The Police club was a wonderful place to explore. It had large rugby fields with high stands around the main field where we could swing on the steel poles supporting the wooden seating planks. It had a club house with a television and amazing beef pies, cokes and chips on tap. Oh how many times after bowling had finished and we had come back from the pool all chilled from the water, would we stand at the back door to the pub and beckon dad to come and give us some money to buy Fanta (my favourite), Cherry Plum (my brother's), Willards salt and vinegar chips (in the blue packet) and cheese and onion flavour (in the green packets). We called crisps chips and French fries, well, 'chips' too! Somehow no-one ever got it mixed up. If a coke was offered we would know chips came in a packet with it and if offered a pie it would come with hot chips – duh!!! We would also whine for a packet of biltong. During daylight hours we would explore the locked and gated small arms range and dig it up for bullets (much to the extreme annoyance of the police who had to fill all those holes in before doing their shoot). We would melt the lead out of the copper jackets and then pour the molten lead into my mom's cake moulds (*much* to her annoyance!) before selling the lead to Harrisons, the gun shop in town that also sold a large selection of fishing rods and tackle. The lead we supplied would be melted down again and turned into weights for the fishermen.

It was during one of these visits to the small arms range that I noticed a golf course on the other side of a row of gum trees. A golf ball plopped on the fairway nearby and my brother and I instantly looked at each other and smiled knowingly. We could steal those and sell them back to the golfers! Well we tried that once or twice but we came off second best after being chased by a rather fit young man. But we were not put off and sauntering along the tree-lined course we soon noticed a water trap. Sitting there on his haunches was Friday, staring intently at the water. He was about our age at the time, maybe eleven or so but smaller than us. We ambled up to him,

'What you looking at?' we enquired.

'Balls' he said pointing lazily at the water. We frowned and looked in the pond's direction, just as a ball ca-ploinked into it, sending ripples into the reeds. My brother and I looked at each other and smiled knowingly again.

Much to my delight the golfers soon appeared but made no effort to retrieve their ball, so we knew instantly we were onto a goldmine! We waited until they were out of sight and then looked down at Friday. We figured he would dive in and go get the ball but he just sat there on his haunches.

'Why don't you get the ball?' my bother enquired of Friday. He looked up at us, squinting against the sun and smiling pearly whites.

'I can't swim,' he mumbled with a Shona accent before looking down at his feet. I think he realised there and then that his goldmine was just about to be raided by two of the best swimmers within ten kilometres. We pulled off our shirts and shorts (we never wore shoes) and dived in to the warm water, scaring the hell out of some ducks and other bird life. The water was a bit cloudy and covered in weeds but the stark white balls stuck out like a dog's ball and within a few deep breaths and plunges we had snapped up perhaps twenty balls. When we waded to the shore we observed a very dejected Friday looking longingly at our hoard. He stood up, shuffling his dusty bare feet while we got dressed and started to walk away.

'No, come with us,' I said gesturing to him with my hand. He hesitated at first but soon a broad smile was on his face again and we trotted off with great expectation to the golf club house.

Our childish expectations were rewarded in a manner far better than we could have hoped for, meeting a man unloading his golf bag from the boot of his car. He bought all of them for what we considered an amazing sum! We dashed off like lottery winners down the fairway, turning in circles, imagining what we would buy with our loot. We soon arrived back at the water trap and there my heart moved for Friday. I called my brother over and we agreed to split our winnings three ways. We counted out the coins, dropping one after another in Friday's open hands, his eyes and smile competing with each other to grow bigger and bigger. He leapt with delight and ran off whistling and singing in a high voice. He spun on his heels once, waving and smiling at us and was gone from sight. It was a glorious moment for me, I felt so good. I did not know at that age how much harder life was for my new black friend called Friday.

Over the weeks that followed we returned there again and again until one day my brother got interested in a girl called Sue at the swimming pool, so I would run to meet Friday on my own. Weeks turned into months from the heat of summer, through winter and then into summer again, with the lazy, chugging clouds up in a sky so blue it hurt the eyes and I would rush to see Friday again, catapult in hand and a smile on both our faces. We would shoot birds and grasshoppers for fun while waiting for a ball to go ploink in the water trap. Or we would dig into the small arms range for more lead.

Over many years that followed, through societal pressures and parental attitudes as well as class structure, my view of black people slowly started to change and I started to feel superior but at the time I knew Friday I saw no colour and I laughed and ran alongside him in those tender years just above puberty. Oh how I miss that heart attitude, how I long for it!

But times were changing in Africa and in Rhodesia in particular, as Britain gave independence to many former colonies. Countries with few whites to the north succumbed to black majority rule without a whimper.

School to adulthood

Although the Congo was not a former British colony, but a colony of Belgium, it too suffered huge upheavals and massacres of white people. I used to sit in the garden with my dad and watch the Dakota DC-3 planes coming from the north containing terrified Belgian refugees huddling together with a few possessions to their name. It sent a chill through our nation and I think this is why Ian Smith one day, not too far in the future from that time, declared unilateral independence from the UK. *We were not going to give in, we were not going to be massacred in our sleep!*

Locally, there were riots and political agitation. My dad belonged to the police reserve and I used to watch with some trepidation as he headed off into the sunset, all dressed up in his dark blue riot kit, with a sparkling white English army helmet on his head, shield on the right arm and a baton and gas mask swinging on his hip. My brother and I huddled into our mom as we watched, wide-eyed, my dad being collected by a big truck with similarly dressed men.

I'm not sure if it was the riots taking place but suddenly Friday was not there anymore. I used to wait by the water trap where I first met him over a year before. But he never came. I never saw him ever again and to this day I wonder, what happened to Friday? Despite the tragedy of losing Friday, or perhaps because of it, I turned to the swimming pool at 'the club' for my main source of activity in those sunny months and years of my life.

As I grew over several years I became so enthralled by girls and my very advanced sexuality found it exciting to just lie there looking at them in their bikinis. The top of the pile was Rita who often pranced past me in a white bikini with a bum most men would kill for. The smell of suntan lotion on hot skins, lying in circles facing each other, maybe six boys and eight girls, listening to Martin Locke playing the tunes of the day on Rhodesia radio or Jerry Wilmot on LM radio. Flirting with our eyes and splashing in the caressing cool of the water, trying to hide an erection when dashing for the changing rooms. Ha!

One incident I will never forget, towards sunset, with only my brother and I left at the pool, I decided to do one final 'bomb' off the four metre diving board. I had the ability to hit the water and cause a massive tower of water to shoot up above me, which acted like rain on anyone below as it cascaded down.

My brother was standing behind me and as I moved forward he decided to push me, maybe to put me off doing a perfect 'bomb', who knows, but I tried to resist by holding onto the railing. My left hand had a firm grip but my right hand slipped off the railing on that side and with forward impetus in full swing I rotated off the diving board to the left and plummeted to the concrete below. To an eleven year old it looked a long way to fall and landing feet first, followed by an almighty crack on my forehead, I momentarily blacked out, bleeding from under my hairline. Brian jumped into the water, the quickest way down of course and pulled himself out to come along side me, dripping all over my face.

'You okay boet!?' he enquired with a degree of panic in his voice.

'Mmmm.' I mumbled and he proceeded to drag me over to our towels on the grass. I tried to stand but my feet hurt like hell and I was dizzy as heck.

'I'll go get dad,' Brian said without looking back and raced off in the direction of the gate of the pool compound. I tasted blood and being dizzy, decided to lie back and wait for the comforting arms and help from my dad. I waited. And waited. And waited (the sun was almost gone by now) and waited!

Deciding I had to rescue myself I headed off towards the gate, which faced away from the club house, quite far away, hobbling on two very sore feet. After what seemed ages I finally climbed up the four steps leading to the front door and passage of the club house, lined with many, many sports photos of teams long gone by and shuffled along, leaning on the passage wall.

As already mentioned, the club had a TV room for kids and as I approached the door, there sat my brother, comfortably ensconced in a big wicker chair, a bottle of hubbly-bubbly in his left hand and a packet of salt and vinegar chips in the other. He caught sight of me and his face formed a picture I will never forget; mouth slightly ajar with a piece of chip balanced at the corner of his lips, eyes wide open, pink skin flushing dark red (my brother took after my English dad, complexion wise, with pale skin and blond hair while I took after mom with dark hair and a skin that could go so dark I was often teased about needing a Situpa [a pass all blacks had to carry]).

'What the heck are you doing here? I demanded, aching all over.

'Sorry boet,' he mumbled, stuffing more chips into his mouth, 'Supercar'.

He was instantly forgiven as it was the unsaid rule that nothing would interfere with our Supercar TV series, a kids film using puppets and an elaborate display of flying machines, especially a car, which gave the series its name, '*Supercar*'. A second episode was just about to start so I sat down eagerly next to my brother. At that moment dad appeared with two hot pies, chips and a hubbly-bubbly each! Food, 'Supercar' and a hubbly-bubbly instantly pushed all misery out of my mind.

Later that night, my dad carried a very sleepy me in his big arms to the blanket in the back of our station wagon. I can still smell the cigarette smoke and soft beer aroma coming off his jacket to this day, fifty four years later…

* * *

We used to turn right to go to the junior school, a five minute walk away, now the time had arrived to turn left out our gate and walk to senior school, seven minutes away.

I was *terrified*! I was about to slide from king of the castle to a serf somewhere in the slums! I practised dressing up in my new Churchill High School uniform, with its purple blazer and cap, diagonally striped purple and grey tie, with grey shorts and socks; feet tucked into shiny black shoes. A satchel on my back, army style!

'How do I stand?' I asked my brother, posing and turning in front of a mirror.

'Like the dork you are,' he quipped, 'nobody cares about that!' But I cared and I wanted to look smart at all times, with my black hair cut short on the sides but combed straight back at the centre, like Elvis Presley, who I admired. I used to sway and jiggle like him, strumming an imaginary guitar when I heard him on the radio.

And Brian was right, nobody cared about how I posed, trying to look like James Bond. I was suddenly in amongst nine hundred boys of all shapes and sizes. Some seemed old enough to grow a moustache; most wore uniforms that had become a bit faded with time and the older boys wore their ties slightly askew but no socks were allowed to slump down and our demeanour was monitored by ever-watchful prefects and honed by the absolute fear of being sent to the deputy head, Neil Jardine, who had a very nasty reputation with his cane, which I soon became a devout receiver of in my five years there.

It was a very good school and generally the discipline was quite strict, we had to raise our caps to all teachers and make way for them in the many passages. We even had to dip our caps to our parents when they collected us in their cars but thankfully I never had to do this as I walked to school.

I would say our school was in the top five in the country and we were harsh opponents of St George's college and Prince Edward in all sports disciplines. The first team rugby matches between Churchill and Prince Edward were so good and fast moving that they drew enormous crowds; both sides had their supporters cry out their war cries, a maroon square of our uniformed supporters adjacent to their square of reddish brown uniforms and off-white boater hats. I must confess that they always looked a bit neater than us as they had to wear long pants and wear jackets and boaters whereas many of us just wore shorts, blazers and caps. The two teams were often chosen to be the curtain raiser to international games between teams like the Springboks and Rhodesia, All Blacks and Rhodesia and so on. We had a superb national team and beat the French and All Blacks one year but then, due to sanctions, got banned from all international sports events. Thankfully we had a giant Rugby nation, South Africa, just next door and the matches with them and their provincial teams were no less entertaining. We marvelled at the size of the Northern Transvaalers, dwarfing our slim and fleet of foot team.

All these games were played on the main field of 'the club' and the bar there would be heaving with visitors and their wives and kids and the smell of wintergreen and the clack of studded boots in the change rooms stick with me to this day; pies being gobbled down and sun and fun for all. I loved that club!!

One of the highlights of the year for me, from a six to maybe thirteen year old, was the Christmas fun day the members of the club put on for the kids, as well as many police reserve families joining in. Father Christmas would arrive in a red and white helicopter, all dressed up in colours to match, big beard swirling in the down-draft, cheeks pink and a massive bag on his shoulder. We would squirm with delight and tug on our parents arms to be able to move forward and as soon as he was clear of the stalling rotor blades, we did just that, mobbing this poor man, sweating in the sun, as our hero. We knew presents awaited us!

While Father Christmas was shepherded away from us, we were guided to the opening of a long tunnel made from Hessian stretched over curved support poles. We entered the run with a bit of trepidation and as we advanced the odd decoration of Father Christmas and the elves and reindeer would be encountered, very professionally done, with some even coming alive as we passed by. I will never forget the magical wonder of it all and sometimes, to this day, I feel it was all real.

After about fifty metres of this we entered a large dome, also covered in Hessian, almost like an igloo and there sat Father Christmas on a sort of throne made out of hay bales. The lighting was amazing, Christmas trees added a lovely scent and before we knew it we were in front of the man! I looked wild eyed at him, not hearing a word he said, lost in the experience and looking at the huge bins that contained hundreds of neatly wrapped presents.

After confirming we had been good boys and girls he dipped his arm into the nearest bin labelled 'boys' and pulled out a present at random for me. I took it eagerly and headed for the exit where we were shepherded into the club hall where cakes, biscuits, ice cream and cool drinks awaited us. I tore my packet open and went apocalyptic with delight when I pulled out a holster with two silver guns, a sheriff's badge and a cowboy hat. I couldn't wait to get it on and suddenly by my side was my dad, helping me.

It was a cap gun, one that you loaded rolls of tape into, with tiny bits of gunpowder spaced every few millimetres. That gun became part of my life and I would race around the garden at home with friends who had similar handguns, spending hours playing cops and robbers. It was my sidearm when we progressed to playing army with Pete over the road and Gavan down the way.

* * *

There was a certain pecking order at high school. The prefects, distinguishable by white shirts rather than grey, double rings on blazer cuffs rather than a single one for us peasants, followed by sixth formers in general, then form fours down to us form one's. We were basically subservient to those above us.

I was fortunate being a big boy, at least a head taller than the others, with a beefy frame, because the 'weeds' in our midst had a hard time with the bullies that existed in sixth form. We generally congregated on a field near the tuck-shop at break-time and this is when most of the offences occurred; stolen pocket money and tuck purchases being the norm. But there was one punishment that was reserved for those weeds bold enough to stand their ground. They were thrown unceremoniously on their backs and held down while their shorts were pulled completely off, at which point an ape-like sixth former shimmied up the rugby goal post, sticking the poor weed's shorts at the very top before adroitly sliding down again. Suffice to say resistance by any 'weed' died out pretty quickly and indeed their very presence became a thing of the past, many hiding under the elevated floor of the woodworking shop.

Things happened in that school that would be deemed dismissible offences for teachers today but back then there was no political correctness (which I *detest*) and few guidelines limiting the amount of punishment a teacher could dole out. Having said that, a teacher could only administer two cuts with a cane, three to four by the deputy head and six by the headmaster. There were some boys like the Brown's (my mate who I used to crawl into the storm water drains with to smoke cigarettes), the Rodriguese's and others who got nothing but six all the time. They were in a select club indeed. Rodrigues once sold the bicycle his mom and dad had bought for him, using the money to take a train to Beira for the weekend so he could swim in the sea and drink wine and smoke pot at the tender age of fourteen or fifteen!

I was generally well behaved but I did have a rebellious streak in me which has lasted to this day. It resulted in lots of 'twos' and a few fours but never a six. The one corporal stripe I got was from my English teacher, Mr Slater, he was old and doddery and had a walking stick that he moved around on. But hold no pity for him; when it came time to give us cuts (which we called 'dooks') his whole countenance changed and a youthful smile would cross his face. His 'dooks' were renowned and everyone feared getting them, just like I did one day for some minor infraction that I can no longer remember. Lining my bum up with a few practice swings ended in the most excruciating pain I have ever felt, with little white stars exploding in my eyeballs. He would wait maybe another minute, forbidding me to rub my arse and when least expecting it number two would arrive! The pain was indescribable as he had the tenacity, even being old and doddery, to land the second cut immediately on top of the first one. To cry would result in serious mocking so I would sit down with tears in my eyes, gritting my teeth almost to the point of chipping them. Thank the Lord I only got Slater's cuts once.

The next pair of 'dooks' was from my biology teacher, Mr Harris. He was a stern, hawkish man that stood six foot three, piercing grey-green eyes looking over horn-rimmed glasses. Mr Harris had bought, at great expense to himself, some microscopes and a wonderful selection of slides that had all types of bugs squashed in them, little Hydra and so on. He went to great lengths to explain to us that the lens must be lowered to the slide while looking at it from the side and then winding it upwards to focus it, thus preventing us from breaking the slide with the lens. Well, you've guessed it, I thought I knew better and promptly broke the slide, the poor little Hydra exploding in my myopic vision. My heart raced!! I looked up in panic and was relieved to see 'Doc' Harris was in the back store room. I quickly took the slide off the microscope and rushed to the front, sliding its cracked frame into a box of perhaps fifty others. I grabbed another one and ran back to my microscope, sliding it in just as 'Doc' came out of his storeroom. My eyes followed him like a set of radar beams and at first I thought I had got away with it. I must have put the broken one in the wrong slot because 'Doc' saw it straight away. He looked up at it against the ceiling lights and slowly turned to look at us, his face darkening, peering angrily over his glasses, massive bushy eyebrows twitching nervously. I tried to swallow but my mouth had gone dry.

'Who did this?' he said venomously. Several heads turned to look at me, which the Doc was quick to pick up on. His eyes bored into mine and he crooked his finger at me. I shuffled nervously towards him and after confessing my guilt he said,

'I'm not going to punish you for breaking the slide, I'm going to punish you for trying to hide your guilt…bend down!'

I turned to face the class. Most of the boys were either smiling or leaning forward in great expectation. Maybe they had never before witnessed a flogging. I tensed up and turned my head to look for the Doc at the precise time he hit my bum. I got a terrible fright, jerking forward. His choice of weapon was one of the curved planks that came off our high, laboratory stools, made of wood. It was curved, just like my bum, making maximum contact. Thwack went the second one and once again the familiar flash at the back of my eyelids.

'Sit down Ballinger!'

I had just survived a beating from the man with the second-highest fear rating after Slater. I was getting a reputation. I was tough! It allowed me a certain amount of swagger rights among my colleagues and even the odd bottle of Fanta slid into my hand at break time.

The third set of two cuts was from my woodwork teacher, a man I came to despise. It happened one day when I forgot to rest my plane on its side and left it on its blade. I got the two cuts from the same type of stool plank the 'Doc' had hit me with but this guy was quite feeble and I had toughened against the pain by this stage. I winced convincingly enough to ensure I got another Fanta the next day at break but really it was no big deal. I got my own back on the very last day of woodwork classes by hitting the plane's blade as hard as I could with a hammer. Vengeance was mine!

My first appointment with the deputy head to get four cuts happened from something stupid I did in our chemistry class. We had superbly appointed laboratories where we were taught everything we needed to know about Chemistry to get into University, if that was the A-level we had chosen. Nestled among a vast array of tubes, bottles, beakers, gas burners and so on was a bottle of phosphorous cuttings, kept in some water to stop it igniting. Through sheer ignorance I teased and cajoled one of the boarders in our class (we had day scholars and a boarding school, for the children of people who lived far out of town, like farmers) to cut a piece of the phosphorous off and take it back to the hostels to show his fellow boarders how it burned through stuff.

The dolt surreptitiously cut some off, planning to put it in a container with some water but at that precise moment our rather sexy chemistry teacher walked into class from the back room. The dolt (I can't remember his name) panicked and shoved it into his trouser pocket. For awhile nothing happened as the phosphorous was denied air but as it warmed up against his leg, it suddenly ignited. A slight pfffft noise was followed by a bright glow in his pocket, rancid smoke billowing out, eyes wide, mouth open and a massive 'neeaaarrghhhhhh' scream vomited into the room. Dolt stood up, turned in circles, all the while trying to get his shorts off before running down the passage to the toilets, a trail of smoke behind him!

Needless to say I became implicated in the whole thing with Dolt's cowardly admission that I had persuaded him to embark in this madness. My visit to Neil Jardine, the deputy head at that time, was filled with fear and trepidation. I got handkerchiefs from my mates and stuffed them into my pants in various flat layers to absorb some of the impact of the cane but Jardine was wise to that and after commanding me to pull them out he administered four very professional cuts that had me running out the office clutching my bum! Ha! I was getting even tougher! I was rapidly descending to the level of Brown and Rodrigues which warranted kudos; people were reluctant to mix it with us.

It wasn't long before I became good friends with Ian Brown and as he lived not far from me we would meet at a suitable storm water culvert and being thin enough to climb through a slot under the concrete canopy we entered our own world where we would regale each other with stories of bravery and defiance, real or imagined, puffing on cigarettes we had bought, stolen or bartered. A few golf balls worth of income went into this venture! I continued to get my share of the cane but as I matured I became more interested in sport and girls so the familiar sting from failing academia became less and less. I never once saw these canings as abuse and I know without doubt that the discipline garnered from those experiences shaped my life for the better and indeed our whole nation was better off for it. We ended up having a very well disciplined and obedient populace that lived life to the full but took our knocks when dished out.

* * *

Sport became a passion of mine. I found out very quickly that I suffered badly from asthma so running, any distance, became my greatest dislike of all sports. So I turned to swimming, which I had already excelled back in junior school, having won the Victor Ludorum and many other cups and prizes at both school and inter-school meets. I developed very powerful arm muscles and soon had a nice six-pack developing which I enhanced by doing rolls on overhead bars where I would pull my chin up to a bar, thrust my legs back and then do a revolution over the bar, dropping down until my toes almost touched the ground, only to repeat it twenty or thirty times. I noticed that with my tan, good looks and muscled body that a few of those exquisite creatures called girls were now letting their eyes rest a bit longer than normal on me. It was a heavenly feeling that only youth can capture before it becomes a little tired from over experience.

I just loved the sun and water on my body and spent inordinate amounts of time at various swimming pools, cycling to Greendale, Les Brown and so on just to be among young people, water, sun and the soliciting smells of suntan lotion, bodies shiny and tanned. They were glorious, glorious days.

By the time I was fifteen or sixteen I had become profoundly interested in underwater hockey. This was played in the deep end of a swimming pool with eight people each in two opposing teams, playing across the width of the pool. We were kitted out with socks (without them, friction of foot on flipper would remove the skin on your toes), goggles, flippers, gloves, a snorkel and a very short wooden stick curving off at a forty degree angle at the end furthest from your hand, rather like a hockey stick. The object of the game was to get a round, flat, rubber coated lead puck into a galvanized metal goal tray about four two metres wide, sitting on the floor of the pool at the juncture of the wall and floor.

This sport required great coordination from its team members and an enormous lung capacity. Our training included swimming a full length underwater in a thirty three meter pool, swimming on the surface back to where we started from then doing another length underwater. After twenty or thirty lengths of this our lungs were bursting but it got to the point where, in a static position, we could easily hold our breaths four or more minutes without struggling but in sprint action underwater, we lasted maybe twenty seconds. We had one guy called Alan, Rita's (cute-bum) boyfriend who we nicknamed 'aqualung' as he could stay down for the equivalent of two breaths for the rest of us. He and Tony Dawson could flick that puck virtually three quarters the way across the pool with such ferocity that on one occasion it was flicked into my goggles, smashing them to pieces, almost blinding me and that was through reinforced glass!

To this day I bear the scars from that game. The knuckle on the longest finger on my right hand is still scarred from when the thick rubber glove wore down from scraping on the tiles of the pool, ending up removing various degrees of skin and my right shoulder has a big scar on it from when I cart wheeled under water to flick the puck forward and a chipped floor tile cut into me like a razor blade. The puck did a lot of damage to the floor tiles of the pool at the 'club' and it involved us having to get aqualungs to go down and replace them, which attracted me to my next sport!

But before I leave my memories of underwater hockey I must relate the one and only tour to Bloemfontein in South Africa, to compete in their inter-provincial tournament. Us Rhodesians were almost classed as another province of South Africa, which was lovely. Without South Africa we would have not experienced any international quality sports events.

I had got into the team, eight of us with one in reserve (see photo) and had trained non-stop for this event. We were superbly fit but had no idea if our tactics and wit matched the fearsome Transvaal and Natal teams.

The pool had an underwater observation room with thick glass keeping the water back from the spectators. It was simply awesome seeing the game like that, rather than from the surface where all you could see was thrashing flippers and heads bobbing up like some shark-feeding frenzy. We quickly realised as we played in the heats and watching others play that Natal was going to be our biggest opposition and we studied their tactics very closely.

Over a period of three days we had whittled down the opposition until we were in the semi-finals with Natal, Transvaal, Rhodesia and Cape Provence being the remaining four. We faced Transvaal while Natal played the Cape Town boys.

I eyed the enormous men in the Transvaal team with much trepidation and when the gong went off for us to race to the puck, it was like encountering a runaway locomotive, the speed and power with which they hit us was staggering! They punched through the front runners and the back line like they weren't there and scored a goal in less than fifteen seconds. We rose to the surface and clinging to the side of the pool looked at each other in horror, coughing and spluttering. But Tony, our captain, did not accept defeat and rallied us with a few strong words. We were emboldened. Tony put himself, a giant of a man, in the front along with a couple of other tanks and this time we broke through. The fight was incredible, with powerful arms on both side pushing and snapping the puck this way and that only to have it robbed by the opposing team. The puck slid from one side to another and then back again. I was getting so exhausted I could only stay down ten seconds but 'aqualung' was there, hovering like a bull shark and in a split second he intercepted a loose puck, turned on himself for protection and flicked the puck a good fifteen feet into the galvanized goal! I could see our team supporters gesticulating with a silent scream in the observation room! And then Alan followed through, picking up the puck and putting it on the edge of the pool, which made it an official goal. That single act of having to pick up the puck, maybe having to push your way through five players, at the end of your tether and taking it up to the surface nearly drowned me and several other players over the years. One would get to the surface, ripping off mask and snorkel, vomiting up a bit of water! It too, is the only time I experienced the prickle of sweat in water, apart from a game of water polo that I tried a few times.

The next day, the 3rd and final day of the competition dawned and I was as nervous as anything, we were in the finals. I had to pinch myself to believe we had beaten Transvaal 2-1 which left us feeling ecstatic and a couple of well deserved drinks went down that night but we were careful not to do anything rash and went to bed early in our expansive group tent.

Now the clock ticked town to the start of the main game; the ladies tournament had just ended and the crowd was large and eager to see if these outsiders from Rhodesia could win. The Natal team consisted of players roughly our size, which was a relief after facing the underwater Rottweilers' from the day before. They mainly had longer hair than us as a lot of men in our country were being drafted into the army. In fact 'Dozy' Donaldson, Butch Wigget and Tony Dawson were all in the police, Tony getting killed a year or two later on his last tour into the bush where the terrorist war was now commencing.

We faced them in the water, one hand on the pool edge, our flipper-feet ready to push off as soon as the referee banged the gong and suddenly my nerves were steady. I breathed in and out deeply to fill my blood with oxygen. I was the point man, I was to go for the puck and if there first I would flick it to a flanking team member and he would decide what tactic to use from there. I got there a split second ahead of my opposition, flicking the puck just over his stick, barging through with massive and powerful thrusts from my flippers, rotating sideways to protect the puck from an incoming player. In that instant I saw Tony Dawson to my right and feigned a flick towards him before thrusting forward to about eight feet from the goal. An instinctive flick of the wrist and it sailed straight into it, landing with a clang! I had scored!!!! But now I had to retrieve the puck and surface with it for the goal to be accepted and I had no air in my lungs whatsoever, I was suppressing the animal urge to breathe but no matter what the cost, sucking my mask and snorkel deep into my face and mouth I was there! I plonked the puck on the edge of the pool. My team mates patted me on my back, our supporters were going wild!

I rotated to the back of the line-up and this time Tony and Butch and Aqualung thrust forward, scoring a goal that looked so easy but those three guys, especially Butch, could motor like torpedoes. It was now 2-0 to us, but that's as far as we got. The Natal boys, known colloquially as 'banana boys' for all the Bananas grown in tropical Natal, regrouped and came at us like steam engines. They may have lost the first two pucks due to over-confidence but after the shock we gave them they rallied and finally beat us 4-2. But we felt very proud of our second place and were treated with respect by our opposition and free drinks flowed our way that night.

The drive down to Bloemfontein was memorable. I was in a Peugeot station wagon with Maurice Mathewman, our oldest player and Butch Wigget and my brother and Tony Dawson. It was my first time to enter South Africa and what an experience to walk into the store at the garage while Tony filled up with petrol. It was full of chocolates, something sanction-hit Rhodesia had not seen for years, not Cadbury's anyway and there were bottles of fresh guava juice as well as pear juice and many other delights. We walked back to the car like donkeys laden down with a prospector's horde, munching our way into the night. We drove into the darkness and I huddled in the back seat listening to the music of the day, Pink Floyd and one I liked the most 'We may never pass this way again' by Seals and Crofts and those by Neil Young, which will forever be in my heart as, by the time I played in Bloemfontein I was eighteen and had just left behind a girl called Carol Dellar from the UK whom I had fallen in love with. We had kissed to that music. She was back in Rhodesia, I was on the way to Bloemfontein and after that I hitched to Cape Town via Durban and caught a ship to the UK.

But I have gone too far forward in my timeline so I regress to a year or so earlier when one of the teams we played against was Kariba, named after the enormous hydro-electric dam (second biggest in the world at the time) north west of Salisbury, set in the majestic Zambezi valley and their team members were electricians and control operators and so on who managed the enormous turbines that generated electricity from the hydro complex there; its cheap power sent all over Rhodesia and into Zambia. What a place!

I subsequently spent many years visiting Kariba, staying at Caribbea Bay on the lake, Kariba Keights Hotel, Kariba Breezes and Cutty Sark among several others. Actually, those trips there were preceded by a visit many years before, at the age of about six, when the dam was brand new and Operation Noah, to rescue many land animals trapped on islands formed from the rising waters of the dam, had just terminated a month before. We stayed in some type cabin there, all very rustic and the smell of the lake and water and the boats going out fishing will stick with me forever. Down at that level, on the shoreline, the lake looked like an ocean, disappearing west to the horizon and setting sun, over two hundred and eighty kilometres long and about forty kilometres wide. It experienced big waves like the ocean and the weight of the settling water was so immense it triggered local earthquakes up to about size three on the Richter scale. The dam wall was a marvel of French design and Italian engineering where ninety men died building it, eighteen falling into concrete pours that could not be halted once they started. Their bodies are trapped there for all eternity.

But now, playing underwater hockey there was a wonderful experience. The pool was owned by the Electricity Supply Commission and was a standard thirty three metre pool with long concrete viewing platforms on the one side that acted as seats and wide areas to suntan on. It was hot, very hot and in later years when I visited with my own family, it was fifty degrees centigrade!

Behind the pool was the Kariba Heights Hotel, which had a simply stunning view of the lake many hundreds of feet below, with tiny boats flanking much bigger houseboats in Carribea Bay's harbour. To the south east of the hotel was the sports club with bowling greens, tennis courts, an outdoor cinema and a club house that appeared to be floating in space because when you looked out the windows all one could see was the lake. The tennis courts were plonked on the edge of a very steep cliff and was most certainly not a place to plop your ball over the fence!

I revelled in being young, free and independent with the exciting promise of meeting a girl I could fall in love with one day and lose my virginity to! I enjoyed the flirting, looking and being looked it. Vain? Most certainly so!

* * *

The frequent visits to play underwater hockey led me into my next craze. One day there was only one guy available to help repair the chipped tiles at the bottom of the pool and he had brought a second set of aqualungs in case he took longer than expected to do his work.

'You had any diving experience?' he said to me.

'No, but I'd love to have a go!'

'Today's your lucky day,' and he promptly showed me what to do, how to breathe plus a few safety tips and before you could shout 'boo' I was hanging off the iron steps leading into the pool, weighted down, goggles and flippers on. I eased my head underwater, gently planing down to the bottom eight feet below but at this stage it was totally impossible in my mind to breathe in so I just held onto my breath for as long as possible. Of course that can only last a minute or two and I reluctantly sucked in a lung full of air. The experience was overwhelming as air rushed into my mouth; what an amazing feeling, breathing under water! I gave a big 'Zero' sign to the other guy and in no time I was chipping out broken tiles with a hammer and chisel while he followed me inserting new tiles with a very thick and sticky glue that works well under water. It was a slow process and I had to make sure all rubble was pushed to the side and a recess left deep enough to take the glue and the tile. I think we did about three an hour.

It's funny, when I got in the pool the water was quite warm but after about thirty minutes I was shivering away much better. No wonder my buddy had a wet suit on, cold is one of the biggest killers of all divers. I learned that later as a spear fisherman at Kariba.

So, I went and joined the BSA, British Sub Aqua club and went all over the show diving with them. I never formally qualified nor got any type of PADI certificate but I self-certified to ten metres by simply watching what other guys did and listening in to instructors.

One of our favourite destinations was Sinoia caves, about a hundred and ten kilometres along the Kariba road. An ancient cave roof had collapsed centuries ago revealing a massive sink hole filled with the clearest water anywhere on Earth. I don't know how they got in there, but tiny fish darted to and fro and were a great source of interest to me when I dived there.

The water is reached by following man-made concrete steps down along what must have been the original underground river, so it was down through a tunnel of sorts until you reached the water's edge. Circular cliffs towered up above us and the aquamarine blue of the water disappeared into the depths like a huge funnel. The water remained constant in temperature so it must be connected to a big body of water.

I'm not sure who has dived the deepest there but the sleeping pool is ninety metres deep and tapers down to a known one hundred and seventy two metres. I used to enjoy getting into my wetsuit, putting on my 'lungs', flippers, weights and goggles while tourists sat on their haunches looking at us in wonder. It was cool down there, even on a hot day, with a very slight mustiness in the air. I just loved that place!

Pushing off from the shore was an experience because the water was so clear it felt like I had pushed off from a high cliff, you sort of caught your breath a bit. After settling down I would sink to about five metres and then pan along the sloping floor, looking at the tiny fish looking back at me, soft ferns gently swaying around and caressing them.

By the time I had reached the maximum depth I was prepared to go to, which on this day was about twelve metres, I looked up and saw maybe six other divers hanging in space above me, like skydivers baling through the air, except they were floating in water. If it wasn't for my bubbles going up it would be easy to think this was a wind chamber suspending people in mid-air. Incredible!

Of course, these trips were accompanied by girls and I simply loved lying around the swimming pool at the hotel, adjacent to the caves, chatting away, laughing and flirting but never getting anywhere which was starting to bug me. We used to listen to the music of the day, splash in the pool and cavort around while the sun beat down and bees licked at our Coke and Fanta cool drinks and water at the pool's edge.

It was there, on one occasion, that my nemesis, Pete Cheney, actually our neighbour over the road at home, was easing away a girl I rather fancied and he sat up to sort of block me away from her. I was furious but the Lord, even then, may have been on my side for as Pete pulled his feet back so he could wrap his arms around his knees, scraped up a six inch piece of rusty wire which went straight through his foot and popped out between his big toe and the next one. Pete was horrified and listening to some dork that said 'pull it out' he did so, accompanied by a fountain of blood and high-pitched screams, rolling over on his side. I have always had a dark sense of humour and burst out chuckling while Pete writhed in agony. A guy with a driver's license pulled him up and with one or more hangers-on they headed off to the local hospital about ten kays away. I was really chuffed as I now had the girls to myself, not that anything came of it of course!

* * *

Another place we loved diving at was Mtorashanga, turning off the road to Kariba, somewhere just before Banket. The trip there was interesting as it took us over a long range of hills that divided Rhodesia into two from north north-east to south south-west. It had an amazingly rich vein of Chrome running through it, so pure it barely had to be refined and despite sanctions against Rhodesia, the West, especially the United States, gobbled it up by the thousands of tons. Of course Chrome is a strategic mineral used in hardening steel that is used in gun barrels and many other military goods. The side of the hills were pock-marked with dozens of little caves where peasants and small operators pulled out the mineral to make a few bucks.

I loved driving through the African bush with its familiar flat-topped thorn trees flashing by, elephant grass towering ten feet or more on the sides of the road, cut down by locals and building companies alike for thatched roofs. And that smell in the rainy season, which cannot be described, filling one's nostrils with life and freedom, frogs hopping onto the road to keep warm, getting squashed under our truck tyres.

'Got another one!' laughed Tony as a big bull frog popped under the right tyre. And even before it was out of sight the carrion were down, feeding off it. Carol, from England would squirm with disgust and cover her mouth as girls do.

I had at last met a girl, I can't remember where and she was English with dark hair, brown eyes, a lovely smile and a body to make the average man whimper. I was highly possessive of her even though I tried to act nonchalant having heard some idiot say once upon a time that if you are too keen they treat you like dirt. So I acted cool but inside I was quivering jelly and cried at night believing that one day we would split up, which of course time and new experiences ensured would happen, but I still miss her to this day. What do they say about your first love?

Mtorashanga is an old, disused Chrome quarry that had filled with water to about forty feet below the ring of rocks surrounding its lip; true ground level. One reached its greenish, but clear, waters via a winding set of concrete steps. We had arrived the first day in a convoy of vehicles at least ten long.

We disembarked, putting aqualungs and kit all over the place. A compressor was positioned on a flat piece of ground, ready to refill tanks, an open-sided tent erected, tables brought out with food and beers and soon a fire was lit for a braai (colloquial name for a barbecue).

Being vain and having a girl I needed to impress lest I lose her (how naive is youth!) I scampered away to a high rock that people jumped from into the depths far below, at least sixty feet below.

'I'll show Carol,' I said to myself as I neared the top of the rock only to freeze solid as I stared at the depths in sheer terror. I glanced down at Carol and she waved back. A few guys taunted me which soon turned into a crowd holding up beers and saying 'jump, jump, jump!!' My knees shook uncontrollably.

I couldn't let them down and would lose Carol for sure if I chickened out so I took a deep breath and plummeted into nothingness. Air whizzed past my ears for what seemed an eternity and then with a bone-crunching slap like someone had hit me full force in the face with an open hand I was in the water, spiralling deeper and deeper into its depths, wind knocked out of me and my bum hurting like hell. I was just about to give up and accept death when my head broke surface. I coughed and spluttered, wiping water from my eyes which eventually focused on the crowd. Few were cheering while many had turned back to their cooking and beer guzzling. Carol was one of them. I was mortified!

We spent the day diving and sun tanning and drinking the odd beer but all the while my bum hurt like heck. I had already squirted some water out of it before diving back in to clean myself off. Eventually I called Tony aside as I was worried my coccyx had hit a rock or something, so we snuck off into the long grass where I promptly pulled my cozzie down for him to have a look.

'Split your bum from your balls to the dopher,' he chuckled, 'but it's not deep and only bleeding a bit.' He stood up and laughed, walking away. I felt relieved but spent the rest of the week walking like a cowboy who had been on a horse for too long. Maybe Carol thought I was trying to impress her!

But diving at Mtorashanga turned out to be one of my favourite pastimes. The water was relatively clear and warm, being locked in the equivalent of a very large granite soup bowl. An interesting part of the dive were some old mine shafts and caves off to the right which I enjoyed gliding through, the bubbles from my mouthpiece becoming trapped under the granite roof just above me.

The more experienced divers went down deep. I was told there was an old aeroplane down there and the guys would take turns sitting in the cockpit. How it got there is anyone's guess but many years later my son dived there and confirmed the story.

On other occasions we had orienteering competitions, similar to map reading I would learn in the army a few years ahead but here a course had been set up underwater that involved compass and diagram reading. Divers would be paired off and they would have to find perhaps fifteen suspended buoys in a specific order in the quickest time possible. It was mainly an inter-club competition and I was made an underwater observer to ensure the course was run correctly and I thoroughly enjoyed the task. However, I was a bit naughty because when the team I supported got into difficulties, turning in circles to decide where to go, they caught sight of me and I pointed in the direction of their next buoy, sending them speeding off like a Leviathan was after them! Needless to say we won but to this day, nearly fifty years later, I feel guilty and tainted.

For me, though, the best times were those feelings of youth, a sense of enjoyment and mild fatigue from exercising so hard plus a braai and beers and cuddling Carol, which I found very sensuous, in my costume. The journey back to Salisbury would often be at sunset, the warm glow washing over my skin and the lovely curvy Carol nestled into me. Wonderful!

I had a lovely time with Carol, my English rose and I found her very attractive with a firm youthful body and a great sense of humour. My friend Chris Gunns and I would often pop around to Carol's friends flat (her name was Rose) on second street and have a meal together followed by lying on the carpet and chatting and kissing while Black Magic Woman by Santana played in the background. It reminded me of scenes I had read about in the book 'Hold my hand, I'm dying', the cars going down second street and life, normal life going on around us, to be shattered in the war years ahead when everything would change.

One night though, I really dishonoured Carol when she invited me for a meal at another friend's house in Eastlea, not far from my mom and dad's place. I had had a few too many drinks before I arrived and even more at the dinner table. I got so tipsy there that all I remember is accidentally pouring a lovely creamy soup down my lap and then proceeding to impress all by trying to make a lit candle look like a cigarette as I sucked on the unlit end! I do not remember getting home or what happened to my dad's minivan but the next day, with a massive hangover, I tracked her down to where she worked in a bank in the middle of the city. With temples pulsing and feeling quite nauseous, I approached her desk to receive a very frosty reception. As far as I could see I had gone a 'bridge too far' with her. I felt terrible, it was over!

However, my mate Chris Gunns suggested the four of us go camping up at Inyanga and he would get Rose to persuade Carol to give me another chance. She agreed.

We set off early one wet and miserable Saturday morning and it was so good to be sitting next to Carol again, her smell and softness so tempting. I remember us coming to the railway crossing not far from Marandellas and it was malfunctioning, with its arm going up and down like a drunk robot and it was cold and windy outside. It didn't matter to me as I was ensconced in this delightful cocoon of warmth on the back seat.

We eventually got going again and by the time we arrived in the pine scented mountains of eastern Rhodesia the sky had cleared, leaving fresh, fresh air sighing through the branches high above us. We set up a tent at the upper of two campsites, the one above a popular, natural pool which nestled just below a gently sloping set of rapids. My mind bulged with memories of all the visits to Inyanga in my youth.

Fond memories of Inyanga included staying at the Rhodes Hotel, which Cecil John Rhodes owned, with its wide veranda and comfortable chairs, overlooking a valley full of pine trees. I loved the cream teas there and the meals in the evenings near a warm fireplace and the smell of the coal-fired ovens in the early mornings as the staff prepared breakfast. My mom and dad always stayed in Rhodes's room while my brother and I shared a second room. We would walk along the shady lane leading to the hotel, bordered by huge Eucalyptus trees, looking for shiny slithers of Mica that littered the area. We would collect it and pretend it was our treasure.

But above all we loved the quick ride down to the aforementioned natural pool at the base of sloping, smooth rocks, over which copious quantities if bitterly ice cold water cascaded. Over the years a large beach had formed there and it became a sort of 'seaside' attraction covered by dozens of people sunbathing and eating picnics before running screaming into the water, which literally took one's breath away. A large pine tree with a rope swing tied to one of its branches was a great source of amusement for people of all ages, to swing off and land into the fast-flowing, darkish water.

I loved lying on the terraces formed around a large octagonal-shaped gondola made of granite piers, topped by a bitumen clad roof, where people more sensitive to the sun could sit with their young children and from there I could ogle at the young ladies in bikinis with the resultant eye candy that occurred when cold water touched nipples. I was a virgin then and still so with Carol, as we set up our four-man tent.

As soon as the tent was up we ran down the gorse-covered hillside along a sandy, meandering path and in a few minutes we were at the pool. We threw our towels down and with a mischievous glint in our eyes Chris and I picked up the two protesting girls, who squirmed and shrieked in our arms, and ran off to the water with them. They held us tightly enough to ensure, along with the water grabbing our ankles, that we would lose our balance and fall into the water with them, which we did.

I'm not sure who screamed the loudest, Carol or me, but we bounced up and down yelling at the biting water! Rose and Chris were no less affected. But after a minute or so I became used to it and my body began to feel warm. I paddled up to Carol and wrapped her in my arms, kissing her. She had an amazingly long tongue. It was all too much for me and I became erect and for a moment we remained locked together before she pulled away, swishing water into my face, giggling loudly. I was sure I would lose my virginity that night, it's all I could think of at the tender age of seventeen or so.

I swam to cool down, which was not difficult, believe me and soon we were sliding down the slippery rocks into the water with much merriment and laughter. Doing what we did reminded me of watching a man have his feet slip out from under him on this very rock, landing full force on the back of his head, splitting it open; his red blood turning pink in the water, flowing away at a rapid rate. Several people rushed to his aid and he was taken off to hospital by one of them. That happened when I was about twelve but stuck with me and I made darn sure none of us slipped in a similar manner, easing into position by crawling like ducks on our haunches to the top of the 'slide'.

Once we hit the water at the bottom, I would let the fast current carry me into some shallow reeds, allowing myself to enter a bend in the river and then another small beach from where I would emerge back onto dry land. This secondary beach reminded me that it was the launch pad of a trip that my brother and I took downstream, about age thirteen or fourteen, on the orange inner tube of some huge tyre. It was incredibly hard getting this massive thing into the water without it being whisked away but we eventually succeeded and on a blinding hot day, with scorching skin and only in our Speedo costumes we raced off along the winding river. It was a heck of a ride and very enjoyable with both narrow and scary bits followed by wider, lazy stretches and we would lie across it like sailors going on a big adventure. I will never know how many miles we went, the last piece of civilization was a golf course along the way and then it was just scrubby bush, the odd pine tree and lots of lichen-covered boulders. I will never forget the smell of that water and the aromas it aroused from the vegetation that it swirled through.

Eventually, for fear of entering Mozambique or some other horror we got out the river and commenced the appallingly hard effort of walking back to the campsite, which on this occasion was the lower one below Rhodes Inyanga Hotel. Fortunately my dad had got worried about us and had travelled along a winding dirt road looking for us and with much relief we tied the inner tube to the roof rack and went back to get changed before going for cream teas at the hotel. The cold water made one feel alive and I was always so warm when I got dressed.

* * *

No sooner had we got dressed and gone back to the camp than we decided to go for a few drinks up at Troutbeck, the pre-eminent hotel in the area, situated way up in the mountains; a firm favourite of mine all my youth.

The climb up the modern road through breathtaking scenery was pure joy and before long we entered pine-draped hills and valleys, with the corresponding scents and fresh air that mountains exude. We coasted down to the petrol station on the right and its non-ubiquitous bakery and gift store that appeared to sell Christmas cards, decorations and presents all year round.

With the fuel tank brimming and our portable tanks rapidly being loaded with cokes and pies, we set off for the entrance to Troutbeck on our left, a couple of hundred metres away, but as we approached the turn-off Chris gunned the accelerator and we shot over the bridge near the dam wall and up the other side, a brief glimpse of the hotel and its gorgeous little dam off to our left; a dam where my mother missed her footing getting into a rowing boat and plop-slid into the inky depths of the frigid water. This had happened right in front of me and I will never forget the expression of abject horror on her face as she disappeared below a white, frothy plume of her liquid 'tombstone'. She surfaced a few seconds later, yelling blue murder with a bit of the dam's prolific weed draped over her head!

'Where are we going?' I asked for the three of us.

'Wait and see,' Chris replied.

We continued up the winding, very scenic and steep road until we were among beautiful dales sprinkled with lichen clad granite boulders and very tall pine trees. The land fell away to the right or east towards Mozambique, climbing higher to our left. After a joyous ride Chris turned left not far after a small bridge, up a dirt road and then left again at the top of the hill. All the while Carol and I cuddled in the back seat, pies warming our innards and the thought of what may happen that night teasing my groin.

A few hundred yards later, along the ridge we had driven along, we came to a dairy farm on the left.

'Wait until you taste their milkshakes" Chris offered up as we bounced to a halt on green grass just outside a small café attached to the milking shed. We climbed out, stretched and immediately had our nostrils invaded by that smell so typical to dairy farms; dung and pee. Cows with big liquid eyes stared dumbly at us with jaws going over and back, over and back.

I had always loved farms and spent many happy holidays with cotton farmers by the name of Daniels that lived west of the main Bulawayo road somewhere between Hartley and Gatooma. The two Daniels girls were gorgeous and I used to sit and gawk at them with both abject misery and hope in my heart, knowing that I would never be theirs. But we slept on the farm veranda one evening, my brother and I and the two girls plus the older brother Rich, who sadly got killed later and I climbed to heaven lying on my tummy while Gail tickled my back. I nearly died from the pleasure of it and certainly struggled to sleep that night!

Carol brought me back to the present. We leaned on the wooden poles of the run leading to the milking machines and watch with interest as litre after litre got sucked out of these lovely animals. I was amused that the main herd stood in a comfortable group waiting their turn. As a human male, I was not sure if it was the relief of udders being emptied or the delightful treat they munched on while being milked. I guess it was both.

No sooner had the milk been taken than it was chilled. This was raw milk, something we did not see all that often in the city. We strolled around to the tables and ordered a large milkshake each plus scones, cream and jam, for such a reasonable price too.

'This is lovely" I said licking my fingers, 'good call Chris!'

I loved the freedom I was experiencing and in those heady days before the civil war broke out, we laughed and enjoyed life and the sun and the goodness of it all. The very farm we were on would be attacked by terrorists and mortared from dark fields only a few years later, rendering the joy we felt now all but impossible during seven years of war.

But I didn't know what was coming on that bright, sunny day and cruised down the hilly road until, this time, we turned into Troutbeck Hotel, a hotel I adored from my childhood. The thing about the hotel is that it was old world with long, narrow, red-carpeted passages running left and right at the entrance hall to quant, old bedrooms each with its own fireplace and view of the lake. In later years a modern wing would be built under the sloping grass that ran down to the dam; built in such a way so as to not ruin the views from the upper, older bedroom wings.

The reception area was a delight with its lovely red, patterned carpets that gave it a year-round Christmassy feeling; an ornate plaster ceiling topping mahogany-clad walls and reception counter made of similar dark wood. There was a fireplace that greeted the visitor, directly ahead and it was reputed that it had never gone out since the hotel was built many decades before.

Carol squeezed my hand tighter and rested her head on my shoulder as we walked through a comfortably appointed lounge, with another fireplace, to a large glazed conservatory that accommodated perhaps twenty to thirty groups of comfortable chairs, the type you sink into and never want to leave. The clusters of lights above us were muted by very ornate glass lampshades made to look like tropical flowers. They were sensational.

We had no sooner sat down than a waiter was by our side and after the order had been placed we retired into our comfortable cocoons and whispered sweet nothings to each other. Chris seemed to be hitting it off with Rose and I could not help noticing, not for the first time, that she had a sensational pair of legs which her tiny miniskirt of the day, brought to full glory.

'Like what you see?' Carol said tugging on my arm.

'I only have eyes for you,' I lied and looked up at the large hill across the lake that towered above us, reflecting its dark shadow over its rippled waters. Fishermen paddled in little boats hired for the occasion and golfers thrashed at elusive little white balls on the far bank. Friday and I would have made a killing here, I mused. I felt bad about not seeing him anymore but knew that society was changing my heart as I grew older, that I had reached the age where I would no longer have seen Friday as my equal but rather someone who lived separate lives from us 'out there'. He did not fit our rising socio-economic bracket anymore. It has taken over fifty years, mainly through becoming a Christian, that I have come back to wanting to be with the 'Fridays' of today. Trying to kill them in the army in later years would strike a very deep divide in my heart.

After our drinks we sauntered down to the dam and breathed in the cool mountain air. My eyes focused on the high, conical hill just to our right front which later formed memories of Huey helicopters circling it before swooping down and along the shore of the dam, along the face of the hotel, girls waving their arms in glee as they sped past. That happened just as the up-coming civil war had ended and the air force pilots were bored and decided to take mainly female tourists for rides around the hill and lake. It would only be a few years until I too was in smaller Alouette helicopters, face streaked with camo cream, rifle resting across my denim-covered legs, going to war. But for now I was a seventeen-something kid who had no cares in the world.

We drove up to Conamara after that, such a beautiful little housing estate nestled around a man-made dam, maybe a few hundred metres wide, snuggled in pine trees with tufts of cotton-wool smoke drifting from granite chimneys. And to the left of that, a small car park on the edge of a sheer cliff to the dry valley below. It was odd that we had so much greenery around us but down below the African tribal lands were dry and barren looking, with loads of conical granite koppies fading into a hazy horizon. We were standing atop a massive watershed, the wind-facing side drenched in vegetation with everything on the leeward side dry and thorny.

Chris and I left the girls there and ran off to the right, ascending a very pointed hillock that offered an awesome view from its summit. We sat there and looked at the dying sun off to the west, its orange embers bleeding into the purple horizon, little cooking fires now lit, adding to the smoky appearance of the valley. I was lost in wonder and full of love for the place, it being my homeland and the joy and majesty of it all.

* * *

By the time we got back to camp it was quite dark so we used the car's headlamps to shine on our tent until we had the gas light burning. Then came out the chairs and I lit a fire in the hearth of a very nice granite braai unit while Chris and the girls prepared a light supper of tinned ham, tomatoes and bread. We finished off by melting cheese over toast next to the embers and then it was time to ease back and get a few drinks under our belts. I never really became a beer drinker so it was a small bottle of Brandy and coke for Carol and I. I'm pretty sure we were all just under the legal drinking age and that gave all of us a bit of a thrill I think, sitting there acting like adults.

We talked and joked and laughed until quite late, dancing light flicking off the trees above, the alcohol buoying our humour and natural urges so by the time Carol and I slid under our blanket on a thick duvet we were quite merry. This *had* to be the moment I truly became a man. The gentle moans and sighs from Chris and Rose spurred me on; my heart was racing. I slid over to Carol, kissing her deeply…first base reached! Ha, it reminded me, as I lay there, of the first time I ever French kissed. I had taken this drop dead gorgeous girl called Pat Eames out to the drag races and after a wonderful day watching these amazing machines and the power of their engines, I invited her out to go dancing. We had a lovely evening and she was very sensual indeed and moulded so well into me. When the evening ended I took her home, kissing her good night. We kissed with mouths closed, a long press on each-other's lips.

'I want a proper kiss,' I said ignorantly, thinking that maybe a proper kiss was kissing for even longer. I pulled her into me, my mouth still closed, only to encounter this magnificently parted mouth with a tongue from heaven lashing backwards and forwards over my frigid lips! I pulled back in delighted confusion while Debbie frowned at me before joining battle again and this time our tongues met, although I hadn't a clue what to do with mine. I went rigid with delight and my breathing came so fast I felt lightheaded. So *this* was a French kiss! My word how wonderful! I had, at that juncture, only seen French kissing in movies and I didn't really understand the dance of the tongues so to speak.

But now, lying across Carol's outstretched arm, her dark hair cascading across the pillow, I operated as a true expert. As reported, first base had been reached. Now, base two, sucking erect nipples approached with much trepidation but I was unstoppable. Clinging to her teat like a Biafran refugee she gently admonished me to be more gentle before battle commenced again. The sex gods must have been proud of me to get to second base so quickly but now and HOW to get to that elusive third base, that amazing unknown quantity that every male virgin fantasised over all his life, the vessel from which we had spent nine months trying to get out of and the rest of our lives trying to get back into!

I started off with some gentle caressing of her closest thigh, moving up to the target and when I got real close, just as I was about to discover and feel something I had never felt my whole life, not even in the school classroom on theatre night so long ago, a firm pushing away of my hand ended the greatest adventure of my life.

'I'm not on the pill,' she said and in that split second I saw in my mind's eye a German fighter aircraft spiralling out of control, flames soaring out the back, a Spitfire zooming away. I had been shot down. First base ended with a pathetic 'Carol?' from me and second base got covered up by her T-shirt.

'Let's just cuddle,' she said turning on her side, 'I'm tired anyway' and with that the man is commanded to 'stand down' but my groin area was bloody *not* standing down and could have been used for a gate post! What torture, the agony, especially with some pretty loud groans coming from Chris and Rose. At any moment I expected her to say 'just kidding' before rolling back to face me but before long I could hear her steady breathing of sleep. I remained pressed against the small of her back and spent the most sexually frustrating night of my entire life lying there, prone, heart beating, the sound effects of a porno film less than three feet away…

The next morning we packed and headed out for part two of our camping trip, to Hot Springs and then a climb to turret towers in the Chimanimani mountain range that runs along the eastern border of Rhodesia, to gaze at the Mozambique plains, flat as a billiard table to the ocean several hundred kilometres away. It was going to be one hell of a climb and far, far too ambitious in my opinion, but Chris was extremely fit and was still doing iron man marathons into his sixties in the far east and Australia, by which time I looked like a chair and did about as much.

We passed through the eastern border town of Umtali on the way to Hot Springs, which headed south towards South Africa a long, long way away. It was a lovely old border town with many old houses built on brick stilts to overcome the appalling number of termites in the region, corrugated iron roofs above and over-wide verandas with iron 'Broeki lace' decorations at pole and beam junctures. Unique in Rhodesia. I read a number of stories where young women in the late 1800s, desiring adventure and a change of life from the bleak weather in England, set sail to Beira, a port to the east of us on the Moambique coast, before catching a convoy of cattle-powered wagons and venturing up to Rhodesia where they settled, married and had children, forming several old clans in the region. Afrikaners also came and settled in the valleys near Melsetter, Cashel Valley and Vumba where deep, rich soils supported magnificent vegetable-growing opportunities.

Umtali became our second trading and export hub between Rhodesia and Mozambique and indeed the whole world, a route now cut off by British war ships when Ian Smith declared UDI in 1965, when I was ten years old. I will never forget being sent back from junior school to our home, where we all gathered to listen to Ian Smith on the radio, declaring our independence from mother Britain. We had seen what majority rule did to countries north of us and we would not accept the same mindless Uhuru to come and destroy our magnificent land.

I simply adored Umtali and later chapters in this book will show why, but for now we had paused for a beer at the Cecil hotel and then grabbing some superb shortbread biscuits at Mitchell's bakery, we were off to the dry and arid Hot Springs resort, about a two hour drive away.

It occurred to me that Carol was quieter than normal and she sat apart from me on the back seat, her face a ruddy, flushed colour. My ardour had cooled a lot and now I was just trying to have fun, putting off 3rd base for some other lovely girl in my life.

We arrived at Hot Springs, having driven through hot countryside sparse in vegetation and overrun with goats, many of which had developed amazing tree climbing skills, to reach the tender shoots of greenery. Goats, being the cockroaches of the animal kingdom, could eat just about anything to survive.

The entrance to Hot Springs looked familiar from the days when we would make day trips there from Umtali, with leafy green trees and grass kept watered by a bored looking individual. We passed through the gate at the back of nearby chalets and ended up in the very dry and dusty campsite, which was reasonably full. The hot water of the springs offered many healing qualities and had a very hot pool followed by a swimming pool with green paint and a concrete surround on one side, grass on the other and lots of flowers. There were change rooms, and a little tuck shop at one end of the pool. That's where we headed after setting up camp and bought a couple of Fantas for the girls and hubbly bubblies for Chris and myself. I also bought a packet of Sherbert that one sucked through a black liquorice straw, bringing back even more memories of childhood visits.

To the west, just a hundred metres away, was the Sabi river either quite flowing or bone dry or just a trickle in it. The latter was the case during this visit as we discovered during a walk later. When we paused at one of the pools of water I told the other three a joke that went something like this:

'Mugabe (the future President of Zimbabwe, whom we all detested, even this early in their struggle) was out walking near a lake with a couple of Chinese politicians, when he asked how Chinese people got their sing-song melodic names.

'Well,' said one of the Chinese men bending down to pick up a flat stone, 'we let the water sing us our name.'

'What do you mean?' Mugabe enquired.

'Let me show you,' the man said before skipping a stone over the water. It made a sound like 'tish-splash, tish, tish, tish.'

'You see, the water made a sound, so the person throwing the stone gets his name or his child's name from the water, in this case 'Xai-plish-tish, tish' he pronounced in a Chinese accent.

'Oh Mugabe,' said in wonder, squeezing his chin, 'let me try, us Africans will get a proud name, a big name!' and he picked up a flat stone to skip it over the still waters, which spoke 'Chim-pan-zeee' off its surface. The Chinese man looked mortified with embarrassment, as did Mugabe who picked up a big boulder above his head.

'No way is my water name 'Chim-pan-zee' we are Africans, we are proud people, I will show you! It will be a name like that of a Lion, a bull Elephant, a honey-badger!' and he threw the boulder into the pool of water, which duly sang his new name in a tower of water… 'Ba---boooooooon!'

Carol and Rose almost collapsed with laughter while Chris chuckled, having heard it before. Of course, the joke had to be told with a Shona accent, which, when mastered, turns it into an amazing piece of comedy, a real gut-wobbler. Carol came over to me and squeezed my hand and kissed me on the cheek, still chuckling away.

That night it was so hot we actually climbed into the hot swimming pool, with the stars shining above, to try and cool down, which worked when we climbed out and sat under the colourful lights with others, letting the evening breeze wash over is.

Our tent was like an oven and all thoughts of mounting 3rd base had deserted me. Instead we were annoyed by the unbelievably loud snoring from a man in a nearby tent, I have never heard anything like that ever again in my life. We all put up with it for about an hour at which point we crept out into the night to sort him out. I was highly amused that two other couples were standing there looking at us and themselves in the bright moonlight.

'What do we do?' one asked.

'Bang on his tent,' Chris ventured.

'Nah' said another, 'he'll just start snoring again later.' We stood there nonplussed when suddenly a lady said she had an idea and slinked away to the trailer in their campsite. She came back a few seconds later with a smile on her face and squints of enquiry on ours.

'Honey,' she declared and giggled. We looked at each other, smiling knowingly. We had fought ants to a bare standstill before retiring to bed, having put ash from the campfire all around our tent to get the black, nipping bastards out. Our victim had a completely sealed tent with big air vents atop which allowed a bit of air to go inside.

The lady very carefully unzipped his tent, which happened to be near his head, now exploding in huge vibrating waves of sound. She unscrewed the plastic cap on the tube of honey and dripped it onto his hair before drawing a long, sticky-sweet line to the nearest ant nest, which were easy to see in the moonlight. We were all giggling like mad and after a few 'high-fives' we slinked off to our tents, giggling away.

We waited with bated breath for about thirty minutes after which there was a pause in one massive snore followed by much slapping and a 'shit!' cried out into the night, followed by more slapping and cussing. We barely heard him land in the pool as we and other tents were crying with laughter! Ha! That'll teach the bugger to lose some weight and stop drinking so much beer! But even then, sleep was impossible for us sliding around in our sweat.

* * *

The next day we turned left out the gate and drove back towards Umtali, turning right at the sign post marked Melsetter, commencing a winding uphill drive that tore the heat and dryness out of our bodies, covering us in a cool blanket of air and greenery that was hard to imagine from the valley below. We turned right just before the village of Mutambara, coasting along amazing, mountainous scenery off to our left, the stunning Chimanimani range.

Our port of call was the whitewashed colonial-style Melsetter hotel where we quenched our thirst before racing to our rooms, depositing our few belongings whither they landed.

We set off to the nearby Outward-Bound adventure school that I had attended a few years before, along a bouncy, neck-jarring road until we reached a small car park.

It was only when I got out of the car that I realised the awesome task we had set ourselves in the heat that was already building up. I knew at the top of this very narrow gorge in front of us, which I seem to remember being called Bailey's Folley, lay the Bundi Plain, a flattish section of land surrounded by jagged, stunningly beautiful and towering walls of grey granite. Nestled in the plain were numerous pools ideal for swimming and cooling off in their frigid waters. But for now there was prickly heat to contend with and insects singing in high screeches that drowned out our laboured breathing.

The steep climb became slippery and dangerous, with parts of the path winding alongside a very nasty fall to a very nasty death. Fear previously felt on my course up here started to rise again. I turned to look at the ruddy face of Carol and when our eyes met she shook her head quickly from side to side.

'I can't do it Tony,' she said breathlessly, 'I want to go back.' I was so relieved because I didn't want to be the first to wimp out and calling out to Chris and Rose, we turned back to the car.

'We'll go a bit further,' Chris said with Rose nodding her agreement. I took Carol by the elbow and escorted her to a flat rock on the side of the path, some way down the hill, where she sat down with a plonking sound.

'You guys are a lot tougher than us Poms,' she ventured.

'I dunno about that, but we are much more tuned to the climate; are you okay?' She nodded and drank deeply from our water container. I sat next to her, noticing not for the first time, the line of her neck, her mouth, eyes, hair and lovely breasts rising and falling as she drew in the air. I kissed her on the mouth, tasting the saltiness.

'That's nice,' she murmured as we continued to kiss.

It was some time later that Chris and Rose returned, Rose looking about as defeated as Carol did earlier while Chris looked as if he could run all the way to the top again. I so admired him!

We got back to the hotel where we cooled off under swirling ceiling fans, downing several cool drinks each. Carol looked flushed against her pink complexion; she looked stunning and my heart ached knowing that nothing would ever develop between us. We spent an uneventful night at the hotel, hitting the sack after a few beers, even though I was under age at the time, it made me feel good. We got back to Salisbury late in the afternoon. I was truly knackered when Chris dropped me at my parent's house and I waved them goodbye before going indoors.

The next day was a Saturday and I was determined to reach third base with Carol. I could not let this lovely girl depart my life without a lifelong connection. I got a condom from a mate of mine and cycled to the place she was staying, with and elderly man called Tom and his wife.

Carol was delighted to see me and after having a cup of tea with Tom we went through to her bedroom for some privacy and a chat. We lay on her double bed and talked into the early evening, just talking and talking and having a good time with each other. My heart was thumping like a bass drum when I reached into my pocket and pulled out the condom, no doubt looking like a puppy wanting its food.

'I don't want to do that Tony,' she announced flatly.

'Why not Carol, our chemistry has been amazing, I thought this would be our next step?' She paused before answering.

'Having sex with you will change us, I have such a lovely feeling for you right now and once we've done it we will be changed for good.'

'But you're leaving soon to go back to the UK…'

'All the more reason Tony, you mean so much to me; actually I could fall in love with you quite easily.'

'What's the problem then?' She looked down at the crumpled sheets before simply shaking her head. She had tears in her eyes.

That was that, third base was not to be. I saw her only once more the following week and then she was gone, not to be seen again for a long time, leaving a huge hole in my heart with the pain of a novice still lingering somewhere in my heart to this day.

* * *

My timeline is out, so, regressing somewhat…school and its adventures carried on as did adventures closer to home with our neighbours. We were kids, no different from others all over the world, playing in the sun and laughing and competing with each other. Our neighbour over the road was Pete Cheney and his mate was Gavan Wales. It was always my brother and I against them.

We played war with our toy guns and put lumps of termite clay on the end of flexible sticks, slinging the mud at each other at incredible speeds that would take an eye out or knock one unconscious if struck, enhanced by a small pebble or two wedged into the clay. I only ever got hit once, contact being made on my left calf muscle and it hurt like hell!! On one occasion about ten day scholars fought a pitched battle against boarders on a field only a couple hundred yards away and what a battle it was! The field was lined with the odd termite mound and it had just rained the night before so we had a ready supply of ammo. I can still hear clay bullets whizzing past my ears at an incredible lick and by day's end we had hit two or three boarders for none in our team. We withdrew victorious at sunset with cusses and abuse following us as we trotted away.

The hostel for the boarders was literally behind Pete Cheney's house. In fact we could see the top floor of the hostel from my bedroom window. When building started there, my brother and I, at the tender ages of thirteen and fourteen years apiece, donned black clothes and home-made balaclavas before sneaking up to the construction site, commando-style on our tummies at about nine o'clock at night. My dad had bought a caravan and the tent with it had no pegs to anchor it down, so, having seen the building yard in daylight, we had seen ten millimetre square-twist steel rods, which when cut would make perfect pegs!

We crawled and slithered forward on our bellies, little whirlwinds of dust climbing behind us until we reached the security fence. A guard sat on a pile of wood about twenty metres away, floodlights silhouetting his big frame. We looked at each other and nodded, our streaked faces hiding our emotions of fear and anxiety.

My brother pulled some wire cutters from his pocket and gently snipped away at the wire until a hole big enough for him to crawl through had been cut. He had to pause now and again when the guard glanced in our direction, face golden brown from a flickering fire. And then he reached the first rod, pulling gently and firmly on it until the end reached me, whereupon I tugged until it was free of the compound. We took another one for good measure, commando-sliding until we were about thirty metres away, standing up slowly and moving off with our booty flexing on our shoulders. Once we reached the cul-de-sac that led to the school grounds we ran like bats out of hell, laughing like deranged inmates from an asylum. I had never experienced anything so exciting or liberating in my life!

By the next day we had hack-sawed the rod into four hundred millimetre lengths, bending each end to look like a hook. We triumphantly showed our dad, who although pleased, feigned displeasure that we had stolen the steel to begin with. My dad was an incredible softie and just smiled a thin smile at us while 'dressing us down'. We chuckled inwardly and drank an ice-cold coke each. In the end we only used one rod and the other lay inside the boundary hedge for many years, in fact it was still there when my dad died in 1992 and the house was sold. Who knows, it may still be rusting away there?

* * *

War with our neighbours was inevitable. Our level of competition rose and rose until one day genuine war erupted. We had built a very nice boxing arena outside my parents' bedroom window and we spent many hours boxing away, not too hard of course, but Gavan Wales was a real toughie and later, if I remember right, became an amateur boxing champion.

Needless to say my brother and I were tired of coming off second best and in a rather cowardly act beat the crap out of Pete one day when he ventured into our territory expecting to play with us.

Vengeance was swift. We came home from 'the club' one day to find our boxing ring totally destroyed and the tin cans forming our golf course holes dug up and our plastic slip'n slide shredded to bits. We used to love pouring water onto the long plastic sheet before sliding along on it on our tummies, drawing many kids from nearby to join in the fun.

My brother and I were horrified! We planned a strike back but kind of went overboard and got Pete's parents cussing ours because what we did was sticky-tape large 'Tom-thumb' firecrackers to the window of Pete's bedroom, lighting it and scurrying off on his bicycle. The window disappeared in shards of glass behind us and we tore off to completely destroy Pete's bike. We cut the tyres, cut the cables, removed the brakes and smashed the headlamp as well as the gyro that powered it, before dropping it outside their gate.

You can imagine, we had gone beyond the pale on this one and after an irate Mrs Cheney had disappeared from ear-bashing my mother, we were called in to face her! How terrifying! With Dutch blood coursing through my mom's five foot nothing frame, with a bite as bad as a Lion's, we stood trembling before her. We realised our fortunes were severely degraded, pocket money suspended until bills were paid, trips out cancelled, 'the club' off limits and so on.

'You silly twerps,' was all my dad said with his usual very thin smile, eyes flicking towards my mom.

'In fact,' my mother hissed with venom, 'get into your bedroom!' We knew what that meant and both of us began wailing in terror. My dad stepped out for a fag while we stepped into hell. My mom withdrew a thick leather belt with brass studs on it. Brian got his first and ran screaming from the room with a red welt on his bum, showing the indents from the buckles in 3-D perfection. I got mine and followed my brother screaming down the passage, holding a bum that was getting hotter by the second.

'I haven't finished!' mom shouted, sitting next to the telephone. She pretended to dial the home for orphaned children down the road, explaining to them that she had two very naughty children and she wanted to leave us with them.

'Mommy,' we shrieked, 'we're going to Beira on our holidays!! Mommy!!!' But she continued to 'talk', all the while her finger was pushing down on the receiver button, but we never saw that.

'Okay, I can drop them off tomorrow?' she said ending her fake call with a 'goodbye and thank you'.

We were beside ourselves now and our next tranche of punishment was to be sent to bed without supper or a Coke, which we got every evening as my dad worked at the Coke factory.

'No mommy!' we wailed as we were guided firmly to the room, door shut behind us, light turned off later by her hand that just appeared at the door. Don't mince with my mother! But much later the door opened silently and two sandwiches and a Coke each slid into the room on a tray, my dad's beefy hand pushing it along ever so tenderly, lest the ire of the dragon be aroused again! Good old dad!!!

Regarding my dad getting angry, I only remember his ire once and it happened when he was shaving in the bathroom. My brother and I were outside with a golf iron and a couple of balls. We could see dad's fuzzy outline through the opaque glass, moving to and fro. I don't know what got into our head's, or more accurately my brother's head, because we decided to either bounce a golf ball off the wall or try and clip it over the roof of the house to land on the grass the other side. I think it was the latter. A quick slice at the ball gave us the hope it would clear the ridge but it stayed at a shallow angle, zooming straight through the window our dad was silhouetted in! A perfect hole formed in the middle of the pane before wobbling and collapsing inwards. Our dad was paused mid-stroke with his razor, eyes wide like an owl, with a 'what the hell!' look on his face. We stared back with equal shock. My brother bolted to the right, emitting a mid-pitched 'narrrr' sound while my dad, still in his pyjamas, accelerated around the corner after him. By the time they had made one circuit of the house I was laughing so much I could barely stand! Sad to say the brass buckles made further indents on our flesh that day and I remain mortified I got included in the discipline. Oh well, one for all and all for one, they say!

* * *

Make love with the neighbours? Isn't the saying 'make love, not war' so true? Well, as we had not included some of our neighbours in this raging war, we kept our peace with them and it was not hard to do so with Marcia Payne. Her house had a swimming pool!

Marcia, one could say, was the proverbial ugly duckling that later became the most glorious swan you have ever seen. But in the halcyon days of our youth we ignored her freckled face and over-bite and oozed and cajoled and charmed our way into her dad's swimming pool at the back of their house.

Marcia's mom could see right through us and in her usual austere way made it plain that she 'was watching us!' whenever we came over to swim, which was mainly late afternoon and into the evening where submerged hanky-panky could be carried out unawares, but mom always seemed to appear when the vultures reached their prey and after a long time of attempting the impossible, I gave up. But it was great fun swimming there in the longish summer days and evenings, when the threat of an approaching storm, flickering lightning from bruised purple clouds and the arrival of millions of flying ants landing in the pool, would hurry us home.

But it was the odd night that the ever-watchful Mrs 'Pain' as we nicknamed her, was side-tracked and it was then that our costumes came off and we would swim au natural! This evolved, with some other boys down the road, into a challenge to see how far we could run down the road opposite the Payne's house (Auld Crescent) before anyone could see us. Well, we would dash off with white bums flashing like the soft white of rabbit rear bouncing off into the semi-darkness. I only had the guts to go two street lamps away; some did three, but my brother did four or more and I will never forget him sprinting back one night with a car illuminating his 'starkers' torso all the way back as he made a wild dash to the pool, just as Mrs Payne looked through the kitchen window to see what all the bother was about. It was innocent fun, a good laugh.

* * *

School to adulthood

School continued at its usual sluggish pace. I made the mistake of following my brother into sciences instead of the arts and paid for it with millions of tears of frustration, especially in my physics class.

The teacher had been there so long that he had lost the energy and desire to teach so he spent most of our allotted time telling stories and jokes, which the losers in our class enjoyed, but I was a serious student and got more and more terrified of my approaching Matric exams (Matric is like AS in the UK and is halfway between 'O' level and 'A' level. It was advanced enough to facilitate university entrance in South Africa, though). The final straw was when he told us this corny joke, accompanied by a sketch, of a jockey falling off his horse, accompanied by the rider, looking over a railing and all you could see was the big nose of the jockey, with eyes wide and the horse laughing in the background. It was too much for me and I went home crying my eyes out.

My brother came to the rescue fortunately and gave me his A level Physics notes, which I studied vigorously and even read them while the 'teacher' continued with his theatrics. I got to know the s, p, d and f orbitals of electrons and so on and was really pleased with myself when our exams came around. I will never forget that day, walking into the school hall with rows of school desks set up, a teacher up front as a monitor and one behind us, so we couldn't cheat and then the paper was plopped down on my desk.

'You *will* read through the questions,' a horn-glassed woman with a severe bun on her head chirped 'and when I say go, you will commence your exam'.

I looked at the questions. No.1 was impossible, the second one was doubly impossible for me to answer and so too the remainder of the twenty questions. I felt my lips go numb and the hair stand up on my entire body! The first question went something like this…

'Explain what a fish sees through the surface of water when it looks at an object above and use formulae and examples to show the refraction of light' or words to that effect. I was stumped! My panic rose and sweat trickled down my back. I looked at the other students and all of them wore the blank, terrified expression that I did.

I started to doodle on my paper and half an hour later I had drawn a picture of a fish looking at a human eye positioned above the surface and *that is all I wrote down in my physics exam!* I cleared my throat and told the monitor I was finished. Looks of terror and astonishment were flung at me. The dowdy monitor approached and flicked up my answer sheet, turning it over once before zeroing in with a dreadful glare.

'Is this all you have done?'

'Yes ma'am,' I nodded in agreement, sweating profusely. At that precise moment I thought of mom with the leather strap and brass buckles and felt the blood leave my head.

'You may leave,' the monitor said suddenly and before I knew it I was out in the hot, dry African sunshine with a chill running down my spine. All the lectures from my mom telling me that unschooled people struggle for money all their lives and 'you will live in squalor' came flooding in. So that's all I achieved in physics but got good marks in Chemistry, Biology and English (which I took up by dropping maths only three months before my exams). Although I detested maths I used to love going to class as the lessons were held at an all-girl school down the road by the name of Roosevelt High. I loved the attention I got in the hallways and was fascinated to see that girls used knives to carve the shape of a man's penis into their desks in the same way we carved naked girls into ours! It was an eye-opener. But in those classes I didn't do a stitch of work and failed every test; I just idled away looking at the girls until my teacher said enough was enough and I must find another subject to study.

* * *

Sport was where I truly excelled, not running or sprinting, nor long-distance but in field events like javelin, shot-put, discus and swimming. I particularly liked Javelin as anything to do with weapons or spears was right up my street.

I'm not sure that the people who taught me any of the athletic disciplines I liked actually knew what they were doing, apart from our universally talented all-round coach by the name of Mr Greenwood. What a gent he was and I can still see him in my mind's eye cycling down Clyde road from where he lived in Greendale, to take up yet another afternoon of athletic coaching but as our school had about nine hundred pupils, he could not be everywhere at once.

To counter the shortage of personnel, we were allocated staff members to come do their bit but in all honesty they knew very little about coaching me in the three disciplines I chose. My only prowess came from Mr Greenwood and when he started to notice talent in me, he came to my rescue more and more and spent an unfair share of time on my labours. I think he had an eye on me representing Mashonaland schools in the up-coming, annual inter-provincial athletic meetings, which is in fact was what transpired when I was about sixteen or seventeen.

School to adulthood

I remember one day, stretching my limbs to get ready for Javelin practice. I had, by now, got the art of pacing forward with the Javelin tucked under my arm before pivoting it into space. All done barefoot, which often resulted in me sliding over the launch line or pirouetting there like a Ballerena, thrashing at the air so I did not fall over said line. But generally, after two years of practice, I had it 'boned' as they say and the distance I threw got longer and longer.

One always gets a fly in the ointment and my school appeared to have a lot of flies, for I was putting in a good show when I half noticed a yellow Javelin coming back at me, or was I imagining it? I no sooner rid myself of the thought when the sharp point of the Javelin landed fair and square between the big toe on my left foot and the one next to it! As the gap in my flesh was somewhat narrower than the Javelin head, it had to force my toes apart to enter into the sandy soil, leaving a nicely removed piece of flesh from both toes. This resulted in me hobbling in circles, holding my foot in one hand while the other arm spun in circles like a lasso demonstration as I tried to keep my balance, eventually losing the battle to gravity.

'Are you alright dear?' a fat Walrus of a teacher shrieked as she charged at me like a bull elephant, 'you alright?' I decided to wind her up by telling her I had lost my big toe, holding my blood stained hand up for her to see. If there is a colour whiter than white, her face attained it and she blubbered spittle, sitting down next to me. I soon put her out of her misery and instead of her soothing my fears she ended up being soothed by me, but what the *hell* was she thinking!!??

I never quite got the hang of discus and found the technique of spinning faster and faster like a clock spring unfurling, a little too hard to master and due to that I mainly used the strength in my powerful arms to launch the disc, eventually achieving a reasonable distance.

But it was shot-put where I really excelled. I found launching those steel and brass balls really exciting and challenging and this is where Mr Greenwood, his hair combed straight back in waves, a bit of gold fleck showing in one tooth, would spend literally hours with me, long after sports ended at four pm or so. It was here that I mastered moving backwards at increasing speed, crouched, one leg back like an ice-skater waiting to pivot and bam a lightning twist at the shoulders and waist, adding massive leverage to my arm as I catapulted the shot into space. Suffice to say I cracked it for all my age groups and I think I am correct in saying that my records still stand at that school nearly fifty years later. In all honesty I had such a strong arm I could virtually throw the 'shot' instead of 'putting' it (a 'put' is not a throw, as throwing involves pulling your hand back as far as possible from your body whereas a 'put' was a rapid arm movement from the side of the neck).

It was during one training exercise that, bending down, facing backwards to the line of thrust, I did not see Mr Greenwood using a tape-measure on my last 'put'. I put immense power into the movement and tossed that twelve or fourteen pound shot further than ever before. It had no sooner left my outstretched arm than I noticed, with horror, that it was heading for the back of his skull where is would crush bone and pulp brain instantly.

'Watch out!' I screamed and thankfully the ever-alert instructor scuttled off to the side with the shot skimming his left ear! I now felt as stupid as the fat lady instructor, going almost as white as she did!

* * *

The long awaited day for the inter-provincial games arrived. Our team would be made up from both male and female (no theys' in those days, ha ha!) from every school in Mashonaland north and south, who would compete with teams from the five other provinces of Manicaland, Matabeleland North and South, Midlands and Victoria. In reality there were really only five teams as Matabeleland north and south became one team as did Mashonaland north and south. I was privileged to be selected for both javelin and shot-put in my age group and as a reserve for discus throwing.

I was as excited as anything that the meeting was to be held in Bulawayo, a five hour drive from Salisbury and I envisaged a lovely train ride as that was the normal way of moving loads of people. I could hardly sleep the night before and rushed down to the athletics field to await the arrival of buses that would take us to the station. My past experiences of school journeys to Bulawayo and Umtali to play Rugby buoyed me along as it would be full of mischief and fun and now that we had girls on board the sky would be the limit!

About thirty or more of us eagerly boarded the tired old maroon and cream buses from the local bus company, some waving goodbye to parents while others were already engaged in youthful chatter and laughter. There were no cell-phones in those days, with young faces becoming immediately glued to screens; it was a time in history where we communicated face to face with our mates and laughed and slapped each other's sides and goofed about.

The first sign of the horror to come was when I noticed that we turned right onto Jameson Avenue instead of going through the traffic lights that led to the railway station. Our convoy filed through the city, which excited the younger kids but for the older, more astute, we realised once we passed the Jameson Hotel that we were on our way to Bulawayo on a creaky old bus that couldn't do more than seventy kays an hour (40 mph). With stops and refuelling this would take eleven hours minimum! I was instantly pissed off and the shorts and T-shirt I had packed for sleeping in on the train suddenly became excess baggage.

'How could they do this to us!' I bleated to one of three people sitting on the rigid, thinly padded seat with a ninety degree back-rest. But we were young and the agony of what lay before us soon faded and fun and games commenced; bombarding pedestrians with bags of litter or on occasions, if they were kids, the odd sweet or two that would result in a near riot as hands clutched at the boiled treats.

After nearly four hours of this we began to tire and I dreaded what lay ahead. We had only reached Que Que, a town that would hold dreadful, haunting memories for me in the future, but I did not know this now. By midnight we had reached Gwelo, where one day I would do my officer's course in the army, a town which also holds harsh memories for me. The only claim to fame of that town, which became bitterly cold in winter, was its huge Bata shoe factory that supplied reasonably priced shoes to just about every person in the country, including the unique and much sought-after 'vellies' (pronounced fellies). Worn by trendy salesmen, who coupled it with their Safari suits, or the farmer who let it become rugged and split with bits of wire or fishing line holding it together, or the soldier or civilian. They were unique and Rhodesians, who eventually spread into the diaspora, still ordered them from as far afield as the UK, USA and so on.

We clambered down stiffly and ordered some chips (the packet type duh), a Fanta, some chocolate (getting awfully tasteless at this stage as proper Cadbury ingredients were hard to get due to sanctions) and swatted the odd, fat, lazy flying ant that fell from the fluorescent lights above us in the garage we had pulled into. Lightning flickered off to the north and a chilly, post-rain breeze blew over us.

I was freezing and dog tired when we scrambled aboard the bus, suitable only for very slow urban transport and now we had to find a place to sleep. Some lay on the stained, diesel-smelling floor, others crimped themselves into a space or wedged themselves at a peculiar angle. We had no sooner settled down than the driver turned the interior lights off and it was at this point I realised I was going to be incredibly uncomfortable all night. I lay down on the seat; my head was just short of a slightly large bum that wobbled against the top of my head, my legs stretched across the aisle, my torso covered by my tracksuit.

I soon got quite sore on one my side so I turned onto my back, as did a particularly tall Afrikaans girl straddling the aisle, who was due to throw discus for Mashonaland, lying opposite where I tried to get comfortable, feet resting next to my upper leg.

As she turned a bit more, wrestling with her own discomfort no doubt, one of her feet landed on my thigh and slowly but surely bounced into my crotch, which aroused instant possibilities of reaching second base without anyone knowing! Ha! I lay there with a mixture of guilt and growing excitement as her foot bounced up and down on my ever-expanding crotch in sync with the revolutions of the bus engine and uneven road. I adjusted my body to get the best rub out of it and before long I was climbing rapidly towards those fireworks and joy not experienced to date, by hand, body, or foot (!) when she suddenly turned again, taking my 'foot job' with her. I was left frustrated and did my best to get her to re-engage but I think she was on to me, well surely she was when her heel thumped down onto my thigh!

We awoke on the outskirts of Bulawayo at six a.m., our mouths thick with food congealed betwixt our teeth, stiff and totally pissed off! I could not believe our school or parents agreed to this horrendous form of transport; had they no idea!!!??

As I sat up slowly I caught the eye of the big Afrikaans girl and she batted her eyelid in a tease, blowing a kiss of bad breath at me, a cute smile on her lips.

'Come see me when you're a man', she mocked before shuffling to the door with the rest of us. I caught a glance of the driver's eyes as I departed the vehicle, noting the drug-induced, bloodshot gaze placed above a toothless grin.

'Thanks Bwana,' he quipped before I jumped down into the heat of Bulawayo, even that early it boded ill for a hot day. Fortunately Bulawayo is set in thorn scrubland and consequently the heat was usually dry.

I cannot really remember where the day's activities were to be held but I think it was Hamilton boy's school. We put our bags in a room before queuing up for some sandwiches and orange juice. I have always liked Bulawayo with memories of fishing and playing rugby here at this very school. I had been skinned alive on a rock-hard field when tackled by two brutes right in front of a stand full of female spectators. Standing up and looking brave, elbow and forearm bleeding heavily and in serious pain, I gave the best steely-eyed macho-man expression that my face could drum up.

It turned out to be a pleasant day, sitting around chatting to so many people of my age. We were blessed in that country, where dialogue flowed easily between both sexes and generally the language was clean. I revelled in it all.

My time came to partake in Javelin and as we only ever faced four opponents, or less if someone had not arrived, there were no heats at all. We threw the javelin three times each and it was basically first past the post. This is why we could do all sport disciplines for basically the whole of Rhodesia in one day.

I did reasonably well and even with a meter or two short of my personal best I ended up in second place. I was happy with that. There was no way I could have beaten the Orangutan from Manicaland no matter how hard I tried so it was okay. I even got a little smile from the Afrikaner girl who was competing in the ladies team.

But it was shot-put where I excelled, even though I was up against boys that looked old enough to grow beards and no doubt they trimmed trees with their teeth on daddy's tree plantation but you know, it's technique, not brawn, that wins the day in any sporting event. I got my movements down to a fine art, thanks to Mr. Greenwood and each of my 'puts' were longer and longer in turn. Two pairs of bushy eyebrows went up in surprise as the 'shot' left my hand, sailing through the air like a bullet. I can't be bothered to look up the weights of those brass balls in a search engine but I know that I started on about ten pounds in early senior school and ended up with lopping great sixteen-pounders in my last year. Today's event was with fourteen pounders. Using my swivelling body like an unwinding spring and a final flick from very strong fingers, at the correct elevation, the 'shot' flew away up to nineteen metres. Today I started out doing about seventeen and a half metres and almost reached my best, eighteen metres by my last 'put'.

It pleased me no end when the human tree-trimmers scowled at me and walked away sulking and my inner smile widened when the Afrikaner's smile was positively glowing. Second base tonight!

The remainder of the day was free so I watched some track events and dozed in the shade of a few stubbly thorn trees before falling fast asleep. I was so tired from the night before and it was late in the afternoon when I was shaken awake for the prize-giving ceremony. When my turn came to get the cup for shot-put I did not know that my hair stuck up at a steep angle 'bed-head' style and a piece of leaf was saliva-stuck to the side of my face. I didn't really know where I was, nor did I care!

After yet more sandwiches we headed off to the banks of buses for the journey home and when I looked at the stylish coaches other schools had provided I sunk into despair; another twelve hours with the pewter-eyed driver and an incredibly stiff back. Nothing else would get stiff either as the Afrikaner girl was not there, as were most of the former passengers. I later discovered that many of them chipped in for a taxi and went down to the train station to buy sleepers back to Salisbury. I was furious but at least this time I had my own seat and slept all through the night to meet, bleary-eyed, my mom and dad in the parking lot at the school.

* * *

I had many such tours away to schools in both Bulawayo and Umtali, the latter small city situated on the border with our eastern neighbour, Mozambique. I loved both cities as they each held special memories for me, Bulawayo for my uncle Ronnie and his kids, wild as anything and the fishing trips they took us on; the wet T-shirt girl being one of them. Or just gliding along the main street with the big dips at every road intersection, the streets originally designed to be wide enough for a span of oxen to turn around and of course the delicious melt-in-your mouth ice creams at Eskimo hut. Without spoiling any memories of people from Bulawayo, my memory of the Eskimo hut is that it was originally a drive-in ice cream and soda shop where you would wait in your car to get served, or was it the Gremlin in Salisbury that did that? Forgive me, I am 65 with a poor memory! But either way it was a great city and when I was an adult in the army I would frequent the Sun hotel, Grey's hotel and the Holiday Inn, the latter where I would once meet the second love of my life after an army call-up to the 'Russian Front' and there I entwined with her, feeling the roughness of my skin against the sheer joy of her smooth softness.

But Umtali holds the deepest memories of all other towns outside of Salisbury. Nestling in a steamy valley just off the Mozambique border, it was the gateway to many wonderful holidays I had in Beira with my mom, dad and brother in our converted ambulance caravan. Surrounded by blue hills and covered in lush vegetation, I adored going to play rugby at Umtali boys high where we got a regular beating in Rugby, although our first team often did well against them. I remember the embarrassment of warming up in front of a big crowd where our goal kicker, 'Rasty Erasmus' was trying to get a few over before the game began and try as he might they shimmied off in every direction no matter how hard he tried, initially accompanied by a

School to adulthood

few sniggers and guffaws but ten balls later the crowd was in stitches! This only pissed the kicker off even more and when a ball bounced back from the tall goal poles he hoofed it with an almighty kick and it duly sailed clean through the posts! He got a rousing cheer so he bowed eloquently, red faced, before the crowd.

I loved the smell of a coal burner there that prepared food for us in the dining hall after the games and the teas were resplendent and only second in awesomeness to Peterhouse high school, where I won the Javelin (well there were only two of us) and Afrikaner-girl batted her eyes at me.

As a kid we spent many, many wonderful times in Umtali on the way to either Beira or the back route to Inyanga, as my gran and granddad lived there in 10th street in a little house made entirely of corrugated iron which clicked and stretched in the sun and when it got too hot we would sit under the sweet-smelling Frangipani and drink drinks. My granddad always quaffed large volumes of whisky and would curse anyone, with Scottish temper in full flow from a six foot three frame, that if he 'wanted water in his bloody whisky he would have already pissed in it!' (his reaction to me after quite innocently offering him water with his Scotch and ice). Gruff old bastard but I loved him in my own way.

My gran was four foot going on three feet and dressed like the old granny in the TV series the 'Hillbillies', hair all tied up in a knot at the back of her head, wearing dresses that were possibly old curtains and a lovely smile to boot. A great cook that she was, plumping up my brother and I, all those shortbread biscuits, oh dear. The thing I remember the most about her was that her one top eyelid opened and closed in tune with her lower jaw when she chewed food; most odd indeed. The last memory I have of my gran is looking at her vomiting into the bath through the splintered door of the bathroom from the cancer that eventually killed her. They jointly loved a brilliant white budgie called Peter that they delighted in and took everywhere in the house. That bird lived such a long, long life but after me accidentally scaring it by slamming the front door near his perch, found him on his back stiff as a twig the next morning. I could feel granddad's eyes boring into the nape of my neck. We got a box and gave Peter a proper funeral that we put flowers on and made a rosary of stones to go around where he lay, to no avail of course as some critter came in the night and gobbled up its ripening takeaway.

The journey to Umtali to play rugby was always by train and that brings back the odd humorous memory for me, especially the times we played tricks on the boarders. It was trick but no treat between the day scholars and the boarders all the time, going away for sport gave neither them nor us any reprieve. Our favourite trick, especially for the new form one kids that rolled around every year, was to drink a beer form a dumpy bottle, wait for our kidneys to process it and then put the refined beer back in the bottle, neatly squeezing the undamaged cap back on. We then let it lie in cold water in the basin in our cabin before sauntering down to find some easy pickings.

These little squirts would look at us seniors in awe and almost fall over themselves to ingratiate us when we offered them a beer and a few sandwiches, which by the way were filled with bits of guts and frogs legs from the biology classroom and then we'd hang nonchalantly onto the cabin door to see their reactions as they guzzled the piss and took a massive bite from their saamies;

mulching jaws paused, gulps ended in near vomit, eyes pleading with us, faces going red while we squirmed with laughter, holding our groins lest we pee ourselves! There was no reprieve for them though, they had to finish the 'beer' and sandwiches or face serious manhandling and to this day my ribs rattle with mirth when I bring forth the pain on those little faces and the spitting sounds erupting from their cabin as we danced down the aisle, fully satisfied. Being a senior had its privileges!

There are so many memories of Umtali I cannot relate them all but one of them was going to the golf course which had a bowling green and there my mom and dad would plonk us while we spent endless hours running the gauntlet on the fairways, ever so green and adjacent to some pretty thick jungle-like vegetation. We would propel our toy planes forward on thick rubber bands and skip along free as anything.

On one occasion we met Steve Lunderstedt and his younger brother who we played with, like four Musketeers. I remember Steve's brother being quite a bit younger than us and we tried some rather awful experiments on him like saying poo tasted good and after he had done a poo on the fairway he picked up a bit and ate it! We howled with laughter and to this day I can see him with a big smile, poo dripping down his chin, giggling with delight. Similar substances also went down that willing neck including millipedes, commonly known as Chongololo's. They tasted just foul and the poor youngster soon had a swollen tummy and tears running down his cheeks.

Another favourite memory, simple in nature but profound for some reason, was meeting granny Lunderstedt. I seem to remember, well this is my recollection anyway, that she lived in a house darkened by wide verandas with diamond-paned lead glass windows. She made us feel so welcome and we would have tea and cakes, sitting on the old fashioned furniture with dated curtains and photographs surrounding us. The lounge abutted a gable wall, where the window was surrounded by creepers and on this day the rainwater was running down the brickwork and dribbling over the diamond-shaped panes of glass sat snugly in their individual lead frames. For some reason the sight of the water running over that pretty window, framed in greenery, perhaps a grape vine, will stay with me until the day I die. I was just so content, as all kids should be. We were unaware of the subtle political changes taking place in the country for that was a lofty sphere we did not operate in. It was our job to irritate mom and make kids eat their poo and at that we excelled!

* * *

Other memories in Umtali include climbing Cross 'koppie' (copse for the unenlightened), so named because it had a very large cross at the top, made of stone and mortar and was clearly visible from several parts of the city. The koppie was fairly high but when I was a kid the climb looked ominous, even more so when my brother told me to look out for Gaboon Vipers (evil-looking snakes with big diamond-shaped heads) that would stop a 'ticker' in thirty heartbeats. I was instantly terrified and spent most of my time recoiling from imaginary snakes in shrubs and the broken pathway. But once at the top it commanded a stunning view of the city and its surrounds and we would sit there, the warm air cooling our sweaty bodies as we drew heavily on a chilled Cherry Plum or Hubbly-bubbly cool drink and some chips or biltong (dried beef). I loved the place and climbed there often, whenever we got the chance.

It was a long walk but once we were down we headed for the main municipal swimming pool with its green lawns and sparkling water, buy another drink and more chips, before diving into sheer, silent heaven, rising with a 'woo!' and then swimming some lengths.

I rather fancied myself in those days but without being too vain I was told by several girls I was 'easy on the eye' and I would spend an inordinate amount of time splashing the reflective black tiles lining the top of the pool sides, set just below the long drain channel that sent the water back to the filter system. Splash and I would come close and look at my reflection. Lovely, if I may so myself and then a quick swish underwater to rearrange my hair and then up again to look at myself to see which hairstyle looked better on me. I was so intent in this vanity that I did not see two girls staring and giggling at me from about eight metres away. I blushed when I realised what was going on and sank to the bottom of the pool for as long as possible before coming up again. They had come closer, one dark haired and one blonde.

'What you doing?' the dark-haired girl asked inquisitively.

'Nothing, thought I had something in my eye' I lied.

'So why all the hair movement then?'

'Dunno' shrugging my shoulders.

'What's your name?' the blondie asked, darkie turning to her and whispering something in her ear, resulting in giggles.

'Tony… and you?' No answer, so I asked how old they were.

'Boys don't ask girls that question' they said almost in unison, in a forward manner.

'Who cares then' I shrugged. Darky (I cannot remember her name) moved hand over hand along the drainage gulley until she was very close to me, looking into my eyes. I swallowed hard when I saw the intensity and beauty of their green colour, light dancing in and out from reflections off the restless water all around us. She smiled and got between me and the steel pool steps I was now clinging to for dear life. Blondie sidled up beside her. My head was gently pulled forward and without knowing or understanding much of what was going on, I felt this gently writhing tongue slowly part my lips and explore the inside of my mouth. I felt my blood pressure rise or fall, who knows what and my head started to fall off my shoulders. I cannot even describe the feelings and emotions inside of me, they were so intense and these girls were no older than me! 'This doesn't happen in real life!' I shrieked in my head but indeed it was and all the while this was going on Blondie was running her fingers up and down my spine. Well you can guess what was happening south of the chord in my costume!

Almost on cue it was some type of signal for her to rotate and climb out the pool, her friend sliding past me. I was literally panting and dizzy I would have drowned had the floor of the pool been deeper than its five feet at this point!

'Our folks are having a braai tonight' blondie said, we live on the first floor of some flats painted blue opposite the Manica hotel, flat number two' and with that they were gone, disappearing into the ladies change rooms, giggling. I feigned a sore toe as I hobbled to the gents' change room, all bent over.

Thankfully we had arranged for mom and dad to collect us towards sunset and before we knew it we were showered and dressed at my Gran's house, heading back into town from tenth avenue and second street, or thereabouts. It was mostly downhill so the going was easy. My heart pounded but not from the effort of walking, I was quivering with excitement. I made myself look good in jeans, a black shirt and 'vellies'.

And this is what I loved about my youth, we were walking out alone into a darkening sky with no parental escort, no cell/mobile phones to call for help and not a glimmer of fear or anxiety in any of us, including my parents.

We found the place with relative ease and stammering with nerves we entered the moderately furnished apartment, windows ajar against the heat of the day and introduced ourselves to a smiling and welcoming lady that I assumed was their mother, which indeed she was. We got a coke each and a few nibbles before the girls took us downstairs to a communal garden where their dad was poking a reluctant fire, sparks floating up in volumes as he thrust in and out with a piece of iron.

'Welcome boys' was all he said and we nodded, calling him 'sir' in a rather stiff manner, which got the sisters giggling. Several other youngish adults, thirties or thereabouts lounged on chairs, biting into the odd snack, take a pull on a drink or blowing cigarette smoke up into the air. I couldn't believe I was here with these two girls, both of whom had scrubbed up rather nicely to put it mildly.

I have always been attracted to brunettes so there was almost a subliminal decision to gravitate to the darker of the two, her tan and youthful glow complimenting the sparkle of her small ear studs and a bit of jewellery around her neck. I loved the look of the ladies in those days, big hair, loose fitting trousers gathered at the waist, wide shoulder pads and excess lipstick, although the dress this night was a little less formal.

My brother and blondie connected and appeared to fade into the background so I sat with, well, let's call her Cheryl and chatted about the things fourteen going on fifteen-year olds talked about, where we went to school, music of the day of which I liked Pink Floyd, Bee Gees, Santana and so on. Our tastes were similar. She made me feel comfortable and relaxed and after a massive steak, potato salad and leafy salads, washed down by another coke and a promise of ice cream, Cheryl looked at her dad's back before pulling me out into the semi-darkened service alley, to the tune of Santana's 'black magic woman' which I adore to this day and pushing me gently against rough plaster started to kiss me with that amazing tongue of hers. I am not literate or descriptive enough to describe what I felt. It was just innocent and beautiful and full of steam and passion and in between each kiss I rested my head awhile and looked up at the stars dotting their Morse codes between leafy leaves and I just wanted to die from the bliss of it. I experienced this again a few years into the future when I stood at the very bow of the S.A.

Oranje mail ship on a breezy night, kissing Anne as the waves exploded into turquoise phosphorescence down below. 'Cheryl' and I kissed a long time, barely saying anything and apart from a bit of a cuddle with her near the fire, under dad's eye, we said very little to each other. We both knew I lived in another city and nothing would come of this but it did begin an exchange of letters that lasted awhile, until one day a 'return to sender' letter arrived at my dad's house. I will never know what happened to 'Cheryl' and would never know why she was so strongly attracted and vital towards me at such an early age.

* * *

The months of my youth turned into years but the life I loved remained so enjoyable that I only ever looked forward to better things. I am saddened by the loss of hope I see in many children today but back then life seemed full of opportunities.

I continued with my love of diving, spear fishing and underwater hockey, which kept me fit and brown as a berry. I so enjoyed spear fishing up at Kariba and entered the odd competition or two. It was a rather chilling experience as the lake was filled to the brim with massive Nile Crocodiles! In fact, one guy rested his spear gun on what he thought was a log in some greenery, but the log took off at a great pace, leaving him gasping for air when he surfaced. You cannot hold your breath when fear enters your heart and mind!

I found it disorientating and chilling when I first entered the water near some island where the experts said 'fish abound'. Well in my patch all I saw was a few guppies staring wide-eyed back at me but what I found most disconcerting of all was the trees of the original forests that still stood upright under the water, appearing petrified so to speak, their leafless branches looking as if they were trying to reach the surface in desperation, like long outstretched fingers. Many had fallen over and had become branchless trunks. They disappeared into the gloom, ever deeper to what must have been the Zambezi river once upon a time. Some even stood stark against the skyline in shallower waters, forming the iconic sunset-smeared backgrounds to tens of thousands of photographs tourists had taken of this phenomenon.

But right now I fanned along the surface with my flippers acting like small propellers, looking down for an opportunity to strike at a big fat bream. Well, as I said, all I saw were a few guppies and their slightly bigger brothers that skipped away from me at lightning speed when I approached. As I explained before, without a wetsuit you will quickly lose body heat and within an hour or so I was shivering, so I slowly paddled back to our launch where five or six others from our team had spread out to hunt. I pulled myself aboard, willingly accepting a cold coke from Dozy Donaldson before rubbing myself down. I was worried about my brother due to the presence of Crocodiles but after a short while I heard air being expelled from a snorkel and, turning in that direction, saw his blond head, face down, moving slowly toward us. I was so relieved!

A few of the guys came back with a reasonable string of fish threaded on wire around their waists; possibly Tony Dawson or Alan Thomas having the biggest haul but it was agreed by all that it was a poor place to try and win a competition so we headed out to another island and there the hunt was more successful. A hard-driving squall that blotted out the horizon soon ended play so we sped back shivering our socks off to the weigh-in and prize-giving ceremony.

I remember watching the boats returning from far and wide while people had a bit of banter, comparing notes, bragging, ate something or guzzled a few beers. We had already offloaded our one sack of fish and had it weighed. I wasn't optimistic we had done very well at all when I saw others teams offload two or three sacks full of fish but all of us went silent when Andre Rabie's boat came in towards sunset. This guy was a living legend in spear fishing circles and today was to be no exception. The bow of his boat had hardly slid up on the sandy shoreline when willing hands offloaded at least seven huge, bulging sacks! The thing that struck me though is that there were only two of them in their team. I think his mate was 'Stretch' Franklin but I may be wrong, fifty plus years after the event. Nonetheless it was nothing short of miraculous what they had speared and they weren't the terrified little guppies we had shot, these fish were monsters that any surface fisherman would have been proud of. I looked at Andre; he was a tallish superbly built man with a shock of sunburned blondish hair and a personality to go with it. He very sadly died in a friendly fire incident in the bush war that was fast approaching our lovely land.

'How does he do it?' I asked Tony while nodding at the pile of fish.

'He goes under the weed and turns around to face the light coming through a weed free area, the fish will be silhouetted while he'll be hard to see, then 'Bob's your uncle". I nodded and looked in awe at the mountain of fish in front of me.

Chapter Two

Beyond School

It was inevitable that at some point I had to grow up and plan for my future. My final Matric-level exams were only a few days away and I had been cramming up to the last minute, not seeing the light of day, which I hated. My fear of having followed my brother into the sciences cropped its ugly head again as I totally lacked confidence in all subjects except English literature. But try as I might to turn the clock backwards, I soon found myself in the hot sweaty hall where I attempted all the written questions to Biology, English, Chemistry and Physics, the latter being a complete disaster. I finished the Chemistry paper reasonably confident but burst into tears when I got home, realising I had given the wrong process for the manufacture of a certain chemical, I had given something very similar. Then into to the Laboratories over the next day or two for the practical papers in Biology, Chemistry and Physics. I did well in the Chemistry tests but Biology was not too good and Physics, well I could not draw the cartoons our useless teacher had taught us for an entire year instead of physics!

I left school in November 1972 and remember cycling to the 'club' to swim, eat a pie and mull over what had just happened. I took my school tie off for the very last time, tossing it on the grass before sitting down and thinking things over. What now? What do I do for a living? Actually, I have never answered this question over fifty years later because life sort of came along and took me by my breeches and did it all for me. I still don't know what my true occupation should have been but I suspect an investigative journalist would have been as close to my heart as anything!

All questions aimed at my parents about what I should do drew blanks from them. I had to make a plan. But for now I spent a few leisurely weeks at the club as did many other school leavers I knew but slowly and surely their numbers dwindled as they got ready to move off to University for the New Year. I was bored and irritable and one day; looking at the local newspaper

I saw Barclays bank was looking for trainee tellers and as a form of racially motivated selection existed I knew I had a good chance of getting the job.

My mom took me to Barbours or some other city-central shop and bought me three pairs of safari suits that consisted of shorts and a matching, open-necked top which would be worn externally over the short's waist. Long socks, up to just below the knee and 'Fellies' or smarter shoes finished off the attire. I tried mine on at the shop and felt a mixture of excitement and dread as I gazed at this guy with slicked back hair, smooth face wearing a darned safari suit! I didn't know whether to laugh or cry, I felt like such a dork!

'I can't wear these!' I shrieked at my mom from behind the change-room curtain.

'You look handsome son!' But I knew my contemporaries who would still be in jeans and T-shirts, laughing their jewellery off, sent me spiralling into depression.

'Mom!' I exclaimed to deaf ears as she proceeded to check-out. I promised myself no-one living or dead would see me in those clothes but at eight thirty the next morning I paraded very nervously in front of the assistant bank manager at Barclays Bank Cecil square branch. Much to my relief I saw that several men, roughly my age or older, wore the horrible outfits. A few female tellers turned to look at me and smiled encouragingly. I guess this wasn't going to be so bad after all!

I soon discovered though, that banking is an incredibly boring business for a trainee and I struggled to pay attention to what was being taught me, my mind wandering hither and thither. The course to become a teller was about six months long and the basics of banking and recognition of fake currency was all part of it.

I did the best I could and soon learned to handle my role at the enquiries counter. Business was slow for me as not much really happened at my post and the summer heat made me dozy and scream for the pool at the club. I was most definitely *not* used to working past one p.m. every day and finishing at four p.m. became simple torture.

But there was one amazing compensation for this dreary role, I got paid! All $250 dollars of it per month. This sounds little but back in the 1970s, to an ex school boy living at home, this was a simple fortune. It sure beat melting lead down and fishing out golf balls for an income. I had recently passed my driver's license and with my dad's minivan and a pocket full of cash a whole new bevy of experiences, fun and mischievousness beckoned to me. Of course my hunt for the lady who would let me reach third base continued unabashed but it never happened, although I did experience some lovely first bases (kissing) in the back of the van. But I was still shy and missed many, many opportunities to find a steady girlfriend. In fact I have never had a Rhodesian girlfriend, ever, even though they were not shy coming forward, it just never happened!

One of my greatest pleasures was to watch drag racing out west of the city and stock-car racing at the showground's Glamis stadium, plus speedway with off-road motorbikes. Most events happened on Wednesday, Friday and Saturday nights and many a time I went there, parked the van, a couple of mates and a drink or two and a braai on the go. Not many stadiums would let you light up a braai and cook meat while you shouted support for your favourite car or rider! I could also go to drive-in cinemas under my own steam now but it was always with my mates and I hungered to end my loneliness within that kind of bachelor lifestyle. Even then I wanted to settle down with a girl.

No matter how much I tried at the Bank I eventually gave up and it happened like this. I was standing at my counter, leaning against a glass partition, absent-mindedly watching a cup of tea being deposited on a shelf behind the teller closest to me. I wondered if I could shoot a rubber band into it. I picked up a bunch of skinny bands first and they all missed, with maybe one or two landing on the saucer. I bent forward and picked up a huge rubber band that had just come off a parcel and pulling hard, taking aim carefully, I loosed it at the tea. The effect was profound when this heavy missile landed in the steaming milky brown liquid, sploshing it all the way up the glass cubicle the teller stood in. She turned to get her drink at the precise moment I fired, only to see it cascading everywhere, an empty cup for sure and a pool developing on the carpet below. She shot me a look of disbelief and anger which made me go bright red and in an attempt to hide my embarrassment I turned away only to look at the scowling bank manager's reddened face! He cleared his throat and moved on after telling me to clean up the mess, apologise to the teller and get her another cup of tea! My resignation was on his desk the next morning!

Bored at home again I wondered what to do next and after reaching a state of frenzy my mother asked Pete's father over the road if there were any government jobs going as he was quite senior in Internal Affairs. To our mutual surprise he came over the following night to tell us there was an opening for a trainee District Commissioner in Plumtree in Matabeleland.

'What?' I said rather ungraciously, 'what's that?'

'District Commissioners run the affairs of the local tribesmen, it's a challenging and rewarding job with a good salary at the end of the day.' Mmm, I thought, me white Bwana with hunting rifle and Leopard skin on my wide hat.

'It starts on the second of January, I've taken the liberty of telling them you are coming. Here's the application forms. Get a medical done and if all is well I will get you the train pass closer to the time' and without further ado went back to his house over the road.

'Mmmm, District Commissioner hey? Has a nice ring to it son,' my mom chimed. 'You *are* going. And that is that!'

I spent my last Christmas at home for many a year, that being Christmas 1972. It was the usual fayre of delicious roast beef, double cooked potatoes, rice, gem squashes, cauliflower, peas, broccoli, roasted carrots and roast onions, covered in lashings of gravy. I think it was so delicious because my mother was not stingy with fats and oils which is where the flavour really comes from and in those days when our export beef was most sought after overseas and in South Africa, it was a meal made from heaven. Michael the cook would take liberal helpings back to his Kia, with a beer or two, relieved from my mother's lashing tongue at last!

My brother, I discovered many years later, dreaded coming to these meals as invariably my dad would pick on something that was not quite right (although everything in my opinion was perfect) and it would upset my mom and then all hell would break loose. My dad would vent his irritation by over-emphasising cutting the meat, really putting his shoulders into the effort whereas a fly walking on it would cut the meat in half. So that peaceful excitement disappeared, as did my brother as soon as he licked the last drops of custard off his spoon. It was such a waste of a potentially wonderful day.

The time to go to Plumtree in the south west of the country arrived quickly and one night I was dropped rather unceremoniously at the train station. I found my sleeper, got the bed fitted by a porter and looked at all the goings on around me, inhaling that all-familiar mixture of steam and coal and oil from the engine a few coaches ahead.

The night was unremarkable and on this occasion there was no dining car so I retired to bed, ignoring my cabin-mate's attempt to strike up a conversation. I just lay there, looking up at the ceiling, the odd orange platform light casting shadows from left to right before blackness swallowed all.

I fell asleep at about midnight, waking at six a.m. to the sight of the sparse thorn bush and dried grass of Matabeleland going slowly by the window, the steel wheels clack-clacking over rail joints. I figured we must be close to Bulawayo as there were people on the odd bicycle heading off to work, then some fences, a few goats and so on. Eventually roads appeared, more traffic and before I knew it we were sliding into the rather barren-looking station at Bulawayo. The engine hissed up ahead, forcing steam upwards in the chilled air.

I dressed quickly, nodded farewell to my cabin-mate and stepped out into the passage before alighting on the concrete platform, smart and resolute in my forever embarrassing safari suit, pale green in colour. Tucking my small case under my arm I strolled down to the ticket office to see when the train for Plumtree would be leaving. It turned out I only had an hour or so to wait and once I had established the platform, strolled outside to look at Bulawayo, its coal-fired power station spewing steam and smoke beneath a bright blue sky. It would be hot today and a bit of prickly heat ran down my spine.

I bought a coke and some rather dodgy looking edibles from a nearby vendor, his goods buried in a big steel box on the front of his bicycle. Actually, the raisin-type bun turned out to be so delicious I bought another one.

The train, powered by a diesel engine this time, departed on schedule and sitting in the rather sparsely furnished dining car, I watched a part of Africa I had never seen before, slip by. I am sure readers who lived in that part of the world will chastise my timekeeping but I think it was only a couple of hours and before I knew it I disembarked into a rather dusty, unkempt railway siding. There was no-one to meet me, well what did I expect a brass band and an honour guard? But it would have been nice to be met by someone, anyone. I asked a local (a colloquial name given to the Indigenous people, in this case proud Ndebele people, an offshoot from the Zulu tribe in Natal, South Africa) where the District Commissioner's office was and the slight point of his forefinger led my eye to a well-kept set of government buildings, whitewashed walls under a corrugated iron roof painted red. Leafy Palm trees bowed in the gentle breeze while the odd stray dog chased little wind devils. A lot of 'locals' squatted on haunches while waiting to enter the premises where all sorts of documentation like birth certificates, death certificates and passports were issued to them, all under the watchful eye of a moustache-brimming African sergeant dressed resplendently in a smartly pressed Marie(tea) -coloured biscuit uniform consisting of a broad-brimmed hat with red band, pegged at one side, held down by a chin strap, open-necked shirt, brown belt, shorts and socks of similar colour almost up to the knees, feet embedded in shoes so shiny I could see my body approach in them.

'I'm the new trainee District Commissioner,' I said to the sergeant. He must have thought I had said 'I am a District Commissioner' because his salute and foot-stomping was so immaculate it would have put many a Coldstream guard to shame on the parade square!

'Sah!' he bellowed, 'the office is there, number three,' he pointed with a muscled arm. I thanked him and sauntered along a polished veranda floor, knocking on the door of room three which was ajar in the heat. A motherly looking white lady in a thin, bluish cotton dress looked up at me and smiled.

'Hello, my name is Ballinger, I'm here to start training as a new District Commissioner.'

'Oh my dear, just in time for a cuppa, she said, 'come around the counter. My name is Elsie Buitendag, my husband is the Assistant Commissioner; they are both away today but you will no doubt see them tomorrow. Sit and have tea and a biscuit and then I'll get 'Lucky' to drive you down to your accommodations.'

'Lucky?' I enquired of myself, and, sitting down on a stool I became fascinated by the stream of people coming in to discuss the need for a death certificate or a birth certificate (plenty of those) and other administrative enquiries and needs like bicycle licenses and so on. It intrigued me that Elsie could speak fluent Ndebele with all its wonderful clicking sounds. Little did I know that learning this language would be one of my tasks but time would present that to me in due course.

Less than an hour passed until a character, straight out of 'Crocodile Dundee', made an appearance in the office. He was short with dark overgrown hair, an unshaven chin below rather unsavoury teeth which became the worst part of the smile he presented Elsie, before kissing her on the cheek.

'Tant, hou gaan dit?' (Aunt how goes it?) he spittled into her ear, bringing an instant grin and blush to Elsie's plump cheek.

'Ag, toe man!) (get lost!) she toyed, pushing his hands off her waist. That's Mr Ballinger there, the new recruit' (nodding in my direction) 'take him to your house.'

Lucky slowly and reluctantly let go of her waist to turn and introduce himself to me, adjusting his round metal-framed glasses to squint at me.

'Lucky,' said with an embarrassing semi-formal bow, taking my hand. A quiff of God knows what alcohol wafted over me. I was about to meet the wildest, most amazing alcoholic in the Universe. German to boot!

'Tony,' I said, towering over him when I stood.

'Let's get this shit outa here' he said picking up my case, 'follow me' which I did, nodding goodbye to Elsie, mouthing a 'thanks for tea' as I exited the now hot and sweat-filled office. I followed Lucky at a heck of a pace to his beat up Toyota Land Cruiser, his shorts pumping just above soiled and rough vellies. His old and shrivelled hunter's hat with long-departed Leopard skin band had a big T3M burned into it by something hot. It would, one day, become my favourite possession.

I cannot for the life of me remember where our accommodation was, no thanks to Lucky's driving, maybe past the hotel, turning left and then bouncing over the railway line and turning left again. There was only one neighbouring house quite far off to the left of the gate and in front of us stood my new home, a fair sized house in brick and mortar under corrugated asbestos roof sheets, floors shiny red of government standard.

'This is the lounge,' Lucky said with an expanse of his right arm. I caught a quick glimpse of rather sticky-looking deep chairs, a few tables and a six-piece dining room suite, 'open plan of course' he continued, hijacking my thoughts. He went into the kitchen to introduce me to the 'cook' who in the whole time I was there never cooked anything but the place was dust free at least, a major opposite of the sandy bush outside. We came back into the lounge with Lucky nodding his head, 'that's Andy's room' and two steps later, 'that's Alvin's room, but no other Chipmunks live here' at which he laughed at his own joke.

'This is your room' and waltzed into a Spartan room consisting of bed, sheets and blankets (never needed in the heat), a wardrobe, a side table with lamp and a chair. 'let's get a beer in us man' he said, dumping my case unceremoniously on the bed. Good Lord, it wasn't even noon yet!

I followed him into the kitchen where an old and sagging fridge stood, its door yanked open by Lucky, revealing layers of Castle and Lion beer. A few scared pieces of cold meat and salads quivered in their ranks.

'Sandwich?' he asked, tossing me a Lion even though I preferred Castle.

'Please,' I said, sitting at the kitchen table and the work of sloppy art Lucky performed on two slices of bread, a breath of butter, some Polony and a tomato but you know what, it was delicious as all food is to a young man and the first glugs of the cold beer tasted like Heaven but in all honesty I am not a beer drinker and I could have ended it at that first, amazing, no taste like it on Earth thirst-quenching gulp.

We passed pleasantries before Lucky announced that he was 'off' but not before at least two more beers had disappeared for my half.

'Wait here for your team mates to arrive and take it from there,' he said in a thick German accent before driving away. I still do not know what Lucky did, to this day, but I think he was an agricultural extension officer who helped the 'locals' know how to farm.

I sat in a deep chair with high armrests and slowly but surely tumbled into a deep sleep, with the hot air blowing gently over me.

The sun was just hitting the horizon when I awoke with a heck of a fright as a Bull Terrier jumped up on my lap, licking my face furiously like I was some long lost master, tail pumping in unison with his flicking tongue.

'Rastus down!' a big, rotund man with curly reddish hair ordered, 'down boy!' (several times) before Rasty found interest in someone's socks. 'You must be Tony?'

'I am,' I agreed, standing like a drugged man, shaking his hand. 'You must be Andy?'

'Correct, Andy Eherke, assistant to the Assistant DC.'

'Oh okay,' I stammered a bit, still drugged from the beer-induced sleep.

'Relax boet, want a beer?' I didn't really, but I didn't want to come across as all stiff and reluctant at my introduction.

'Castle,' I nodded.

His squat, tubby frame no sooner disappeared into the kitchen when a very handsome guy in his late twenties dimmed the light of the door, jet black hair slicked back, brown legs and arms matching his dark green safari suit.

'Alvin? I enquired, offering my hand.

'The very one boet…beer?' Darn, no wonder such a big fridge was needed.

'Andy's getting it, thanks.'

Then 'Mr Beer' himself arrived in a cloud of dust, alighting the stairs very nimbly considering the three beers at lunchtime. Rastus shot through the lounge like a bolt of lightning, almost bowling Lucky over!

'My boooooy,' he drooled in German (assumed by me), kneeling down to hug Rasty, his tail going crazy.

And so the foundation has been laid for a story covering six of the best months of my life. It would turn into a book if I had to write it all down in dialogue format.

The next day I was introduced to the District Commissioner and after a very quick glance up and down, smiled at me, revealing a gold filling in his upper left jaw. He was a handsome man with dark hair and tanned skin, a cravat hanging loosely in the vee of his safari suit top. Comparison with Clarke Gable would not be remiss of me.

I was assigned to issuing passports and was led by Alvin to my quaint little office, all on its own, out near the flag pole. It was hot and a bit dusty but an adequate ceiling fan stirred the liquid air. Alvin sat next to me and for the next few hours showed me how to check the requisite documents, fill out the passport in my best handwriting and record the issued document in a big ledger. I eyed the ledger with some trepidation because it had been brought across from Elsie and her handwriting was immaculate and stylish. That was not one of my greatest strengths!

After a formal introduction to the foot-stomping sergeant, who would serve me gallantly, collecting pies and cokes from nearby shops, for months ahead, it was the end of the day.

It soon dawned on me that I had no transport and although I could easily have walked to our rooms I never did in the whole time I was there. It was an unwritten rule to head for the hotel for a sundowner and that's exactly where Lucky's front car wheels led us.

We formed a twelve-something circle on the veranda while more beers, gin and tonics were ordered. I think I only ever bought one round there the entire time, they just seemed to flow!

I was pleasantly surprised to see the odd girl there although most looked a bit older than me, but the game of glad-eye and flirting soon commenced. I had just started on my second beer, feeling all grown up and part of the crowd when a big 'Dutchman' (Afrikaner) came out the hotel from the car park at the back, Elsie on one arm and two gorgeous twins my age in close tow.

'Buitendag,' he said in a gravelly voice, proffering a hand that looked like a coal scuttle. 'Deputy District Commissioner.'

'Tony Ballinger' I said trilly, fighting off waves of pain from a crushed hand.

'I hear you know Elsie and these are my two daughters...' their names could have been 'Dimble' and 'Numb' for all I knew because my ears closed, jaw dropped open (as did theirs, just a little) and Jannie Buitendag's hand clamped even harder over mine. 'Sit, sit,' he commanded, making sure the girls were as far from me as possible.

'A round of drinks,' he said to a hovering waiter and when I said beer he said to the waiter 'make it a coke,' and then to me 'you're only eighteen in May.'

I have *never* been so embarrassed in my life, especially when the twins' hands covered their mouths, giggling. I swore there and then I would get this big Dutchman back by hopefully spoiling his very delightful and well-protected girls and that is exactly what I set out to achieve. It enabled me to smile back at the giant of a man.

But you know, Jannie was a real softie and was the typical Afrikaans family man, devout, strong and very protective of his *volk*, his kin and I guess he extended that feeling to me, this wayward youth in the middle of the

African bush; he would take me under his wing. But that did him no good as far as 'Dimble' and 'Numb' were concerned, they were still my targets but oh, how to get at them with their Rottweiler of a father in attendance.

I spent many happy times at his house, being the willing recipient of Elsie's amazing cooking. There are few nations' women that know how to cook like Dutch women do, their cakes, koeksisters (sticky-sweet pieces of flour plaited together before being baked in the oven, with a few variants of honey and raisins added or just the plain original one dripping in syrup), roasts, pies et- cetera, etcetera; all main dishes done with lashings of lard and meat. No wonder the men were such giants, a few of whom resembled Jaws in the James Bond movies. And the eye-dances with the twins were electrifying and I could not decide who was the prettiest.

'You're coming with me tomorrow,' Jannie said one evening, 'have your bags packed for a couple of days away; I'll pick you up at seven a.m.'

I left the dinner wondering what was in store for me but went home and packed a few change of clothes and some biltong (dried beef that some call jerky) just in case I missed a meal or something.

Jannie was true to his word and picked me up in his lumbering station wagon spot on seven. I threw my bag in the back and jumped up front. It was a sparkling-blue-sky type of day. We bounced out the gate and then headed who knows where, possibly slightly north, north east into typically stunted Mopani scrubland, a tree that grew just a bit higher than the car roof making navigation without a compass impossible. The dirt track consisted of thick, congealing clay and I was amazed the old car could keep going, it was rough and every bounce in the road shoved a broken seat spring into my bum, snagging a bit of my safari suit shorts. I edged closer to Jannie to escape the annoying barb causing him to look askance at me.

He didn't say much as we trundled along, watching the sun climb into a whitening sky. The trees marched past our windows and in them would be found Mopani worms that fed off the leaves. The worms were massive, about the length of an adult male's thumb and in some cases as thick as the thumb. The locals would pick them off the leaves and roast them over an open fire, producing shrivelled appendages that looked like harvested foreskins but they tasted like peanut butter. I came to enjoy munching them.

About three to four hours later we reached a brick under shiny new corrugated iron building where Jannie dropped me off to wait for Andy and Alvin to arrive later. After a final wave of his hand Jannie's car bounced off into the distance, leaving me in a very sparsely furnished house and an African cook with a huge, beaming smile. I accepted some tea in an iron mug, standard fayre in the bush and sat down in an old comforter with even more springs escaping than Jannie's front car seat.

It gave me time to think of the twins and all the girls I had encountered back in Salisbury and the girl in the alley in Umtali. My mind fixated on Wendy Wigget, who I have traced down over fifty years later. She was my alternative to Rita (with the cute bum, at the 'club's' swimming pool) and indeed that is where I met Wendy. She was stunningly cute with blond hair and blue eyes with teeth and a smile to die for. She had a naughty sense of humour and in the time I knew her we were inseparable. My clearest memory of her was frolicking in the shallow end where I would go under water and holding her firm would blow bubbles into her belly. It sent her into peals of laughter and a throaty giggle, but under her elder brother's eye all three bases were strictly off limits although after going to the cinema in town once I managed to fire off a quick first base, which judging by our mutual reactions could have 'led somewhere'. Sigh!

The sun set like a ball of molten steel deforming into the horizon, leaving behind an intense heat the likes of which I have only experienced once or twice in my life, it must have been at least 49 or 50 degrees. Bugs screamed in the trees like banshees, their trill deafening. Mozzies started out on their nightly vampire buffet while flies went home to bed, to hopefully be sucked up by some nasty thing slithering in the night.

I was outside panting in the heat when a Land Rover and Jannie's station wagon exited a cloud of dust, misting out the dying embers of the sun.

'Thank (bleep bleep bleep) today's done,' said Andy when he escaped the heat of the Land Rover, nodding at me and heading straight to the fridge. Alvin and Jannie chatted as they approached me before easing gratefully into two easy chairs. Andy appeared with four beers and ignoring Jannie's distaste of me drinking alcohol passed me the coldest beer I have ever touched, running it over my forehead and neck. I glance at Jannie, half expecting a comment but he just smiled at me and said 'cheers'. I can honestly say the first few gulps felt like Heaven had touched base on Earth and I eased back into my chair to listen in to the banter of the other three men. It appears they had been on a pay run to a nearby African purchase scheme where local small-scale farmers sponsored by the government got paid for their crops.

Andy lit a fire, more for cheer than warmth and we circled it looking at each other in the orange, flicking light. It was an interesting evening of banter under the African sky, stars twinkling, dark out there, the odd wild animal whooping in the distance, no people for a hundred kilometres. It was exquisite and I felt so relaxed and at ease.

At about eight p.m. the smiling cook put supper on the table which consisted of huge steaks, each with streaks of fat running along the edge, nicely browned, mashed potato, peas and carrots and lashings of gravy. For any young man food is consumed with relish and that was borderline the best meal I've ever eaten. I got a piece of bread and after pouring a bit more gravy on the plate, wiped it clean. Jannie was treating me like an adult and even brought me a second beer. I suspect his strictness was for the benefit of his ladies but I was grateful nonetheless.

Time waxed on and at about ten thirty we all went to the stretchers cook had erected, covered in two sheets only and a pillow. But even one sheet was oppressive in our rooms, which accommodated two people. At about midnight Andy said 'shit!' and dragged his sheet down the passage. The bath was turned on and I could hear him sploshing the sheets in the water before coming back sopping wet to bed. I decided he had a good idea and while getting into the sheets was a bit chilly on my hot skin, it very quickly warmed up and by one a.m. the sheets were bone dry and a repeat soaking took place. I slept fitfully until the sun started to brighten the eastern sky and by then it was a little chilly, the dry sky not holding warming water vapour,

Watching the sky turn mauve, then pink, then orange then pale blue through the curtain-less window reminded me of the film Zulu where Chard went around waking his sleeping men and the sky in that scene was similar to what I was experiencing now. Birds started to sing and the orchestra of crickets became silent one after the other when they scurried back to their earthen grottos for safety. The cook was already hard at work and soon the smell of bacon cooking aroused all four sets of nostrils. I got up, washed the vital pong-manufacturing parts of my body, brushed my teeth and packed my bag while others followed suit, hair at erect angles and yawns voiding most of their faces'.

After a hearty breakfast that consisted of enough bacon to feed a division of men, toast piled high and to-die for flavoured eggs, tea in a tin mug, we set out for the day.

'Where you taking that?' Alvin asked when he saw me carrying my bag to the car, 'this is our base for two more nights.' Feeling a real 'wally' I retraced my steps to the bedroom before running outside, just in time to see three .303 rifles being loaded into Jannie's vehicle.

'What are they for?' I enquired

'We have loads of money on us to pay farmers at an irrigation scheme we are going to today, you can never be too careful,' Andy replied. Mmm, I loved weapons and was hopeful one would be allocated to me, which it wasn't as the three of them had passed basic weapons training from the Police.

We headed out in a two-vehicle convoy to a couple of sturdy barns not too far distant. Off to the right was a dam with some concrete water chutes and gullies that fed water to irrigated lands. The ground was divided into patches as far as the eye could see and in the distance stood a conical hill; whether it was inside Rhodesia or Botswana I knew not but the land to the smudged horizon looked vast with less of the scrubby Mopani trees than earlier on.

We had no sooner disembarked when an army convoy of about eight vehicles, a water and fuel bowser in tow, trundled past us. Rather bored looking white troopers gazed at us as they passed by, with a lone passenger in a door-less cab giving us a thumbs-up. It felt comforting they were out here as the first real shots of our very long civil war, the bush war, had just been exchanged the year before on December 21st 1972 at Altena farm when the owner Marc De Borchgrave was gunned down. Although the war had been limping along since 1964 they were mainly incidents in very remote areas and the day to day life of most civilians did not change at all. Perhaps another reason for our three rifles was for self-defence and I had just not been made privy to this information.

It was stiflingly hot again and much to my irritation we had to do the pay run inside a barn with virtually no access to air. Added to this was the pile of humanity waiting outside to get paid for their crops and flies and babies crying, with mixed aromas of fermented beer, baby poo and armpits adding cheer to the occasion. Four tables had been put side by side with hard chairs slid under them. Three uniformed District Commissioner levies brought in a large steel trunk from the back of Andy's Land Rover, chained and padlocked for security. They also sported an old, delightful, .303 rifle each.

The first table was where I sat. To my surprise I had to count the money out based on chitties presented to me by each farmer. Their crops had been assessed by 'Lucky' two days earlier and each farmer had been given a slip of paper with the crop type and its value in Rhodesian dollars. My time at the bank came in really handy and I had no problem pulling out correct sums of money. The eyes fastened on that cash box and what was coming out of it looked like school boys at their very first strip show. *Nothing* went unnoticed.

As soon as the farmer had received his wad of cash he went to Alvin at table number two, who entered the plot number and amount paid, which he duly signed for, if he could sign, which few could. Alvin had to put his signature alongside the farmer's signature as evidence and then said farmer moved to table three where Andy sat. Andy spoke the local vernacular fluently and after what seemed a long diatribe aimed at Andy, the farmer stood erect in horror and handed his money over to him. A ripple of anxiety and consternation swept through the crowd as the nearest farmer passed the news back and like wildfire everyone knew that farmer number one had had to give his money back to the white man at table number three!

What Andy had explained in the local language of either Tswana, Kalanga or Ndebele was that the money to plant the crops (which was a first to many a farmer here) was a loan, repayable over three years and every time the farmer produced a crop a third of the money would go towards the loan. Now, this is logical to you and I westerners but to these dear local folk it was confusion of the highest order! They had forgotten, either deliberately or not, to forget this agreement and before long there was a long, bickering argument going on between Andy and farmer no# 1 which was making many others fidget, sweat and go pale. It also had an effect on me as there were only six bolt action rifles to ward off maybe two hundred very excited gentlemen.

The beauty of the loan and repayment system was that if you worked hard you would do well but if you sold your hand-drawn plough and the seeds collected from the barn (next door) to buy beer and chase prostitutes then you would get nothing and be kicked off the scheme. To pun it, you would be weeded out and only true farmers would remain, which in fact is what happened. Farmer no#1 had been lazy and had produced a shoddy crop so the money he got paid only equalled the first of three tranches of debt servicing but to ensure there was no mutiny that would result in us being butchered, a standard one hundred dollars was given to the farmer for trying, but added to the debt!

The next few farmers had done really well and had produced respectable crops, donning their caps to Andy before walking outside, smiling and carefully counting more money than they had ever seen before. I did not fancy their chances of escaping a mugging but in those days there seemed to be a code of honour among people and we only heard of the odd robbery. And of course the success of these men helped the remaining farmers calm down a bit; maybe the white man could be spared a machete or two after all! The fourth table, of course, was occupied by Jannie and he stuffed the retrieved bank notes into another chest; from whence it had come I had no idea.

It was late afternoon by the time we had finished and I was drugged from fatigue, sweat and anxiety. Alvin told me to follow him and we walked down the road a bit to the earthen-walled dam where we stripped down to underpants, diving into its cool caressing waters, much to the amusement of nearby fishermen who had never seen a semi-naked white man before. To say the water was divine is an understatement and I revelled in it, going under into silence and then emerging to float in my back. The water smelled as all dams do in Africa, slightly muddy and in all probability was infected with the parasitic worm called Bilharzia which would burrow through your skin before ending up in your bladder where it would lay its eggs and start its reproductive cycle all over again after being peed back into water. But I didn't give a toss I was loving this and following Alvin's example we went over to the slime covered chutes and tobogganed down its green alleys having a whale of a time.

A honk on the Land Rover's hooter brought us to our senses and we scurried back to the vehicle like two kids, dressing on the go. We had both steel chests in the back plus the ledgers and before we knew it we were back at the house we had stayed in the night before, where we stored the money and cracked open some beers. Jannie was already there and the outside fire lit, which this time I welcomed as my body temperature had dropped, despite the heat of the day.

It was lovely to chew the fat and we laughed at some of the scenes we had witnessed during the day. The thing I miss the most about living in a foreign land, as I do now, is that people I know in the UK do not share our slang or style of talking, which is clipped and partially guttural without any hint of political correctness, spoken straight from the heart or one's ass to the recipient, which would often lead to swift verbal and sometimes physical punch-ups but after tempers cooled the guys would slap each other on the back and crack open a beer. It's just different here and perhaps the reason I am writing this brief memoir is to remind myself how it was. By ten o'clock I was dead beat and hot again so we repeated the previous night's sheet-wetting and slept quite well, to be welcomed once again by a gargantuan breakfast. No wonder I was putting on weight already!

It came as a pleasant surprise to me that today was indeed Saturday and it was decided we would go to a nearby river that had dried up to the point where only pools remained and they were literally filled to the brim with bream, which produced a rather muddy-tasting white flesh. However, soaking it in milk the night before transformed it into a perfectly acceptable fish when fried in beer batter.

Three or four fishing rods appeared from nowhere and Andy set about showing me how to fasten four hooks to a line onto which we pegged tiny titbits of biltong. We chose a grassy ridge along a steep embankment and with a quick flick the hooks and weights went flying into the water. What I have to say is without exaggeration but as soon as the hooks hit the water all four of them had been taken by a bream of varying size, some small and some big. To reel them in was no easy task and before long we had a growing pile of fish flapping about on the grass. Andy asked Alvin to get some sacks out of the Land Rover and within three hours we had filled four sacks. It got so easy we didn't bother baiting the hooks but just flung them into the hungry mass where the fish bit anything they saw. It was a complete massacre.

After a while Andy got a bit bored so he took the cackling, brandy-soaked 'Lucky' to the opposite side of the pool and started hammering away at some ducks with 'Lucky's' shotgun. He got a couple before the rest got away but not to be outdone 'Lucky' took his gun back and aimed at a circling bird, loosing both barrels. Well, no skin off 'Lucky's' nose but his aim was a bit low and the next thing Alvin and myself were being peppered by little balls of shot, some of which were not too kind. Alvin shrieked at 'Lucky' who in turn put his hand over his mouth, bent over and cackled like an old witch. I was thankful Jannie had gone back to town with the three armed levies and the money because if he had seen this display of weapon handling he would have gone ballistic!!

I will never forget the expression on our cook's face when we returned with two fat ducks and two hundred fish. His eyes looked like ping-pong balls, as we staggering under the weight of them. Fortunately Andy had bought his own deepfreeze, which was massive and now I could see why. The cook gutted the birds and fish before loading them into the freezer, the latter still with their scales on; there was just too much to do before the heat 'offed' them and I am pleased to say Andy gave the cook about ten large fish which he took home with glee to share with his extended family.

* * *

The days and weeks passed by with great enjoyment. There were several things that stand out in my mind. We had quite a few parties at our residence and single female teachers would join us as well as some nurses and single men from the police etcetera. We would darken the lounge to candlelight, put on records, dance in sweaty heat and simply enjoy our youth, which I guess this book is about really, recapturing my youth. I drank too much for a young man and do not remember many details from these parties and had no real idea if there was any female interest in me but I was still shy of eighteen and even though I looked a bit older, nothing stuck.

The one night the party was in full swing with most people outside, flames flickering from a braai, the moon a lopsided smile in the sky surrounded by glittery diamond lights. Lucky was going all out, turning in circles to the music on one foot, a half empty bottle of brandy in his hand, fag in the other; yet despite his skeletal frame he always seemed to have a lady to dance with. I was feeling very merry on my fourth Cola Cane, an alcoholic drink mixture of cane spirits and Cola with a reputation for killing many brain cells; in fact it was banned some time later for being too powerful.

It was while I examined the goings-on through semi-double vision that Andy came into full view, pushing a motorbike, Rastus flicking circles in excitement. It was common for Andy to go for a ride and take Rastus with him on the pillion. Andy very unsteadily put his leg over the bike, gestured to Rastus to climb on board (accompanied by inebriated clapping), pounded the kick-starter a few times without luck (guffaws, sniggers and laughter) only to realise he had not switched the fuel supply or ignition on. That remedied the bike gunned into life with an almighty roar (dog tail washing-the-drum motions amid cheering, wolf whistling) and Andy was off like a shot! But he mistook which side of the fencing pole was the 'gate' (there wasn't one) and which side was the fence, now hidden in the darkness. He chose the fence! His bike hit the strands with an almighty twang, impaling it at a ninety degree angle to mother earth, catapulting Andy and Rastus into space, landing with a yelp (Rastus) and a grunt (Andy) along with meat-bomb on road sounds.

Well, the crowd of spectators, myself included, literally collapsed with laughter and I mean deep, belly-wobbling laughter that went on and on, it was just so wonderful to laugh like that, especially at someone else's expense! The laughter was still going on when Andy ambled back into the firelight, a sheepish smile on his face and an even bigger one on Rastus's, no doubt the latter thought that was meant to happen and he wanted more, more, more!

The next morning I had to report to the doctor, a rather attractive German lady, as I had turned a strange shade of green, thanks to possibly eight or ten bottles of Cola Cane.

'You have alcohol poisoning,' she remarked in a cloned Arnold Schwarzenegger accent.

'I do?'

'Yes, I want you to go and buy some freshly squeezed orange juice and Vitamin C tablets and drink three litres of water by lunchtime.'

I thanked her and did as she instructed but after one disapproving look from Jannie I was sent home to sleep it and the log-chopping headache off. I have never had a hangover like that!

Andy too had taken the day off and despite a graze along his forearm he looked okay although his little piggy eyes were blood red. I enjoyed almost as much mirth when I saw him saunter past me in the lounge with a pair of shorts, T-shirt and takkies (running shoes) on. Rastus did forward and back circles to and from Andy and then they were out the gate. I spilled coffee all over me laughing at Andy's ungainly gait. His huge stomach oscillated to and fro, throwing him off balance so it was four paces forward, oscillate, pause, four more steps, oscillate and then with alcohol still coursing through his veins one more oscillation put him on the dirt road, belly up like a beached whale. It was such a funny sight I laughed uncontrollably. But kudos to him, he actually got up and staggered of out of sight only to reappear about forty minutes later with Rastus bloodied and whining. He had thorns and porcupine quills coming out at every imaginary angle around his head but his smile was still there, ready for more. We spent a few hours tugging the quills and thorns out of his head with a pair of pliers, narrowly avoiding slashing teeth if one was just that bit more painful to remove. What a dog he was, I loved that animal so much and would play rough and tumble with him plus chase-the-stick. His perma-grin-smile reminded me of Tinker and I would pull his head into my neck and tickle the back of his ears. I think I missed him more than any human when I finally left Plumtree. I can still see the patch of black fur over his left eye, to this day, a true canine pirate indeed!

* * *

Another memory, simple but profound for me was making friends with the game ranger at a nearby park, I cannot think where now, maybe Matopos but his name was Rich (surname escapes me). He was a handsome man with dark hair, a few years my senior. Well, he was more of a friend of our group from Internal Affairs than me but he treated me like the others, even though I was the youngest.

One night we managed to chat up some nurses or teachers at the hotel and long story short we decided to go and see them a couple hours after they got back to their accommodation. I can still see Rich and I going up and down on a see-saw outside their room, flicking stones at the window, laughing our heads off.

After a while the window sash slid upwards and the face of one of the girls appeared in the gloom.

'What you want, it's midnight?'

'Just wanna see you,' Rich replied.

'Go home you two!'

Then the face of the other girl appeared and her opinion was different.

'No, let them up,' and that's what we did. I had no idea why the window was so high off the ground but Rich put me on his shoulders and launched me towards the outstretched arms of the girls, now giggling away excitedly. My arms were still pretty strong from sport and it wasn't hard to pull Rich inside at all.

It was both embarrassing and exciting to be with the girls. A small lamp was switched on, a record put on a turntable, coffee was made (laced with a bit of brandy) and we sat back and chatted to the girls, laughing easily and enjoying the promise of what may lie ahead.

But by one a.m. we were all yawning and the girls said they were tired and had to work in the morning. Rich, by this stage, was on the bed of the girl he fancied, more to his age than mine and before long he was fast asleep, spooning her. I was paralysed with inexperience so I just sat on the floor looking up at the other girl, I know not her name.

'Come on,' she said simply, 'you'll freeze down there by four in the morning.' I sprung up like a jack-in-the-box and lay on the bed, my face looking into the hair at the back of her head as I spooned her. Feelings and emotions swept through my body. To feel her, smell her and absorb the warmth of her body was to die for, she smelled so lovely and womanly, oh, I could not sleep for a long time it was so exquisite, I just lay there listening to her breathing, a few gentle mews leaving her lips as she began to dream. So this is what it was all about I thought to myself, how lovely.

* * *

On one particularly hot Saturday a group of us drove out to a house in the middle of nowhere. It just seemed surreal that a brick under tile house could exist in the remote bush. It had a veranda along one side with a railing of ornate iron with full blooded roses smiling in the sun.

We sat under a couple of umbrellas and chewed the fat but as the heat of the day kept going up we decided to drive to a nearby dam where a braai was lit and easy chairs laid in a big circle. The aspect of friends sitting around a braai chatting is to me the epitome of life in any hot climate, it's just so lovely to be among friends of family. I miss it in the chilly climes of the UK where I live, where people seem more isolated somehow and getting together difficult to plan with the irreverent weather.

I looked at the dam and decided a swim was long overdue. Fortunately I went everywhere with a small bag in which I stored my floral 'Speedo' costume (cut tight into the crutch, not baggy like beachcombers) and a big towel. I changed behind one of the parked cars and walked slowly towards the water which was a bit cloudy and choppier than I first realised. I was still in good shape from my underwater hockey days so the attendant looks of enjoyment from the ladies was most welcome. I sheltered my eyes from the glare of the sparkling wavelets to try and see if there were any croc heads breaking the surface. A brief look at my audience and an 'oh well' under my breath I waded deeper and deeper into the water until I had to start swimming. It felt wonderful to have the cool waters caress my skin like an attentive lover and I propelled myself forward with ease.

About half way across I paused and looked back at the team nestled under the big thorn tree, smoke rising up leisurely from the braai and even at this distance a faint waft of meat cooking reached my nostrils. A couple of them waded in the shallows.

At that precise moment something skittered past my leg, giving me one heck of a fright. I put my face into the water and nearly died of fright as this dark shadow hovered beneath me! I was just about to scream in fear when I suddenly realised it was my own shadow! Ha! A similar thing happened in the Canary Islands later in the year when I had gone out too far, only to be terrified by my shadow on the sandy sea floor fifteen feet below!

However, I could not stop the surge of fear and bolted for the side of the dam I had initially started out for and was hugely relieved when I arrived safe and sound. I had totally misjudged the expanse of water and looking back the group looked small, almost like ants. What to do now? Dare I go back the same way? Could I suppress the fear I felt and just take my time getting back? I knew I couldn't so I started the very slow and painful process of walking back along the shoreline where stone and thorn did their best to make my journey horrid.

It must have taken me forty minutes to get back by which time the meat was gone, apart from a sausage and one a warm beer was kept in reserve for me. But I felt buffed and young and warmed by the sun and it turned into yet another lovely day in the freedom of Africa.

* * *

The following week we went to see Rich, the game warden, based I believe at Matopos National Park. He lived in a colonial-type house with brick walls and veranda under green corrugated iron roof sheets. Large boulders, typical of the area, painted the backdrop and a troop of monkeys could be heard gibbering away in some high thorn trees. A nice place indeed for a bachelor to live in.

I had, by this time, fulfilled one of my life-long dreams of purchasing my own rifle and, socialising with the very people that issued the license I had no trouble getting one for my Bruno .308 which I simply adored and revelled in the bandolier of shiny ammo that I brought with it.

Rich's eyes lit up when he saw the rifle, I will never know whether from interest or the gall he may have felt for me bringing a rifle to a National Park, without permission. Whatever the reason for his facial expression he soon smiled and invited the four of us inside where at least fifteen people, slightly older than I, stood or sat in various attitudes of indifference while chatting away to each other. We plonked our contribution of drinks down on the table and it didn't take Lucky very long to zero in on a bottle of brandy, his eyes lighting up like the proverbial child on Christmas morning.

I swivelled slightly and noticed, to my dismay, a distinct lack of females but oh well a boy's day out can be just as great, can't it?

'Let's see whose rifle has the best velocity,' Rich said suddenly at my elbow, much to my pleasant surprise, 'I've got a 30-06' and with that he disappeared into the room next door. I walked to the door of the room he had walked into and just managed to catch sight of a rifle cabinet stacked with rifles and shotguns.

'Expecting a war?' I prophesied without knowing it, for that is how Rich died, as the target of a terrorist's bullet.

'You never know,' he replied selecting a Winchester .30-06 in immaculate condition.

We passed through the crowd of onlookers in the lounge, attracting several who followed us outside. We didn't have to walk very far and soon came up to a wooden firing construct at the head of which looked like a shooting range, the target being a massive granite boulder at least four storeys high.

'The plan's simple,' Rich said, 'we fire on the command to fire, counting down from three and the first bullet to hit the rock is the winner. You must fire at that orange patch of Lichen and I'll take the whitish patch to the right.'

'Ok,' is all I could say but behind me the onlookers murmured a bit louder and I could have sworn I heard a bet or two being placed. 'what's the prize?'

'We've got some young ladies from the teacher training college and a few nurses arriving just now and the guy who wins has first dibs at a girl that we both fancy.'

'Agreed,' I nodded, a squirt of adrenalin pulsing into my gut.

We went forward and selected a sitting position each, loading one round each from the magazine.

'Best of three rounds,' Rich said, then, facing Andy, 'will you do the countdown? After saying 'one' you must say 'fire', okay boet?'

'No problem,' Andy said and then getting into the full swing of the event told us to take up our positions. We pulled the stocks into our shoulders, tensing slightly against the recoil. I had the patch of Lichen fair and square in my sights and then Andy started to count down to 'fire!'

I pulled the trigger but nothing happened while next to me a thunderous clap smacked my senses. I looked at my safety catch and it was still in the 'safe' position. I rested my forehead on my arm and sighed while all sorts of derisive remarks were made from the crowd, Rich and my so-called three supporters! 'Lucky' held his bottle above his head and did a little pirouette, giggling in a high-pitched voice.

'One-nil,' Rich said without compassion. I started to object but he wasn't having it. We reloaded and positioned ourselves once more.

'Fire!' and we both pulled the triggers simultaneously. A split second passed before two resounding 'thwacks' echoed back from the boulder, sending a troop of monkeys on a mad dash for safety.

'Tie,' the crowd chorused. I was in the game again. I glanced sideways, noticing Rich's lips were compressed into a thin smile. He loaded a round with a blue tip.

'Fire!' shouted Andy. The discharge crashed in unison but one 'thwack' echoed off the rock-face about a good half second before the other.

'Rich!' they all shouted and I sat upright looking at him grinning from ear to ear. Now I knew a .30-06 was faster than a .308 but at this range the travel time should be almost simultaneous; I was hoping to overcome my disadvantage by pulling the trigger a fraction of a second earlier than Rich.

'You bastard!' I spat, 'there's no way your round could have reached there so quickly! What have you been up to?'

Rich smiled and pulled another blue-tipped bullet from his pocket.

'Just a 'few' extra grains of powder,' he chuckled, his wide grin forcing laugh webs at the corner of his eyes.

'Bastard!' I repeated, 'you cheated so it's two nil to me!'

'Whooaaa,' went the crowd, 'sore loser' and other jibes...

'Nope, I won fair and square boet, no mention of charge was made...' and with a chuckle he stood up, rifle stock under his right armpit. 'Just light fun man, let's go shoot some Vervets (monkeys), one of the little bastards keeps raiding my fruit trees and other stuff, plus they wake me up before dawn doing the tango on my roof.'

I was well pleased and followed closely behind him. Everyone else lost interest and so Rich and I set out on a lone hunt. It was great being with Rich, I really liked him and his easy-going nature and we threaded through the rocks looking for our prey which had become elusive due to the crash of rifle fire. Walking with rifles, as we did, would soon become a familiar thing for me when I soldiered through the Rhodesian bush war. That was only a few years away. Already the once peaceful and happy land we knew and loved was slowly changing, with men going on call-ups into the army and the sense of safety driving in the countryside fast evaporating. Perhaps those wise enough started to emigrate, what we called the 'chicken run' and slowly but surely things started to change and it would never recover, eventually sliding down to the evil rule of Robert Mugabe and beyond.

But for now I was young and the war only a mild nuisance at this stage. We went this way and that through rocks, dodging thorn bushes and avoiding the crunch of leaves under our shoes, as far as possible. Movement in a tree about sixty metres ahead caught my eye just as a panic alert was sounded by the Alpha male. Rich gestured to me to take the shot and leaning up against a tree I steadied my breathing, waiting for the fidgety target to settle a little and when it did I squeezed the trigger. I just caught sight of something dropping to the ground.

'Nice shot,' Rich said patting me on my shoulder. I made safe before working my way forward and then I was there, looking down at this poor little animal, eyes mostly shut, a red patch in its chest, blue balls signifying it was the Alpha male.

'Good shot,' Rich repeated, but I felt awful looking down at the little, crumpled body, its wives and offspring screaming madly in the distance. I had come of age with regard to killing and I didn't like it anymore, this was not a frog exploding in my mom's bathtub, this was a lovely little animal that loved life. I felt a real shit.

'They won't bother me again,' Rich nodded and as I stood there I wondered how much man had pushed animals back and back and back in *their territory!*

By the time we got back to the house a party was in full swing. A seventeen-seat coach, packed with girls, had arrived and now everyone was on the grass outside, talking, laughing, smoking and drinking while 'Ventura Highway' by America wobbled the woofers of large speakers. I got a drink of brandy and Coke and then slowly wove my way through the crowd to see if there was anyone that took my fancy but while a few of them did I felt dejected somehow and chose to go and 'talk' with 'Lucky' instead. 'Talking' to 'Lucky' was a misnomer actually as he got really close to your face, his round John Lennon style of glasses almost touching your cheek, his breath a mix of a distillery and breakfast cereal, some of which lingered at the corner of his mouth, his right arm around my shoulder. But you know what I loved it and just sat there laughing my head off at nothing which inspired 'Lucky' to talk even more crap.

The state of inebriation of all of us was enhanced by what Rich had concocted, a fruity punch made *inside* several watermelons. He had cut a hole in the top of each of them before removing a portion of the fruit. Into each melon he poured a mix of Brandy, Whisky, Cinzano, Gin and any other substance he could find before plugging it up and then leaving it in the sun to ferment! The percentage alcohol must have been fifty percent because after one glass, washed over chunks of ice, it was an instant brain killer. A lovely sense of numbness crept into my senses and suddenly 'Lucky' was making perfect sense and with our arms wrapped around each other we hugged and laughed until we ended up on the grass, no doubt killing any interest any of the girls may have had in me and all I remember (vaguely) is that it was very dark when we drove home and how we got there is anyone's guess. I slept until lunchtime the next day, duplicating the alcohol-poisoning treatment from not so long ago and accepted a lift to the club to have a swim.

I ordered a 'bloody Mary' and sat with my legs in the cool, blue inviting water, looking into its depths. A ripple caressed my calf muscles and looking up there were the 'twins' in front of me, 'Dimble' and 'Numb' in bikinis! I looked rather quickly to the side to see if Jannie was zeroing in like a class nine torpedo, falling into the pool in the process, but he was nowhere to be seen. I surfaced to face two smiling, pretty young women and I smiled too, well who wouldn't?

I spent a memorable afternoon with them, laughing and happy, splashing each other in the pool, blowing bubbles in each other's bellies and so on, just getting to know them. I loved their Afrikaans 'eccents' but evening approached and soon their sheriff arrived and with a curt nod Jannie took them home.

I spent another month sitting in a stuffy office swatting flies, eating too many pies and cokes and decided at the end of the month to hand my notice in lest I end up like Andy, fat and sluggish and perhaps another version of 'Lucky' to boot.

My final month passed very slowly and when the day came to go down to the station with the three of them to say goodbye to me I felt really tearful and wondered if I had done the right thing. The recent memory of the twins moist eyes made it much harder to go. But in the end I waved to my three remaining 'Musketeers' through the window of the train and they waved back until they were small dots. And then they were gone, forever. Another season, another chapter of my life story had come to a close.

* * *

I went through school with Alan Roodt, a tall, wiry guy with a smile that never seemed to leave his face and when I got back to Salisbury from my experience in Plumtree, the fun I had had with him during my school years picked up again. Our mischief was always innocent and he was my best man at my first marriage to Diane Faulkener nee Saint nee Dymock.

After school and on weekends, Cliff Kelly, Barry Munro, Alan and I would pile into his green Mach 1 Mustang (we could get driver's licenses at sixteen in those days – far too young in my opinion) and do what kids did! We would go to the drive-in movies on Friday nights, to both the drive-ins, the one on the Umtali road and the other in Mabelreign. We could tell we had arrived at the Mabelreign drive-in because the police had erected a scene near the entrance of a head on collision between two vehicles, with dead and dying people (dummies) lying next to it, one through the windscreen and others on the ground, covered in very real looking blood. It was put there to remind people like ourselves that speed kills, not that it impacted Alan one jot as he would normally leave a hundred metre streak of burnt rubber on the tarmac! Man that Mustang had power!

In those days there was a basic charge for the car and a fee per passenger to enter a drive-in cinema, so it was common for one or two of us to squeeze into the boot at the ticket gate and why we were never searched is a complete mystery because once we were inside, along with other cars pulling up near us, people popped out of boots like jack-in-the-boxes all over the place! It was just good fun and we goofed on the swings and slides up front with a 'doctored' drink in one hand and an ice cream in the other, much to the annoyance of the small kiddies there.

Occasionally a girl would come with us and the windows would become a bit steamy. Although only innocent kissing it was never me doing the kissing!! I was starting to feel like I had the plague but you can see from the photos in this book that I was a good looking young man so why, why, why? Could I not read the signals? Was I too shy?

As the three of us had access to vehicles as kids we repeated the above scenario quite often, except I had my dad's Morris Minor minivan. There was no boot in that type of vehicle, but it did have a spot for a blanket! And Barry had, if I'm not mistaken, a Morris 1100 Sedan, the one with a sloping rear window. Once again no boot! Our parents were letting us down buying cars that could not hide passengers in a boot; how dare they? Ha!

Now that I was without work and back in Salisbury living with my parents, the fun reignited. Alan belonged to a boat club at Lake McIlwaine, about thirty kilometres outside Salisbury on the road to Bulawayo. It was the main source of drinking water for Salisbury but also supported a national park, a hotel and several boat and yacht clubs. I cannot remember its name now but it was opposite Admiral's cabin and was probably the most popular there.

On the way there one day, along the Oatland road, which at the time was dirt, we zoomed along in Alan's Mustang. A bunch of locals and their kids waved at us and we waved back. I looked at Alan and a wicked thought crossed his eyes.

'Watch this,' he said before accelerating backwards, then braking. He reached into a bag and threw a huge wad of sweets onto the dirt road behind him. The 'local' children ran up to get the sweets, shrieking with delight, at which time Alan put his foot flat, allowing a few hundred horsepower to spin the back wheels, showering the kids in dust! Alan laughed so much he nearly spun us off the road and I too joined in gut-wobbling laughter as we gyrated down the road.

For many years I thought that was funny as no harm had come to the kids and they got some sweets to boot, but times have changed and it was not a nice thing to do. But the rebel in me, at the time, thought it was great fun and not many months later Barry Munro and myself repeated it up at Inyanga in his Morris 1100 but I laughed more from the lack of tailspin than I did at the kids getting covered in dust!

One evening we went to the hotel at Lake McIlwaine as a large party was going on there and it was great to see so many young people and pretty girls all in one place and I was soon 'happier' than normal but, forever unable to start a conversation with a young lady I sauntered down to the boat jetty where a few couples were necking. Lights fractured off wavelets and a cool breeze blew off the water.

It was while I was sitting there, reflecting on life, that I witnessed a very funny event. One of our well known radio announcers staggered towards a boat that had two massive engines, anchored by the bow and stern cleats. He stumbled and fumbled along, trying to get keys out of his breast pocket, his partner ten sheets to the wind and about ready to go to bed on the grass. They eventually made it into the boat with border-line avoidance of immersion into the cold, dark waters and after more fumbling the man started the engines, which screamed a mighty roar in neutral. Donning a sailors cap Mr Broadcaster put the engines in gear without reducing the revs and the boat took off like a bolt out of a cross bow; but there was one thing missing, he had loosed the front bow line only while the one at the rear had been partially undone on the boat cleat, causing it to unravel like a hissing Cobra and wham, the unravelling rope came to a dead end in a big knot. Naturally the boat came to an instant standstill, the rope smacking the water in a mighty whiplash. As this happened my eye just caught sight of both of them flying forward off their seats, landing with a thump and a crash in the lower part of the cockpit! The boat's engines were still screaming away and the bow swung left and right, seeking escape. I cracked up laughing as a few others did and after making sure they were okay we went our way, chuckling to ourselves. The moral of the story is to undo the tie-lines on a boat before you take off, or rather not drink to oblivion and then try to drive a boat, take your pick!

* * *

It was actually at this stage that I met Carol and she is mentioned earlier in the story because it's easier to talk about events in blocks rather than in a linear timeline, which would make the book easier to understand but would be incredibly long, weaving in and out of similar topics. For example if I told a linear story, the mention or referral to underwater hockey and events relating to it would have to be mentioned innumerable times whereas lumping all underwater hockey events (and others) into a story-block gets rid of that complication, but it does mess with the overall timeline. Complicated, I know!

Despite getting to know her and the fun that that entailed a yearning for adventure never ceased to grow and getting back almost full time into underwater hockey enabled me to get fit and trim down again as my drinking had started to get to exceell and that is the last time I saw him; he died a few years later in a contact with terrorists, a lovely young man gone, leaving a grieving wife behind, who I think was pregnant at the time.

Chapter Three

Africa to Australia via Europe and back again

Although this book is primarily about my youth, coming of age and my married life in Rhodesia, my journeys after Durban are worth mentioning as my experiences were varied and interesting. I had always loved my 'uncle' Armour and 'Auntie' Jean, whom we had met up in Rhodesia where he worked as a land surveyor and now he was back in Durban with his wife and four children, two boys and two girls.

I arrived there in great anticipation of lovely, relaxing times ahead as I had saved virtually all my bank and Internal Affairs income so money was not an immediate worry. But I did not know that I would meet Veronica, my 'cousin' and meeting her turned into a life-long 'fatal-attraction' relationship for both of us, that still digs my heart-strings to this day but not so for her anymore. I put their relationships to me in Italics because they were distant blood relatives of ours on my mother's side. I think Aunt Jean and my mother had the same grandparents or something to that effect and so 'Aunt' was an affectionate title given to Jean and 'Cousin' to Veronica. It would have been legally and morally acceptable to have married Veronica.

Although I was only eighteen at this stage of my life and Veronica was about thirteen, we had instant chemistry towards each other. She was physically very mature and looked more like a sixteen year old than thirteen and she had these big, wide enquiring green eyes, gorgeous lips and a very nice body. Okay, not something kosher to talk about, maybe, but I was a boy then, just a few years older than her.

I spent a terrific two weeks there, surfing with Veronica and pretending to be a lifeguard at Durban's main beach as I had a lovely body and stood there looking at the bathers with sunglasses and a tracksuit top on. I had more than one kid come up to me and ask where first aid was as 'those bleddy blue bottles have stung me my maat!' and I would point at the real lifesavers over at the tower, chuckling inwardly.

I went out at night to Umhlanga rocks and ate prawns at Gordon's prawn and then eased through the various sophisticated hotels on the beachfront, forever hopeful! I did meet Barbara Bray though and we swam a lot the next day and met up in the evenings and kissed in an alley but her father was very protective and in the end told her she could not see me anymore. What's new? I thought to myself.

The two weeks went by and then it was time for me to head off to Cape Town. Luckily an old friend of 'uncle' Armour was about to head off to George in the Cape, situated on the coast, three quarters the way to Cape Town. The only downside was that I had to ride in the back of their pickup which had vegetables in it and something that smelled rank but I couldn't find it.

I am pretty sure I saw tears in Veronica's stunning eyes and my heart was skipping when I hugged her goodbye. Our paths were to cross several times in the future with many knee-wobbling 'close calls' but we never made love, as much as I wanted to do most of my life; she left me breathless for some reason. I climbed into the little brown van and waved at her through the back window until I had lost sight of her. I felt really low right then but after three hours of bouncing around in the back I fell fast sleep only to awaken at lunchtime at someone's farm.

I sighed, asking myself if this was our destination and after a negative to the same question the old man driving, said, 'just stopping for a break with our friends here.' I eased my stiff body out and stretched, running my tongue around my mouth.

'Come in for coffee and bikkies,' a handsome woman of about fifty said, which would be most welcome in my forever empty stomach. We introduced ourselves and then sat for possibly the nicest coffee I have ever tasted.

'Gee that's lovely coffee,' I remarked.

'Thank you, we actually grow the Chicory that's inside it.'

'Chicory?'

'Yes, it's a plant root which is roasted to take the bitter edge off a dark-roast coffee. We blend our own here,' then looking up at a young lady who had entered the room she said, 'Donny, why don't you take Tony on a little tour of the farm?'

We looked at each other and there was instant welcome in her eyes, her mouth widening to a small smile. As for me, yes she was a bit of a wow. I wore pale blue jeans and sandals made from old car tyres with a pale yellow T-shirt and a surf board on a necklace around my neck. Yes, I *am* vain and

Carly Simon would be proud of me but I knew she had few visitors like me on her oupa's plaas (father's farm) and so I followed her outside into the bright sunlight, the cheeks of her bum pumping up and down. She too wore pale blue jeans and a long-sleeved white top knotted at her belly button.

Oh boy do I fall in love easily, you may have noticed by now but we instantly clicked as we walked along in fields of Chicory. She bent down and pulled a plant up, snapping a root in half, handing it to me.

'Lick it,' she said and immediately regretted it, it was so bitter it made my lips curl and I spat my saliva out in a hurry. She reeled with laughter, her hand across her mouth.

'Wow, how the heck does that make coffee taste nice?'

'Come with me I will show you,' and off we went to a big barn. As we approached it a lovely aromatic smell danced in and out of my nostrils. 'This is the end product after roasting the root,' and she held up a palm full of powder. Its taste was so mild and its aroma so delicate I could hardly believe it was the same product. But time marched on and after a couple of hours in her delightful, youthful company we headed off into the dust once more, her arm waving until we were out of sight.

Sliding doors ... what would have happened if...?

* * *

That night we ended our journey close to East London and climbed the steps of a very spooky wooden house that creaked like mad all night. These were yet more friends of my hosts and I spent a fitful night looking at the bedroom door to see if someone entered with an axe or if something would float in with a long coat and hat on! I was totally exhausted at a surprisingly early breakfast and almost fell asleep face-down in the very tasty oats porridge made for me.

Well, I slept like crazy until we reached Plettenberg bay where we stopped for a snack at the Beacon Hotel on central beach, an amazing place to stop really as the hotel is built on a spit of rock where the spray from big waves would splatter against the windows. The sea was warm there and clear and it wasn't long before I was doing broad strokes parallel with the beach. Then back into the van and an hour and twenty minutes later, having traversed beautiful scenery (the garden route in South Africa is exquisitely beautiful) we reached George, our final destination. A jet of adrenalin squirted into my system when I realised I now had to hitch-hike to Cape Town nearly four hundred kilometres away. The old boy let me out the back of the van and I said my thanks to both of them, giving her wrinkly cheek a kiss and him a firm handshake.

'The train station is over there son,' the old man nodded towards brick buildings, 'maybe you can get a ticket for Cape Town?' I could have kissed the old boy and giving a thumbs-up headed over to the ticket office to see what was available. I was in luck, a passenger train was departing at two pm so I bought a ticket and a pie and sat waiting on the platform.

At roughly two fifteen a steam engine, pulling perhaps fifteen coaches, sighed and hissed into view, not bad time-keeping for Africa really. I showed the conductor my ticket and was given a cabin to rest in until we reached Cape Town at about nine that night. I plonked my bag high up on a rack so no casual passer-by could see it and then set out to explore, checking my balance as the train moved off with a bit of a jerk (we threw the jerk off later!) and soon found a very pleasant dining car and observation lounge right at the rear of the train. It was filled with tourists and holiday-makers and after buying my favourite drink, an Appletiser, I squeezed into a seat right next to a big window. I had a nice guy to chat to the whole way and later on the setting sun squinted through mountain saddles, covering the most breath-taking scenery in various shades of gold. I will never forget it.

When I got to Cape Town I was met by some relatives and taken to their comfortable suburban home where I stayed for a week. I can't remember their names but one or both worked at the Argus Newspaper and so for a few days I was employed by them as a filing clerk which was great as I earned some extra money. And then the day arrived for the greatest adventure of my life to date; to get on board the S.A. Oranje, a Royal Mail boat that weighed about thirty six thousand tons, carried one hundred and ninety one first class passengers and five hundred and ninety one tourist class passengers. It was a dream come true and I breathed in the smell of her and the waters of the dockyard as I clambered up the steep gangway.

I dumped my bag in my cabin before racing out to explore the ship, finding myself at the stern with loads of other people my age or thereabouts. This was more like it! I stood there in a party mood as the ship was eased away from its berth by two little tugs and before we knew it we were moving northwest with Robben Island off our starboard bow. I revelled in watching the big screws churn up the water behind us with seagulls darting here and there to snap up the remnants of the odd fish killed by the passage of the ship or food waste being thrown overboard. And the smell of the air, it reeked of freedom!

The heady excitement gave way to slight fatigue so I wandered inside and soon found a comfortable lounge near the upper decks and joined a group of people I would spend most of the two week journey with. We were all thrilled and excited when large unbroken rollers came towards us from the port side, as we were heading further north now, waves almost as high as where we were sitting but because the swells were far apart all they did was lift the ship up in a gentle corkscrewing motion, leaning to starboard before rolling back again. It was an awesome experience that captivated all of us in the lounge and the odd wooooo! would escape someone's lips when all thirty six thousand tons heaved over. No doubt these waves were part of the current full-moon tide and would crash all along the Cape in steaming anger. No wonder it was called the roaring forties around here and it was time well spent watching these massive mounds of water angle towards us, some so massive I genuinely felt scared. Apparently the Captain did not fear as he had no intention of turning the ship bow on into the waves and so we wobbled along for a good few hours.

It was a marvellous two week trip and I experienced being dunked in the pool during the crossing of the equator, coming first in a fancy dress completion where we dressed up as the South African censorship board, one board member being Old Mother Hubbard and I represented one of the films they heavily censored namely the 'Last Tango in Paris' and I wore a sign around my neck that said 'Last Mango in Parys' (Parys being a town in South Africa) and I was dressed up like a Mango!

I spent most of my time sunbathing and eating great food as well as swimming and dancing in one of the two nightclubs, watching shows and so on. Nothing but nothing beats a good sea cruise. Yes, well I tried to get some girls interested in me but on this occasion I was just having fun although a girl called Anne appeared to fancy me and one of my sweetest memories is taking her by the hand to the very bow of the ship and, leaning over, looked at the explosions of phosphorescence against the steel hull as little sea plankton shivered off light after being disturbed. It was wildly windy and the stars shone as if from some imaginary bridal train in the heavenly host above. I pulled her close to me and we kissed deeply. I could feel the warmth of her against the chill air and in a way I cannot explain, it was like everything around me simply vanished, all other senses just switched off. It was electric. But nothing came of that and I didn't pursue her, much to my own surprise.

* * *

Arriving in Southampton was a dream come true. My dad was English and as a result I used to look at a map of the UK for hours on end, wondering what the place was like and I had heard that English girls were willing to come forward and were liberated.

My tan certainly drew stares and smiles and my word a double-decker bus painted red just passed by and a police bobby in peaked cap wandered down a street. Ooohhh, red post boxes and phone booths, it was just like in magazines and the girls wore knee-high boots with short skirts and the jackets had fake fur lining, long hair escaping train-driver, newsboy and Gatsby hats, just stunning, like the movies!! I spent one night in London with the crowd from the ship, minus Anne and we went to a three-storey high discotheque which was such an eye-opener and after plucking up courage to ask a girl to dance I was shot down in flames by being told to 'fuck off'. I almost staggered backwards. Then two black guys asked where the toilets were and after listening to my tale of ignorance they nodded at each other and said, 'fucking South African,' and then to my face 'we don't need you in this country, fuck off!'. I was so taken aback by both verbal assaults that I stood there with my mouth open. It looked like fisticuffs were about to start when Vernon, a very big and powerfully built guy in our crowd asked if all was okay. One look at him and the two boneheads pushed off. I was dumbfounded, I thought the English were like nice little ladies in a corner sweet shop but I soon discovered those little old ladies had chiselled teeth and a long, forked tongue. So much for my introduction to the UK and it began a lifelong love-hate relationship with the English. But the gall of the two blacks telling a white man to leave the UK has stuck with me to this day. (I feel it only fair to say I have made some superb English friends since I came to live here in 2002)

The next morning I caught a train to Brentwood, East of London where I met all my dad's relatives and ended up lodging with our very sweet aunt Dot and her dear husband George. I was fascinated by the English countryside that rolled by, so green and interesting, I had only ever seen such green grass in Cape Town and on a patch of cardboard that belonged to my miniature railway set, made in England.

My aunt was very generous indeed and fed me like a herd of pigs day and night and in next to no time I felt my jeans getting a wee bit tighter. But before they arrived home from work to let me in, I walked over to a field nearby and just stared at the leafless Oak trees, traffic passing by in the distance, red double-deckers among them and so I sat down under a tree to try and picture my dad's youth here and also knights of old and

German bombers soaring overhead and so the two hours I waited passed very quickly and when it was time to get up I discovered two or three things about English fields, don't sit on the grass for you *will* get a cold bum, a wet bum and most assuredly would have sat on a dog's turd, which abounded everywhere!

My aunt managed to get me working on a building site where a new medical centre was being built and I soon discovered what physical labour was, something few whites had experienced in Africa. I remember, for example, a truck load of three hundred by fifty kilogram sacks of cement arriving and calling *three, yes three* labourers to offload it we set about doing so, having to carry the sacks to a dry section of the building about thirty metres away. This took hours and I was totally knackered at the end of it with my face and clothes covered in cement dust. I must have looked the same as Harry, his face was streaked with sweat but he seemed fine, a short lad he was too. I so enjoyed the bath that night, only to learn my aunt was horrified I bathed every evening ('we have one bath a week' she had chimed) so I paid her extra for the hot water.

The next day when I saw Harry he still had a lot of the cement dust in his hair and the sweat streaks were there also, like the remnants of an old waterfall down a rock face. I caught a wiff of him too, not pleasant.

Now, being a virgin and a foreigner to boot I was the target of many pranks and at tea break one day, Harry asked me to buy him some Kit-Kat and a few packets of 'three'. I wrote down the order of a few other guys and walked maybe sixty metres to a 'granny on the corner' type shop. I placed the order, picked up a Mars bar for myself and then asked for a few packets of 'three' from the old lady smiling sweetly at me. Well, the smile disappeared, heads swung in my direction and her filed, saw-teeth flashed as she hissed menacingly 'this is not a chemist young man, you can get your bloody condoms there!' Good old Harry, I discovered he could run pretty fast when I got back to the shed that acted as our canteen!

All good things come to an end as mine did one Friday afternoon when I was caught warming my hands around the fire where scrap timber was burned. I had just finished a long day of carting concrete in a wheel barrow to a foundation trench and I was tired and now sweaty-cold so I decided to warm up a bit and anyway it was only twenty minutes to clocking off. Well, some tosser in an overcoat, like you see in English police detective movies said, 'Oi, you lazy git, all you ever do is warm yourself, pick up your cards on Monday' and so I was fired on the spot, which to this day I feel was grossly unfair as I had worked as hard as anyone. I had also heard that old-timer expression of 'pick up your cards' for the first time. In those days employees carried a card with their details on it and you would buy a holiday stamp and attach it to the card every week when you got paid and in this manner ensure you had money to take leave when you were due it. Paid leave for construction workers was unheard of back then and the card system was what worked before commercial computers had been developed. I was now unemployed (again!).

I spent most Friday and Saturday nights up in London, being wowed by the night life and teased by all the XX and XXX movie posters. It was a world far from swimming in the concrete chutes of Ingwiza dam and the thought of it made me very homesick. As for finding a girl here it would have been easier to get to the moon without a rocket as London is a very lonely city. In fact all I attracted was gay men, literally every time I went to London a gay guy would be after me. What's wrong with me?

Anyway, my Uncle Jeff had an idea. He ran a small business fitting roof trusses and other basic joinery and carpentry work in houses and employed aunt Dot's son-in-law, Norman, as a Carpenter/Joiner. He offered me a job as a labourer, which was very kind of him and we would set off early in the winter mornings to erect roof trusses and attach the branders to them, then sort out skirting and any manner of things. Now Norman was a comedian of note and one thing I love about the Brits is their sense of humour. He often had me in stitches but the one time he made me laugh so much I stepped on some loose scaffolding and fell onto the snow below, cushioning my fall. It was a simple thing that made me laugh, a bit naughty really and it was when he put the metal end of a hammer between his thighs, up near his crotch and pretended to masturbate the handle, tongue hanging out, making loud sexual noises while down below an old granny, bent over, pushing a walker, head covered in a scarf, fumbled by. It was just so funny the way it happened and how I caught it with my eye, that I became paralysed with laughter, stumbling slightly before falling eleven feet into the snow below.

I soon got tired of being a Carpenter's assistant and going home to a pleasant but boring house in the evenings. I started to scan the newspapers for work and in one of them was a big advert for staff at Pontin's holiday camp in Prestatyn, North Wales, so I sent in my application and was accepted almost immediately. I bought a train ticket, said my thanks and goodbyes to that fine family group and headed into the unknown. My dad's family were awesome, they had grown up in Symonds Yat in Herefordshire and when their parents had died from TB the five of them were split up and sent to different foster homes all over the country. This must have been appalling and led to serious insecurity in all of them to their dying day. I saw it in my dad so often and I think it was transmitted to me as I lacked confidence during my officer training in the army a couple years hence, almost being booted off the course because of it. My dad's siblings only reunited many years later and unanimously decided to settle in Brentwood to be near each other.

The countryside was so pretty as I journeyed in a fast train to Liverpool and from there I caught regional trains and a bus until at last I was at the holiday camp. One cannot describe an English holiday camp of that era unless you've been to one. It was a mixture of loudspeakers, piped music and staff in wicker hats and striped jackets, rows of basic accommodation and a barbed wire fence all the way round. In my opinion all that was missing were guards in coal-scuttle helmets shouting 'Raus' or 'Schnell!', restraining vicious German Shepherd dogs on a leash. I entered this strange world, my employee pass shown at the gate and then I was escorted to my room which was in a barrack block, two beds inside, a wall heater, a table and that was it. Bogs and showers at the end of a long corridor. I was next to the bogs so I often had loud explosions in stereo coming through the flimsy walls.

Now, without waxing on about my time there, a few noteworthy things happened. I joined as a 'Linesman' without having a clue what a Linesman was, only to discover it was a glorified name for a Dustman. The local council did not service the camp so the owners had bought their own truck and we passed along the back of rooms to collect bin bags from the couple hundred dwellings. We threw the bags onto the back of the truck and carried on until all were done, then drove out the gate to the dump. I was fascinated by what people threw away and at the dump I got an almost new suitcase, a pair of brown leather shoes with the price tag still on it and a nice carry bag to name a few of the items.

As always I was restless (I still am today age 65) and so I kept my eyes open to do something else. My chance came from an angle I did not expect and that was the indoor camp swimming pool complex. I spent every minute swimming after work and was still a fit and powerful swimmer. I think I impressed the senior lifeguard because he came up to me and offered me a job as a trainee lifeguard. I was thrilled to say the least and after waiting a few days for the transfer I started work in an environment I love, well not the steamy smell of chlorine but the water itself. The staff set about training me to save a swimmer and resuscitate him/her and I just loved it. After a few weeks I passed my test and was allocated the viewing chair to watch the large pool below me.

I saved three people in my six months there. One was a rather tubby gent that headed to the deep end from the shallows, bouncing up to the surface and then sinking to the bottom before coming up again and this proceeded calmly until he hit the four metre deep diving well, where he sank like the Titanic in its death dive and never came up again. I rather maliciously watched him thrash around a bit to teach him a lesson and then, disrobing, dived from the tower to help him. His eyes were wide in panic and his mouth was opening and closing like a fish in an aquarium. I knew he would try and latch onto me, which he did, but I had been trained to cope with that and pushing hard on his jaw I eased him up and rotated him, getting my arms under his armpits, his face in my hands. He relaxed then and I frog-kicked to the edge of the pool. To get him out I put his hands one on top of the other on the poolside, with my one hand on top of them and then lifted myself free of the water. I then turned and pulled him out and being a chubby little kangaroo I was happy for helping hands that appeared from nowhere. Fortunately he was breathing okay, if a bit rapidly so no saliva-sucking air-blowing into lungs had to take place, thank the Lord. The thought of it made me want to puke.

The second save was a young girl who panicked in the deep end and the last one happened by the grace of God. I was just about to lock up the pool when I heard a faint splash and a whimper behind me. I turned back out of curiosity only to discover a boy about three to four years old thrashing around on the bottom of the shallow end of the pool. I dived in clothes and all and took him to the side where he took a deep breath and commenced crying and screaming at the top of his lungs. I did my best to placate him and in so doing did not see his mother approaching like a Lear jet ten feet off the ground.

'Joey!' she shrieked, 'Joey!'

I said he was okay and calmed both of them down, which took a while and then after profuse thanks she led the sniffing child away. I have no idea whatsoever how that boy got into the pool but if I had left the building five seconds early he would have died.

One of the lifeguards was Andy Ligemar, a county long-distance runner, who may have even run for England if my memory serves me well. We became fast friends as his humour was so similar to mine and after work, where the sun only set at eleven p.m., we would run along the beach for miles and miles, it was just amazing that I could run like that, maybe it was being at sea-level that did the trick as Salisbury in Africa was thousands of feet above sea level and with my asthma, a battle of a place to breathe in.

On one occasion we stormed along the beach but I knew in my heart that Andy was just doing me a favour by pacing me and getting a little bored he zoomed ahead of me and up and over a sand dune. I followed in his footsteps only to meet this horrifying apparition of a screaming man running back at me, mouth and eyes wide open, arms outstretched with what looked like black clothing or flesh hanging off him, like an atomic bomb survivor. The smell hit me the second he passed me and all the while his scream carried on, fading slightly as he ran to the sea a few hundred metres away. I started to laugh in my belly, welling up to a loud guffaw that climaxed as a high-pitched laugh I am known for. I was laughing so much I stumbled and rolled down the sand dune. Poor old Andy, a man who did not like humanity, griping about the shitty little kids in the pool all day, had run clean through a broken down barrier straight into a slimy, foul-smelling, disused waste recycling pond full of human shit! Ha! The proximity to the dunes had allowed sand to blow a crust over the pond and Andy, mistaking it for a level piece of sand, had run straight into it!

I had barely recovered from my fit of laughter by the time I met him coming out of the waves. His skin still looked brown and he stank like, well, shit! He saw no humour in this and informed me in a highly agitated voice that he was going home to 'bloody shower!' It goes without saying it takes many showers to get rid of that smell and he was not too popular at work over the next few days where everyone sat apart from him in our tea breaks. Poor old Andy. (I was clearing out some stuff recently and came across his address, I must write and see if he is still in the area?)

* * *

There is a line that goes, 'a bus never comes then suddenly several do at the same time' or words to that effect and that is how it went getting to third base.

I went to the night-club located in the camp one night, having a drink and to cut a long story short I met a shortish girl with dark hair and a plain, unremarkable face and we had a few drinks together. Her Name was Sharon. She worked in the kitchens and had seen me coming and going to the male staff block. We got a bit tipsy together and she invited me back to her horse-box. We kissed each other after closing the door behind us and then turned the light off, undressing each other by the light of a passage lamp outside. After all my years of struggle this was finally it, the runner was about to get to the sandbag before he was struck out and that's exactly what happened. I experienced delights and the fulfilment of wonder like never before and discovered this was way, way better than what I had imagined! And as I lay cooling down next to her, trying to imprint the sensations on my brain, she started to cry quietly. Now, I had just lost my virginity so what did the tears mean?

'Are you okay?' I asked nervously, maybe I had hurt her?

'I'm pregnant,' she answered between sobs. I went cold inside. I was an ignoramus about female bits and pieces, knew nothing about dogs 'on heat' or a woman's 'period' so I immediately thought I was the father but how did she know!? Does something click in their brain?

'How do you know so quickly?' I stammered in disbelief

'No you daft clot, I'm two months gone' and she sobbed a bit more, 'I'm lonely and there's no father for my baby to look up to.'

It took me a few minutes to calm my swirling brain. It's not mine, thank the Lord (thoughts from an ex virgin, by five minutes). She went on to explain what had happened and after she had calmed down and had a sip of another drink we made love again and I even smoked a cigarette afterwards like in the movies! I was no longer a virgin – hoorah!

I had a guy called Billy staying in my horse-box of a room and he was short with spiky hair on top, long on the sides. He wore shoes with four inch heels for obvious reasons but was a chatty and likeable fellow. He was going out with one of the maids and he came back to our 'kennel' one day with his girl and another called Pauline, a tall blonde. We consumed a few drinks and by early evening Billy and his girl went out. Pauline and I didn't and third base × 2 was achieved. I was getting good at this!

Then Heather came along (the third bus so to speak). I have no idea why she was at the nightclub one night, but it was with two friends, one of whom I knew quite well from staff meals and I was invited to sit with them. Heather was short, slim with a head full of auburn hair, green eyes and a lovely smile. She looked about twenty eight, certainly older than me. There was instant, mutual attraction and when Sharon, who had given me third base the week before came and sat uninvited at the table, I felt quite irritable. Heather sensed there was something between us but instead of standing aside she went for the kill and asked me to dance, which I did willingly. I felt awful about Sharon and when I glanced at her at the table she looked crestfallen, but in those days I was a selfish, inward-looking swine. Maybe I still am? Besides, Heather felt so lovely in my arms and she stared intently into my face as we danced in slow circles. By the time we had finished dancing an hour later, Sharon was nowhere to be seen. I did not know it then but I was about to enter another life-long relationship with a female.

At the end of the evening I was invited to Heather's house and soon discovered this was a discreet rendezvous. I had to sneak through the front door after she had turned off the porch light. Stolen fruit tastes best they say, in this case it certainly did. I can't say I am particularly proud of that time in my life as I now consider sex and the marriage bed sacrosanct. But back then as a relatively wild eighteen year old this was heaven and mimicked the movie 'Summer of '42' which haunts me to this day. There is something sweet and amazing about a sexually raw young man being taught the ropes by an older woman. I pretty much learned everything I know about pleasing a woman through that experience.

As Heather's house was quite far away, over an hour by bus, she used to come and see me when I knocked off work and we would carry a blanket into the wind-swept dunes, under grey lowering clouds and a crack of moon smiling at us, and make love for an hour or two. It was such a telling and profound experience getting to know her and we would drive all over, to pubs far away and isolated places or the back of her car and I fell so deeply in love with her, it was absolute hell when we parted some months later. The last time I saw her was when I was sharing a very basic flat in Chester with Steve Orrock, a wild man full of absolute fun. He had a smooth face with the hint of a moustache, long blond hair and a skinny frame and he would put on a skirt and high boots and walk hand in hand with me down the streets of Chester. The looks of puzzled enquiry on the faces of passers-by have stayed with me to this day; 'was he or wasn't he a female?' And that time, we were so sick of eating boiled cabbage with butter as our staple diet, that we walked miles to a farm to steal some chickens. We crept in towards where they were kept but all of a sudden a light clicked on and two or three dogs the size of small cars pelted towards us! There was only one route of escape and that was through a cow pen that had a fox-proofed barrier on it, granting safety from very long, gnashing teeth. I dived over the fence only to land in a massive cow pat and mud at least a hundred and fifty millimetres deep! Thwack, splash landed Steve and we burst out laughing, steam rising from our mouths. Then the long walk back to our flat where much laughter took place when we looked at our reflections in the darkened bathroom window.

It was into this mad-hatter's environment that Heather came to say goodbye to me and we switched the lights off in the lounge, lit a fire and lay on the carpet while orange flickers danced on the ceiling. It was a very passionate farewell and we both cried. (I still get her Christmas cards every year to this day).

* * *

Admiral Tait junior school. I am top right, at least a head taller than all the other boys.

My brother Brian (right) and I.

Posing in my mother's garden much to the delight of the neighbour's daughter.

The Rhodesian underwater hockey team in Bloemfontein. I am top right.
My brother is top left with Tony Dawson between us.
Below my brother is Alan Thomas, known as 'aqualung'.

Carol and I with admirers near Inyanga.

In Port Elizabeth shortly after visiting the
Chicory farm.

Supper on The Oranje on the way to the UK. Vernon is on the right, closest to the camera. I am just to the right of the blonde standing.

Sharon, my third base, in dark top.

Sharon and I with friend at a wedding.

Lifeguards at Pontins Holiday camp, Prestatyn, North Wales 1974.

The couple that collected us from YWAM, Perth.

We were so grateful reaching the end of the Nullabor's dirt roads we kissed the tarmac!

From Perth to just west of Sydney. I spent three days in this car, travelling across the Nullabor desert where no tar roads existed at the time.

Jess in Sydney.

The train engine we used for shunting in Sydney harbour.

Me looking out the cab door of an engine I am about to wash and wax.

My Holden Station-wagon. I had to accelerate going downhill because the brakes kept coming on by themselves!

Jess on the motorbike we hired in Bali, shortly after the ridiculous competence exam.

'Roast' our pet piglet being prepared for dinner, killed in revenge by the Lobsang's owner, left, because I would not let him sleep with Jess in exchange for his sister.

At my aunt's horse ranch just outside Cape Town.

Jess on the patio wall at the cottage we rented on the north side of Bali. It was here a male audience waited patiently to see her emerge naked from the ocean.

The 1275 GT mini my brother miraculously loaned me to take Jess for a drive to Mazoe dam.

Jess with a friend from the Edinburgh Castle, taken when I was on guard duty at the School of Infantry.

Me holding the butt of an 'MAG' machine gun at our graduation demonstration at the School of Infantry.

My brother pointing at my Lieutenant's 'Pip'.

Totally exhausted, having just completed a 'battle march' at the School of Infantry. Me with cap on, standing. Pete Wells is to my left and sitting is Dino Quinn.

Ant Marsh's motorbike that I smashed up on the way to see Jess.

2nd Lieutenant Ballinger.

The Elephant Hills Hotel burning down, having been hit by a wayward Strela missile intended for a tourist plane flying over Victoria Falls.

The 'Ellie Hills' still smouldering. Only a few hours after this photo was taken, waiters were serving beers from the sole bar that survived the fire!

Guys in 1 Independent Company dressed up like tourists so they could mimic civilians on the booze cruise, ready to repel any terrorist attack on the pleasure boats.

The 'Ellie Hills' ruins which we used as a forward firing observation platform.
Notice spray from Vic Falls in the background.

Me with my first wife Dianne in Johannesburg, near Wemmer Pan.
Not sure who the older couple are.

L-R: My grandfather, Uncle Ronnie, My dad, me, my mother, Dianne, Sandy and my brother Brian. Kneeling is Michael, our long-suffering cook.

My second wife, Coral, on the right, at her friend's wedding.

The best day of my life, 4th January 1986 when I married the loveliest woman on Earth, Coral, my beloved.

The car port built by my brother and I. Despite a bit of damage, its still standing 34 years later.

Building our new home. This is only part of it.

Dad with Rowan and Amanda. All three of us went for rides around the neighbourhood at the same time on that bike!

My son Rowan, left, daughter Amanda in the middle, with friend Kezi.

My granddaughter Izzy Ballinger.

Some of my workmen putting in the finishing touches to the waterfall leading into my swimming pool, where I spent so many happy hours.

The tea room up at the dairy farm past Troutbeck Hotel, shown to me by Chris Gunns. Seated with our best friends, the Philipsons and Coral's twin sister.

Onard (my foreman, who stood with me when my workforce marched on my house) marrying his sweetheart, Tabitha, our maid. What a blessed marriage ceremony it was.

Utter contentment on my face, at the peak of the good times, before Mugabe destroyed the country.

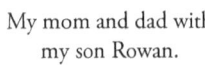

My mom and dad with my son Rowan.

The small house I built after selling my main house. We struggled to find space for all our goods.

The stunning view from our lounge and viewing patio.

On set at Inyanga, making a movie called 'Congo' for a Flemmish film crew. I laughed my socks off when I saw Coral dressed like this.

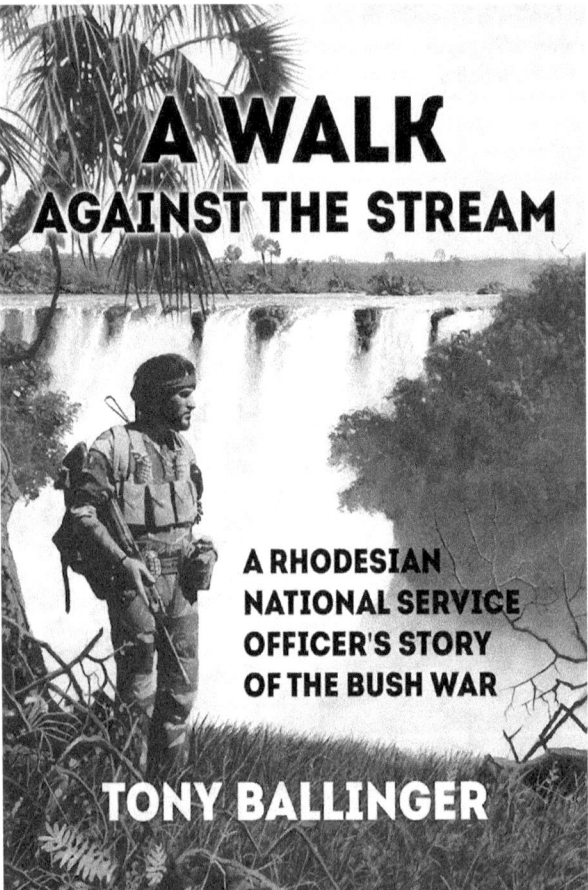

'A Walk Against the Stream' gives far more detail about my experiences at Victoria Falls than the current book you are reading.

The next day I travelled by train back to London, to stay with, of all people, Carol Dellar at her parent's house in Maida Avenue, Chingford. It was a sort of anti-climax seeing her, from my point of view, but she seemed genuinely happy to see me and we went off to a pub and reminisced about Rose and Chris and our camping trip to Inyanga, but after a few drinks silence fell over us and we headed back to her parents place where I spent a fitful night thinking of Heather and our time together.

Carol's dad was none too pleased with me when I told him my flight to Australia departed at eleven a.m. from Luton and it was now eight a.m. He still had to get me there and get back to a meeting before lunch so our kiss goodbye was quick and perfunctory although I did feel a brief, tight squeeze from her as we parted ways. I was off to Australia, having seen a plane ticket advertised for £175, which included a week's cruise on the RHMS Patris from Singapore to Freemantle, near Perth. I didn't realise it then that the Patris was an old mail ship called the Bloemfontein, sister ship of the Windsor Castle and the SA Oranje.

* * *

The flight to Singapore was uneventful except for a brief stop-over for fuel in Colombo, Ceylon, now Sri Lanka and my claim to fame was vomiting at the bottom of the steps as I came down the ladder from the plane. I was a coward in the air and had swallowed a full bottle of liqueur over the Swiss Alps, resulting in much merriment imposed on nearby passengers but as soon as I left the cool of the plane, to be met by a sledgehammer of heat, it just came up. I apologised profusely to the young lady at the bottom of the steps whose smile did not flinch an iota, even though a bit of bubbling splash landed on her one shoe! I have never felt so ill!

Singapore was incredible! The wall of heat was the same as Columbo and the surroundings were lush green with colourful flowers everywhere. Back then if your hair was not short (males only) they would put a bowl on your head and cut off everything below the rim of the bowl. I, however, was starting to lose my thatch that early in life (something that has irked me all my days) so I kept it shortish on the sides, anyway.

We were ferried from the airport to the harbour where our ship lay at anchor, as described already, an old mail ship that used to ply its way between the UK and South Africa. The cabin I was allocated could have been from the Oranje, a year or so previously, except this time I was even lower down in the bilges, somewhere near the propeller shaft by the feel of it.

I was so tired and weak from the flight that I went to the sunbathing area at the stern, sat down on a recliner, ordered a drink and fell fast asleep. Luckily the shade from a nearby gangway crept over me or else I would have been burned to death by the sun.

The ship sailed towards evening and it was a lovely trip down to Fremantle where we docked about a week later. My main memory from that journey was the pudding we were offered one evening. The ship was owned by a Greek line and the chef was retiring after many years' service and I think he decided to go out with a bang. He made perhaps twenty floats of ice cream, shaped to look like the ship, poured brandy around the base and, dining room darkened, the waiters entered in one long line, flames licking the hulls of ice cream. It was *spectacular!* And on the very last night he made an entire Acropolis out of ice cream and Meringue and all this for £175 from the UK! Needless to say I was first in the queue, literally and took great delight removing a pillar of Meringue and ice cream from the front portico, causing the roof to collapse. Yummy!

It was a slightly grey day when the ship slid into Fremantle, Western Australia and there I met the second bit of bias towards me as a Rhodesian. Although I travelled on a British passport (thanks to my dad being a Pom) it had 'born in Rhodesia' stamped in it and this caused a lot of teeth sucking, frowns and drawing in of breath from the immigration officials as they all gathered around to look at me like a specimen of plague had just landed before them. They opened a book as thick as a New York telephone directory and consulted one-another about what to do with me. Much to my chagrin, I was kept waiting until all fifteen hundred passengers had disembarked and then, literally shrugging their shoulders, a big metal date stamp was brought down with a crash on a blank visa page of my passport.

'Welcome to *Oustraalea*,' a big boy said smiling at me and, retrieving my passport and bag, descended the gangway to the relative freedom of *Oustraalea*. I had fortunately made friends with a couple on the ship and they suggested I share their taxi to the YMCA in Perth, which is what I did with a degree of gratitude as I had no idea what to do. However, even at that young stage of my life I was beginning to realise that 'someone up there' always looked after me and no matter what situation I entered into there was always a solution. I would never be allowed to flounder or starve.

We headed into Perth and I fell in love with the place, it was just like Salisbury in Rhodesia with a beach where our western suburbs would have been. The houses looked the same, the weather was the same, the people dressed the same and even sounded similar to us. In fact I have almost always been mistaken for an Ozzie or a Kiwi most of my life in European and British circles with many saying 'aw sweet, what a *lovely* accent' when I spoke 'Rhodesian', being just a bit softer than the South African accent.

The accommodation at the 'WAM' was okay, very basic and I had a full free day to go to the beach, ogle the lovely girls, pawn the brand new radio I bought in Singapore and go for a boat ride on the Swan river, which bisects the city. I slept so well that night but I still had no idea what to do with myself. I needn't have worried because, over breakfast, my mate from the ship came in and said to his female partner that he had found a lift to Sydney which had been their destination all along.

'You wanna come with us?' they asked almost in unison and being caught totally unawares I stared at them with my mouth slightly ajar. 'You wanna come with us?' they asked again, smiling.

'Why the heck not?' I said excitedly and before we knew it we were collected by an attractive young couple who were heading to Brisbane. They had a massive old 'yank tank' of a car and the five of us fitted in with room to spare. The thing was a bit of a gas guzzler and that's why they had come to the YWAM to see if any people were heading east and help pay the petrol. I can't remember what we chipped in but it would have been a lot less than a plane ticket and in next to no time we were off.

I will never forget the three and a half days it took to cross that vast expanse of land. There was no highway back then and after a few hundred kilometres east of Perth the tar disappeared and we traversed the Nullabor desert in fine talcum powder-like dust that got into *everything*, even sealed suitcases and every now and then at a gas stop we would stand under a coin-fed shower and wash ourselves down. The photo of the two girls kneeling down to kiss the tar is an indication of how bad the dirt road was. And we soon reached a place near the Blue Mountains where the couple and my mates from the ship turned north, heading for Brisbane. They had dropped me off at a railway station in a town the name of which I could not pronounce and there I waited for a passenger train. While I sat there I relived life in that car for three days non-stop with drivers' changing places, lying in weird driving sleeping positions, using thighs as pillows and so on. How odd to have a strange girls use my thighs as a pillow!

That quirk of 'chance' or fate or planned design I described earlier came around again. While on the Patris I met a guy who really liked a T-shirt I had bought in Soho in London and I traded it for a non-descript, yellow T-shirt from UCLA, University of California, Los Angeles. I did so as my T-shirt was a bit rickety and his was brand new. Anyway, when a train eventually pulled up, for Sydney, I climbed aboard and found a seat designed for day travellers. Sitting opposite me was a thirty-something guy with smooth pink skin, balding and a ginger beard. He kept staring at me which made me quite uncomfortable as I had had enough of gays in London and was just about to say something when he said, in an American accent,

'When were ya at UCLA?'

'UCLA?' I frowned

'Yeah, the T-shirt.'

'Oh no, you got it wrong, I swapped this with a pal of mine.'

'No kiddin' I used to go there, it was a great university.' And so a life-long friendship started right there with Harold. 'Where ya goin?'

'Sydney,' I said trying to sound like an International jet-setter.

'Got a place to stay?' I recoiled inwardly in case he was 'one of them', 'cos my girlfriend and I share a condo with another girl called Jane, ya'll welcome to stay until you find your own place?' I nodded inwardly thanking my unseen protector.

'That would be great,' and we made our introductions. I could rest easy now and enjoy the winding route down through the blue hills, which were staggeringly pretty and then through Paramatta to the main train station before catching a bus to Glebe, a compact suburb of mainly older houses not too far from the harbour.

Harold's girlfriend was called Mary, a tall girl with almost Native American looks, beautiful, long plaited hair cascading down her back. There was hope for me if Harold, who was at the side entrance of the house of good looks, could get a stunner like her but as I was to learn in the three weeks I stayed there, he was a great character with a dry sense of humour that could be easily missed, but not Mary, she caught every joke he made and the two of them would often cackle away privately without Jane and I having a clue what it was all about. It fascinated me that the English language could be spoken in so many ways. In fact, years later when I did white-water rafting down the Zambezi river, I enjoyed the American guide so much I offered to buy him a beer back at Victoria Falls and he accepted by asking me to join his group of guides. Well, you would think I was in the darkest part of Africa because I could not understand a single word these white Americans were saying to each other as they joked and laughed in their easy, laconic drawl.

Jane (another life-long friend alongside Mary) had a slightly round, cherubic sort of face with a few freckles on her cheeks and hair plaited in two Gretel-like sticks either side of her head. Her greeting was rather formal in one of those gritty outback accents where one fancied Crocodile Dundee would pop out the woods and say 'G'day mate!' But Mary's greeting, apart from an approving smile, came after looking at Harold and saying, 'Brought another stray home?' accompanied by a wink at me. Harold, you see, had a bad habit of collecting all these lost souls and bringing them home. I fitted in though and slept on the couch for a few weeks and felt right at home among them. In fact Jane and Mary still communicate with me to this day but Harold fell off the radar a long time ago. We used to go for walks up in the Blue Mountains where we caught freshwater prawns, big things with serious nippers and we would cook and eat them just near the stream and we had a few memorable parties. Jane eventually hooked up with a guy called Jeff, whom she married but I once asked her why we didn't hook up and she said she 'didn't think of it' but would have been fun. Now she tells me!

My money was now running low and I was beginning to panic a bit but Harold dropped a newspaper in front of me one day and pointed out a vacancy he had circled in blue ink.

'They're looking for trainee train drivers,' he said, 'that would be a bloody good job if you can get it.'

I immediately filled in the application form and posted it off, express mail. I could not believe my eyes when a letter arrived about a week later with a positive response inside it. I was thrilled, I had always wanted to drive trains and two days later I was in a queue of about forty other young men. After a very basic elimination process, like being able to spell 'dog' or 'cat' we were down to about twenty five males. Tests carried out over the next day or so eliminated about seven more and all of a sudden I was accepted, all my details submitted and I was officially welcomed as a trainee train driver, which took about four years to fully qualify if you stayed the course. I was ecstatic. From the word go my salary was incredible, as many wages seem to be in Australia, which is why their standard of living is so high. To top it all I could walk to work and so started a fascinating year-long adventure on the Australian railways.

I started at the yards at seven the next morning where I was trained how to recognize signals, couple and uncouple engines from a train and many other things relevant to the post. I took many varied trains to their destinations with many varied drivers most of whom were great guys with a terrific sense of humour and they all seemed to want me when I had to replace a sick Fireman, my technical title, even though we drove huge diesel engines made in the USA. I loved starting those beasts, I would go into the gut of the engine unit, prime the engine with a long pump handle, flick the battery power on and start the engine by pushing a green button, red for off later. The noise required ear muffs and I kept a picture of myself poking my head out of a small access door halfway down the engine for many years before I lost it, taken when our two engines pulled a prestige train, like the Blue train in South Africa, to Brisbane.

A few memorable journeys were taking passenger trains up into the Blue Mountains west of Sydney. This entailed using coupled diesel engines to the foothills and then exchanging them for electric engines, which were more powerful. I remember on one trip up there that I forgot to read out the signals to the driver as the line entered a tight turn to the right. The long nose of the engine prevented the driver from seeing the signals so I was supposed to relay their condition to him but I was far away in my thoughts and just stared at the red lamp without its meaning sinking in. At last the driver could see the lamp and applied emergency brakes, much to his great annoyance. I felt embarrassed and stupid but I guess I didn't feel as bad as all the passengers getting chucked around behind me.

I often had to catch a train back to Sydney as a spare hand and I normally had a doze in the conductor's wagon at the back of the train. On one occasion the heater had gone off and believe me it can get darn cold in those mountains, where snow often falls and I was so cold in the leaky cabin that I cut the tie cord on a big mail bag, tipped out the mail and climbed inside to keep warm, doing the reverse when I got back to Sydney main.

Well, my favourite time was shunting in Sydney harbour where we would make up trains for their destinations. One night, we had been going back and forth for an hour or so, with me pushing the dead-man's button every sixty seconds, which is all I had to do apart from uncouple the odd unit, the driver told me to take over as he was 'off to the pub over there mate' and before I could protest he was out the cab, nipping across multiple lines, ducking under a fence and into the pub in three seconds flat. It did not seem to bother him I was an unqualified driver and had no idea what I was supposed to do even though he had said 'nothing going on for an hour, mate'. Then, sitting in the driver's seat, I see the green shunt controller's light come on twenty or more coaches down the line. What the hell do I do now? I blew the horn to see if the driver would reappear but nothing happened, so, having watched how the controls were operated on many occasions, I eased the brakes, slid the gear lever forward into position and elevated the revs more than I should have. Now, because there is an incline in Sydney harbour what I should have done was take the breaks off only, to let gravity do its thing, but by accelerating, the wagons took off at a heck of a rate.

To add insult to injury the train brake hoses had not been connected by me and only the light, little 'Noddy' engine I was in was available to stop a dead weight of maybe six hundred tons or more. Needless to say the little green light up ahead suddenly flicked to red with the operator waving it like crazy, which indicated emergency stop! I pulled the throttle back and applied maximum brakes but all that did was allow me to be dragged down the hill at a fractionally slower rate. The sight of the linesman up ahead running for cover bode ill for me and then it came, a massive, echoing, crashing thud as the furthest wagon ploughed into something, the shockwave progressing along the train like a snake flexing its spine and then boom my 'Noddy' engine was brought to a halt instantly, throwing me forward and almost over the control column. I have never heard a bang like that and sailors on nearby ships came out to look as did people at the pub and a few townhouses. I just caught sight of the driver's legs pumping like crazy as he ran back to join me. I thought he would tear a strip off me or go for my throat but he just smiled and said,

'Still gettin' the hang of it mate?' The Linesman did not even come forward to see what was wrong, I could not believe it.

I needn't have felt so bad when, a few nights later, I watched a drunk switch operator pull the switching lever under a massive container of refrigerated milk, sending the front set of bogies to the left of the points and the rear bogey to the right of the points, which made the container crab along until the angle of the two lines was so divergent that the whole thing came off in a spectacular cartwheeling crash, popping the lid off, sending many hundreds of litres of milk down the hill. To my surprise rail operators appeared from nowhere and I was encouraged to join them, mug in hand, to drink as much milk as we could without bursting. It was delicious. Then, like clockwork, a little recovery unit arrived and in next to no time the wagon was back on the correct track, lid tightened, wheels tapped and checked and off it went! The fact that the end user would be out about seven hundred litres of milk didn't seem to bother them! Only in *'Oustraalea*!'

* * *

The night run I hated the most was taking cattle to the slaughter house. The line was long and flat and after gunning the engine a bit before putting it into neutral, the train just coasted along on its own momentum. This afforded a degree of silence as we slid along like a big serpent under a shocked, white moon. And at the end of the line, steam reflecting in the night air, loomed a dark, ominous structure. The smell around us changed and even before we smelled it the hundreds of cattle behind us had and now they were groaning and mooing as if pleading with us to not do this. I felt a real shit delivering them to their deaths but thankfully it never put me off steak. We would leave the wagons there and travel light back to the depot.

The death of cattle was not the only death we carried on the trains. As part of our duties, when we got back to depot and if our shift had not ended, was to clean out the engine's cab, fill the toilet's dispenser with paper, top up the tank that fed fresh water to the sink, waxed and polished the side of the engine and sprayed the 'gubbins' under it. It was during the latter exercise, when an engine had pulled in, that we had to steam clean off the remains of a young man who had committed suicide somewhere along the line. A bit of scalp with dark hair was put in a bag and the coroner came to collect it. Thankfully this only happened once. However, if there were no engines to wash we would walk past the 'wogs' (Aussie for Italian and Spanish immigrants) washing the passenger coaches and pretend to speak Italian by adding 'A' and 'O' to every word. A yank called Larkin excelled at this but as some of the 'wogs' were very pretty young women, not the type of Spaniard that grew a beard, his charms went into overdrive and he occasionally did okay.

Beyond the washing area was a canteen that normally served good pies but on one occasion I got a ham sandwich with maggots in it! Anyway, we would jump on an even tinier 'Noddy' train and zoom down to our rest room which was an old day passenger carriage that had had the seats removed and tables and chairs, bunks, some easy chairs and a television installed. The occupants over the years had plastered the walls with an amazing selection of pornographic pictures and it was impossible to miss them if you lay on your back in a bunk.

Around about this time I bought a car, an old blue Holden station wagon from one of the Aussie train drivers and he and his wife would often invite me over for a meal. They were a really nice couple. (A funny story with that car happened when the guy that sold it to me gave me some brake fluid from the train depot when the car brake fluid got low. What he didn't realise is that the train brake fluid would cause the rubbers in the car braking system to swell badly, preventing the brakes from operating properly. This became very embarrassing one day, in the main street of Sydney, when I had to leap out and bleed the brakes before moving on again! It got so bad that I had to rev the engine going *downhill* and then nip out at every red light to bleed it yet again! I eventually dumped it at a red traffic light near a cinema, much to the consternation of the police who sought me out over the matter. Ha!).

I had also moved out of the house that I had been sharing with Harold & Co and moved into a one-bedroom flat. I found it so lonely I looked elsewhere until I found a lovely condo complex three storeys high, with a pool and sauna on the roof. I was earning an amazing wage and I volunteered for overtime whenever I could and that paid double time. I also 'worked' public holidays and got triple time. I put 'worked' in italics because all I did is sleep in the staff restroom to earn several hundred dollars for the day and this was back in the 1970s!

I needed a woman, it has been the bane of my life that I am highly sexed and so the hunt started again. I did not have to look far because a very pretty Japanese girl with the cute name of *Michiwo Miwa* lived in the flat directly above me and we met in the sauna room after a swim. I think she wanted to practice her English so she invited me around for a meal after we had showered and I arrived with a bottle of wine at about seven pm that night. Michiwo was dressed in one of those body-hugging silk outfits, dark blue with tropical bird designs printed onto the fabric.

We ate a very pleasant, traditional Japanese fish and rice dish which was delicious and I even tried Sake for the first time. The Sake and the wine did what it was designed to do and before long we were on the bed enjoying our youth and our bodies. She was a good lover but a terrible kisser, it appeared to me that 'French kissing' was not known in Japan so I had the very enjoyable duty of teaching her how to kiss properly. I have always believed a man must give gold and take silver in bed and so we had some pretty enraptured evenings together. We also took long drives along the coast, stopping to eat fish and chips or just hold hands as we walked on the beach.

It saddened me no end when I knocked on her apartment door one day and she opened it just wide enough to see a young man sitting in the background. Apparently she wanted to learn every dialect of English so after a 'sorry' from her I was sent packing, no explanation, nothing! I became determined to replace her but didn't succeed until I came up with a cunning plan. I often went to the University to listen to jazz, which I particularly like and on one visit I saw a big notice board with all sorts of things for sale and accommodation requests on it, so, grabbing some paper nearby I wrote down my details for ladies wanting to share a flat. It was so bold of me I still can't believe I did it and why was it bold? It was bold because my flat was a very big open-plan bed-sit with no dividing walls and two separate beds, a table, a lounge suite, kitchenette etcetera all in one big room.

Well, I had a train of young girls come and see the place and their reactions varied from horror, to terror to peals of laughter but early one evening Claire knocked on the door. She had a pleasant face, nice-ish body and an easy smile.

'How much is it again?' she asked and I repeated the information from my notice at the University. 'If you can knock it down thirty dollars you have a deal,' she said extending her hand for a shake. I was gob-smacked but there it was, I had a female flat mate in an open-plan flat!!

I was taken even further aback when it came time for her to take a shower the first night she stayed with me, whereby she quite happily disrobed in front of me and waltzed across the room to the bathroom stark naked. I feigned total disinterest as I sat cross-legged on the couch, reading a magazine. She was far better endowed than I had imagined and a big gob of adrenalin shot into my lower belly, I had no idea what I had let myself in for quite honestly and with that amount of openness it only took until the following night to join her in her 'bedroom' which was three metres from mine across an open patch of carpet! She was pleasant and I enjoyed myself but there was no 'rumble in the belly' so to speak so after a month or two she left to go and live with her boyfriend who apparently she had had all along! It was too confusing to figure out so I just chalked it off to another life experience.

It was one evening when I was visiting a popular wine bar that I met her. I thought wearing jeans with tears at the knee-cap and a pale yellow T-shirt against my tan would look good but apparently this fad, which I created for myself, had not caught on with anyone else and in fact would not do so until the 1980s. I often wonder if I started the craze in that wine bar as I certainly got enough attention, including that of Jess Strang, an American girl with long blonde hair, brown eyes and pale skin, moulded into a nice little body thank you very much.

'Too poor to buy jeans, huh?' was her introductory line and although she was at a table next to mine, she invited me to join her and her friends. It was a pleasant, easy-going evening with people from all over the world. I could sense that Jess had taken to me and by the end of the evening we had swapped addresses (there were no cell phones back then) and we had agreed for me to collect her at the university or hospital, I can't remember which, at noon the following day, Saturday.

I arrived dead on time due to my excellent map-reading skills and before long we were chatting and heading into town to watch the 'Towering Inferno' movie which had rave reviews. The cinema we were going to had special speakers and other technical effects so we could feel and hear all the noise going on in the movie. Back then it was a bit of a cliff-hanger and it wasn't long before Jess was gripping my hand, which I totally enjoyed. The act itself was sexy but the fact that a woman took the lead was even sexier to me. Or maybe she was just scared but my ego would not acknowledge the thought. There was only one place to go after the movie and that was back to my flat where we spent a lovely warm evening making love, with rain heaving down and thunder crashing outside. I have always loved the sound of rain outside a bedroom ever since.

We spent maybe four months together before I realised I was falling for her but those feelings coincided with me wanting to move on again.

'A penny for your thoughts,' she said, sitting on a rock next to me one golden evening at the beach. My mind had been far away on Rhodesia and I suddenly felt very homesick, I wanted to go home and I told her so.

'Come with me Jess, please,' I said without thinking and was most surprised, after a long pause, when she simply said 'okay.'

I have often wondered what life I would have had in Australia if I had stayed there. I had a fantastic job, was about to be promoted to Senior Fireman, had loads of money coming in, a nice flat and a girl I was starting to love, what had home to offer? It reminded me of that movie 'sliding doors' where a simple thought or action can change which door you walk through in life. I was so confused, but there is something about Africa, she is a delightful, cruel mistress and you cannot be rid of her.

Just before I resigned from the railways I took Jess up into the mountains by train. It was nice to be a passenger for a change. We had booked into a bungalow-style lodge for two nights and after squaring away our clothes we made a cup of tea and jumped into a huge King-size bed. It was so comfortable that I could feel sleep enveloping me like a lover but the lover next to me had other ideas! Jess put her cup down and rolled to face me, putting my cup next to my bed before kissing me deeply. I love women being dominant in bed and as she bore down on me her blond hair cascaded over my face, surrounding it like a soft towel. It was the first time she told me she loved me and I felt the same. I loved her. And that was the difference, my heart was in this, it was no longer just physical. It was some of the most tender nights of lovemaking in my life.

The next day we went to the bottom of the Blue Mountains on the world's steepest railway line, so steep that you sat like an astronaut does, almost on your back and you could soon see why. The car we were allocated inched along and then suddenly the bottom fell out at possibly seventy five degrees angle, which took a lot of toe-crunching in your shoes to get used to but before long, like a roller-coaster, we reached the bottom flat section. From there we walked hand in hand to a really stunning waterfall with a large circular pool of water and like others there, had a swim.

* * *

We left Australia on Garuda airlines the following month, experiencing two horrible things in the flight. First of all, when the plane was being pushed backwards by a little tow vehicle, the hydraulics on the front wheel of the plane gave way and the nose came crashing down on the tow-driver's cab, crushing him instantly. The panic inside the plane was absolute but within myself I felt no fear, pulling Jess back down to her seat while attempting to climb over other seats to escape. We eventually reached the back door chute where we took off our shoes and slid down to waiting arms. Jess was as white as a sheet as were many other passengers. We were guided back to a waiting room where we were given food and drinks and listened to a few announcements and apologies from the airline staff and airport manager. We were asked to wait until all our kit had been transferred to another plane but this was too much for some people who picked up their bags and left the airport.

Three hours later we were on another plane heading for Bali in Indonesia but halfway there the plane suddenly dropped thousands of feet and everything not tied down started to float in the cabin; food and drinks (just served), flight attendants (serving), passengers, small cases you name it, all to come crashing down when the wings of the plane finally found purchase on the air. A lot of wailing broke out and this time I was as white as Jess and knocked back three brandy and cokes in rapid succession. I hate flying!!!

Bali, in 1975, was paradise and there was only one commercial hotel on the island but we decided to stay in a 'Lobsang', a traditional B&B in Kuta beach, which consisted of a dark room, with one candle, two very dubious beds, no cupboards, no chairs, no table and no glass in the windows. We felt very nervous having arrived after dark and I spent a fitful night waiting to be hacked to pieces for someone's supper. But I need not have worried because in the morning we enjoyed a nice fruit breakfast and noticed lots of other young people like us moving in and out of their Lobsang's but we were too far from the beach so we caught a 'tuk-tuk' and found a much nicer place, well this one had a door to the room but still no table, chairs, glass in the windows etcetera. We were immediately befriended by a tiny little pig that had the run of the grounds, which we immediately called 'roast' and after securing our kit as best as possible we set out to explore the place. It was lovely, a tangle of huts and dogs and chickens and peasant life going on all over the place with lots of toothless smiles and bows and nods from the locals and after a few minutes we were on the beach, its stunning white sands spread out like a stretch of desert, palm trees bending over to inspect the turquoise-pale green-dark green and blue waters lapping at our feet. We dived in and wrapped our arms around each other, smiling and kissing and I really felt in love at that moment.

We soon discovered that we would need transport to get around so I hired a motorbike but before being allowed to use it I had to do a competence test at the local police station. I arrived with a passport-sized photo and stood in a short queue waiting my turn, watching with curiosity. I wondered if I had to sit a written test or an oral test or what but nothing like that happened and in a short while I was summoned forward to sit on a Honda 125cc and gesticulated at to proceed. Fortunately I had been watching the others so I sat on the idling bike, kicked it into gear and proceeded to weave in and out of fifteen evenly spaced orange traffic cones, turn around and repeat the exercise on the way back, without putting my foot on the ground. I succeeded admirably, smiling at Jess as I glided to a halt. More gesticulating to go into a room where I handed my photo to a man behind a desk who promptly scribbled on a card, attached my photo and stamped it with a resounding bang, a smile on his face, the card presented to me with a great flourish and even more smiles! I was now legally allowed to ride a motorbike in Bali!

'What the hell was that all about?' I laughed into Jess's face as we headed back to the motorbike depot. She shrugged, hugged and laughed a deep laugh. But I soon found out why that was all I had to learn. There *were* no road rules, no give-way signs, no traffic lights. The sandy tracks that served as roads were replete with pigs, kids, adults, carts and goats darting across your front tyre and I very quickly saw the reasoning behind the competency test, it was to ensure you could miss all these mobile targets when going about one's business! Jess squeezed me from behind and we laughed all the way back to our Lobsang.

I very quickly decided that it was too hot to wear jeans so I bought a Sarong, a colourful length of cloth, that I secured at the waist, packed my T-shirt, put on sandals and walked around like a local. It was so liberating! We swam a lot and would rush home during the mountainous storms and try and find a place to make love, which was usually standing up in the shower, which at least had a door, balancing under cold water which came from the butt attached to the wall outside. The only downside is that we had to put up with the odd mosquito larvae wriggling on our skin while trying to reach the divine heights of lovemaking and so our attempts usually ended up in peals of laughter as we swatted them away, breaking our rhythm.

We did some exhilarating journeys on that island on the back of our little bike. Petrol was almost free, Indonesia being the major oil producer it was and we toured pretty much the whole island, up to the central volcano where a still-primitive tribe 'buried' their dead upright on wooden poles, to the jungle, to the fascinating architecture of ancient temples and to the north where the Dutch had settled, building houses with typical high, ornate, white gables. We rented a very nicely appointed bungalow and had an entire volcanic-sand beach to ourselves, with sunsets so beautiful you could not but know God exists.

It was there that we experienced our first unusual event. Jess had by now, thanks to the sun, acquired almost platinum blonde hair and one can imagine, in a land of many millions of dark-haired people, that this was something worth exploring. Well, we swam naked as our beach cottage was so isolated and no doubt the odd prying eye saw what we were doing because, in a relatively short period of time, we had a bank of male spectators sitting on the beach. I am positive their intentions were those of simple fishermen, simple peasant folk but it was a bit unnerving the first time it happened. In this instance I covered myself with my hands and went and put my Sarong on, accompanied by many smiles and nods, heads quickly turning to Jess to see what she offered, the latter up to her neck in water amid signs the tide was beginning to distress her. She looked spooked and I teased her by indicating with my arm that she should walk out naked but a scrunched up face and a positive NO mouthed at me was her final answer. Now Jess was a mild creature but I did not want to find out what her wrath was like so I went inside and got a large towel which I waded out and gave her.

'You swine!' she said slapping my shoulder, 'wanna get me raped?'

I had not thought of that and looked nervously back at the group of men. But nothing happened and we got back to our cottage without incident and the men soon dispersed, no doubt a bit disappointed or maybe happy they had actually seen a woman with blonde hair up close.

Our second experience of this male curiosity was when we were sitting under a grass umbrella on the beach and a funeral procession came down to the water's edge. The men carried a wrapped body on a float, covered in stunning garlands of local flowers. Each man had a type of hat on and wore short, knee length Sarongs in a black and white check design. The moment the men in the procession saw Jess they peeled off and stood around her, feeling her hair, chatting animatedly among themselves. I had been idling time away in the water and when I became aware of what was going on she had disappeared behind a wall of brown flesh. I got a fright and ran to her aid, getting a bit loud in my defence of her but they smiled and bowed gently before moving away. I knew they meant no harm but it scared both of us. We eventually calmed down and ended up witnessing a rare, traditional water burial where the float was lit on fire, pushed out into the golden sea, pinky-orange clouds covering the calm horizon and all the while the men sang a beautiful dirge in lovely deep voices and the ladies rocked to and fro in their colourful, full length dresses, flower necklaces and hibiscus tucked behind an ear. It saddens me that today the island of Bali is modern with cars and hotels but back then it was pure nature and I think something precious, like in many parts of the world, disappeared forever under a tidal wave of greed and modernization.

The third and final time Jess's rare looks (in those parts) resulted in our privacy being invaded was when the host at our accommodation offered, in broken English, to give me his sister for the night if he could take Jess; a trade so to speak. We declined, obviously, much to the confusion noted on the man's face and whether or not he took offence was unknown but we suspected it was taken when we came home to find 'roast' as our dinner that evening. I felt sick munching on his hind quarter while Jess refused to partake at all, insisting we go to the nearby local restaurant where they did simple foods and the most amazing, ice-cold fruit shakes. I drank so many of them, they were so delicious, that I was often seen running like an Olympic sprinter for the bog, which in this place and all others on the island was a hole in the bathroom floor, something I detested as the runny poo often splashed on my ankles. I would not have made a good bomb-aimer!

Our final experience of note was that we discovered 'magic' mushrooms and after quaffing a few in a special soup we walked down to the beach. On the way I noticed I started to feel a bit numb and that, my only way to describe my vision, was that I had entered a living oil painting. The edges to everything became a bit smooth and the colours were enhanced five-fold. Motion was different and when we got to the beach I noticed with some astonishment that the waves were translucent black, the white frothy crests were now purple, the water a very deep green and the palm trees just like a scene from Gilligan's Island, all blurry, moving in jerky slow motion, a thick oil paint effect. We collapsed on our backs on the beach and watched in mute fascination the movement of the clouds, as they danced and formed patterns, it was incredible. And when we went in the water, real or imagined little fish pecked at our skin in an expert defoliation exercise but I will never know if fish were there or it was just something weird going on with my nerves.

Jess and I were curious about the hut at the far end of the cove, it looked so magical, with smoke jerking slowly out the top, palm trees crossed over the front wall like swords of an honour guard. It was not too far away but the exploding colours of the sunset, now changed so dramatically, made us take our time. It was fully dark when we got back to where our towels should have been but were now well and truly stolen but we felt so good we went back and made awesome love in Jess's bed and somewhere along the line I remember a couple of young faces watching us fleetingly through the open window but we felt so good we didn't care.

After a full, glorious month of dining under the stars, watching the riveting Kechak dance every night and walking on moonlit beaches, we caught a plane to Singapore for the next leg of the journey. It was lovely repeating a few of the things I did previously in Singapore, with Jess and our highlight was going to 'Boogey street' down near the harbour, the fourth largest harbour in the world. The main street through there was filled with bars, cafes, restaurants and many other wonderful sights. It was set ablaze by many colourful lights and we found a place to eat where squid and many other alien foods, like big spiders and so on, delighted me, but not Jess, she stuck to noodles and vegetables and basic fish.

The main attraction of course was the parade of transvestites that wandered down the street towards midnight. Now these 'gals' were not the garish, half-bearded creatures that you see in western night clubs, these were just stunning 'females' that would take away the breath of most straight men. They did not wear fancy dress or anything like that but rather wore miniskirts with high boots and slim-fitting tops. Their faces were beautiful and if you passed by one in the street you would have been none the wiser; that is far eastern men for you, silky smooth! And men, especially sailors, were quite happy to go with them and that was their main function, as prostitutes. It was funny though, seeing them walk off arm in arm with a man only to pause and do a piss in the open, men-only urinals that were positioned along the road, each cubicle as high as a man's waist so they could see life carrying on while they did a pee. Very practical!

Our plans were to get to Thailand and then fly to the UK. I wanted to go east through Hong Kong and the USA but as Jess was an American she persuaded me to go west, something I will always regret really as I loved the USA. In those days visas were a mere formality and in fact when I had arrived in Australia I could work without any legal requirements and I dare say could simply have stayed there after filling a few forms out.

* * *

From Singapore we drove over the causeway into Malaysia and this is where I discovered the people in that part of the world do not like drugs and every passenger on our rickety coach had to take out every single item in their suitcases and lay it out for inspection on the tarmac. I dreaded the thought that some 'Midnight Express' situation would unfold and that I would be hauled off to jail because a smuggler had put his wares in my case. But it was all okay and Jess and I sighed with relief. We drove on through, what was then, very thick jungle and I shuddered to think my own countrymen had fought here with British troops to quell a communist uprising; it turned out to be one of the most successful campaigns against guerrillas' (terrorists) ever fought.

On advice we ignored Kuala Lumpur and went straight to Panang Island where we booked into a very comfortable YMCA, which allowed us to share a room. We did very little there except catch a bus full of locals (read: chickens, ducks, pigs and a few people) down the coast and were so horrified by the bus driver's antics that we asked to be let out in the middle of nowhere from whence we walked to a beach near a fishing village. There was nothing to do there but swim and we did not enjoy the cloudy (looked like milk had been spilled in the ocean), tepid waters and after floating backwards into a rock full of crustaceans that cut me open, we went to the village and caught the bus back, with the same lunatic driver now scowling at us but thankfully he drove a bit more humanely.

From Panang we went a bit north and then caught a passenger train to Bangkok in Thailand. It was a long, slow ride but thankfully they had first class accommodation (very, very cheap to us) and so Jess and I just sat in our cabin drinking tea without milk, (they had probably chucked it in the ocean!) and watched the endless miles of rice paddies going by. It was so hot and so mesmerizing that we eventually fell asleep, missing entirely the call to show passports at the Thai border and it was only as the inspectors were leaving the train that I asked a passenger what was going on and so Jess and I had to scramble after them with our passports. They were not too amused as they had to get their table and date stamp set up again and we almost missed the train when it started to glide away from us.

The remainder of the trip was uneventful and we arrived in the steamy, hot, busy, massive capital of Bangkok where we found a nice four star hotel for next to nothing, observing all the western men with their tight-thighed (Thai-ed?) girls hanging on their arms (which still goes on today) and I soon discovered that sex was as freely available there as buying a coke. But we were exhausted and slept for nearly twenty four hours, to emerge to the wonders of eating bird nest soup, turtle soup and so on plus any bug that crawled or slid or spat at you (before being dropped in boiling oil). I loved the grilled Octopus legs on sticks and would walk around munching them before popping the odd spider in my mouth (not bad actually) or a frog whose eyes stared at you in cooked horror as you pulled its legs off and ate them. Boy, what a shock to the system.

We took a trip to the massive Temple of Dawn in those boats that have a rod leading to a propeller at the back and climbed to the summit of the temple of fertility which had hundreds of steps with a pair of dildos on either side, all the way up! And feeding a little elephant was so cute but in hindsight very sad as its mother was tied to a short chain just behind her, swaying with the sway of the tormented. I hate it!

Ten days later we underwent a very scary taxi ride to the airport and before too long were winding our way towards Moscow on Aeroflot, the main Russian airline. It was a good flight but as there were only twelve people on board, Jess very kindly enabled me to enter the much sought after 'mile high' club, which was wildly erotic. Then Moscow, where it was freezing, about minus ten the day we landed and I was still in Jeans, a T-shirt and sandals. To make matters worse we sat in a transit coach with the door wide open, waiting for more passengers to alight while the driver sweated away in a steamy enclosure, jacket off it was so hot in there.

Customs and immigration was straight out of a Bond movie; big men in fur hats patrolled with Kalashnikovs slung. The lady who took my passport was dressed in a white uniform and had a classic Lotte Lenya accent from 'Russia with love.' I was shivering uncontrollably from the cold and the whole scene suddenly had me giggling and no doubt the guards and the immigration official thought I was on drugs. Her accent made me chuckle when she tried to pronounce my name, something like 'Beeeala -anger' or sounds to that effect but after an extra careful search of our bags we were free to enter mother Russia.

I was so cold by the time I got to our hotel room (read: Siberian death camp) that I bathed for forty minutes before climbing into rough cotton sheets spread on some type of cot, under thick blankets, which was surprisingly comfortable and with the freshly bathed Jess lying on top of me, we made love to the sounds of the couple next door banging their headboard against our thin partition wall.

The next morning, after one of the best sleeps of my life, we dressed warmly and went down for breakfast. We were only staying at the Aeroflot hotel because there was no direct flight to Heathrow from Bangkok in those days and we had opted for a day in Moscow and a connecting flight the next day. The breakfast was black bread (read: for Siberian prisoners), coffee (lovely actually), butter (lovely and thick) and jam and that was it. I stared at the kitchen door for ages hoping bacon and eggs would be wheeled out but nothing happened and we eventually headed out to meet our tour bus.

I was fascinated by these hardy people rushing to and fro in the snow. I did not see anyone eating their children or carrying them by their feet, I did not see Russian women with beards and men with teeth missing. So much for Western propaganda. In fact they were quite handsome and the women breathtakingly beautiful with high, Slavic cheekbones. The main street had stores, yes a little sparse by Western standards and you could probably grow an inch of hair waiting for oncoming traffic but they looked happy and took great delight swimming in an open-air hot spring with steam curling off in all directions.

The thrill was Red Square with all its incredible architecture and then on to the University of Moscow, reportedly big enough to take seventy years to visit one room a day, it was towering and massive. So that's where they taught people to hate us and build atomic bombs I thought, rather stupidly. All in all it was a fascinating and apparently happy place. I knew where to shove any future ill-feelings towards these rather stiff but friendly people although, ironically, in less than a few months I would be in the army in Rhodesia where black men carrying Kalashnikovs, made in Russia, tried to kill me. But I did not know that then.

* * *

We landed in London where I tried to get a visa to go to the United States with Jess and see her family. Despite every trick in the book, even telling them we were engaged, I had no proof I would leave the USA after my holiday and that darn 'born in Rhodesia' raised its blasted head again. I was absolutely crushed because Jess's dad had arranged for us to take a Corvette Stingray (my favourite car) around the USA, gas included and 'have a good time' and here I was pleading with a tight-lipped fascist bitch who just kept shaking her head. I left the embassy in tears.

Our ship to South Africa, the Edinburgh Castle, another mail ship, was due to depart in just under three weeks, and from Cape Town we planned to fly up to Salisbury to stay with my parents. We were at a loss about what to do and after thinking about it Jess decided to go home and see her family as she would be with me in Africa for who knows how long?? We waved goodbye at Heathrow, as a flight headed west to New York in four hours' time and then, deciding against going to my aunt and uncle, who I loved (but boredom lurked there) decided to head for Heather's place. I felt rotten as I knew I would be unfaithful to Jess but Heather was very special to me and towards the latter month or so with her she had introduced me to her husband who worked permanent night shift as a tanker driver for Shell. I cannot remember how we were introduced, some cock-eyed excuse was made up and slowly but surely he accepted me and came to like me and said if I was ever back in the UK to come stay with them.

The journey up to Wales took me back two years, everything looked so familiar. I no longer had to sneak into the front porch when the light was turned off but got there in a taxi and knocked on the door quite openly. Bob was asleep and would wake at about six pm for his night shift. Heather answered and after a wide-eyed look at me pulled me indoors, taking me by the hand to the lounge where she sat next to me, tears welling in her eyes. We kissed and fondled each other but could not go beyond that as her kids were due home soon and then Bob would wake up for work.

Bob put on a superb act of having a frozen shoulder when he woke up as he guessed, quite correctly, what would happen when he went to work that night but he had regular Avgas deliveries to make, from the refinery to the airport and back again, until his shift finished at 8 am the next day so he had to go no matter what. I felt terribly ashamed, guilty and happy-excited, all at the same time and I could tell by Heather's slightly short-tempered, breathless attempts to get the kids to bed early was her way of showing she was dying to get into my arms. And it happened at about ten pm when we sat next to each other in the lounge. The smell of her was intoxicating and we made love until a couple of hours before Bob got home, repeated every night except when Bob was off duty. I remember him shouting at her upstairs one night and she told me in the morning that he was complaining about the house getting dusty and he never had an ironed uniform to wear and 'what the hell was going on?' It was understandable really because as soon at Bob fell asleep in the day time we were at it like rabbits again, keeping one ear cocked for a creak in the staircase. It was wrong of course and I find it hard to be so flippant about that time in my life but it happened and it formed a deep, deep groove in my memory. I felt even worse when I got a letter from Jess, because she expressed her love for me yet again and hoped I was being as faithful to her as she was to me. But knowing Jess's appetite I wasn't entirely convinced she was being faithful too and we were probably cuckolding each other. But, I said, soothing my conscience, she was only my girlfriend and our future was not guaranteed. I could not give up Heather for that. I wanted both of them, I think that was it really. (In defence of Jess's character, I really do believe she was never unfaithful to me but as she had suggested 'swinging' with other couples on more than one occasion, I never became totally convinced, at the time, of her honour. As Jess will be getting a copy of this book all I can say is sorry for lying to you about Heather).

That lasted several days and then I had to go to Heathrow to meet my brother whom I had bought a ticket to the UK for. We met up with all the Uncles and Aunts and cousins for a meal and after a day or so with dear Aunt Dot, we decided to hire a car and take a tour up to Loch Ness. Big problem though, we were both under twenty one and that was the minimum age for car hire. We were gutted but my friend in the sky helped us along after two American girls overheard our plight and offered to hire the vehicle for us. They were planning to go to Scotland also and it suited them to share the costs. (The UK is pretty expensive to average-income Americans). My mood swung from being gutted to being elated and so we set off in a tiny Mini Minor which propelled the girls into fits of laughter because it was so small and had a 'stick shift' (Americanese for gear lever) and in no time we were off on a direct line to Scotland, stopping only for fuel and the odd touristy sights on the way. We really clicked with these two girls possibly because they were only twenty three or so and therefore not out of our league. In fact (oh dear, sighs the reader, here he goes again) the dark-haired of the two was quite attractive and we hit it off well together. I think I had an advantage over my brother for two reasons, I was by then an expert in most sexual matters and I knew what tickled Jess's American humour so I applied a bit of charm and it worked wonders.

We stayed in several B&Bs, went for a cruise on Loch Tay and Loch Ness and one funny thing still tickles my brother and I to this day. Brian got so tired of people not understanding his accent when he asked for directions, often cupping their ears and saying 'Wot's that laddie, og aye?' that he practised his Scottish accent and after pulling up to an old, wizened man to ask, in a perfect Scottish accent, where the next B&B was, the old boy cupped his hand behind his ear and said, 'Wot's that laddie, og aye?' I just cracked up, doubling down on my midriff so suddenly that I pulled a muscle but unable to stop laughing I entered that high-pitched cackle that I am famous for, setting the two girls and Brian off. We just cried with laughter and all the while this poor old coot was standing there, puzzled, scratching his bald patch.

Our last night was spent at a quaint B&B under thatch, set amidst stunning scenery and the girl (call her Cathy) and I wandered through a very pretty garden at sunset, letting our fingers briefly touch over the top of Foxgloves and when I turned to look at her, with the sun magnifying the beauty of her eyes, the knowing was in them and we stood silently looking at each other.

'I've enjoyed your company,' she said, just above a whisper in a mid-western accent. I swallowed heavily, 'come see me if you're ever in the 'States.'

'Likewise, if you ever come to Africa.'

Another sliding door?

Chapter Four

From the army to emigrating to South Africa

The Edinburgh Castle left Southampton harbour to Cape Town in early March 1976, the exact reverse journey from over two years previously. The ship was due to be mothballed or scrapped and this was her last journey. A number of passengers weren't too kind to the loose furniture and knowing it would be destroyed, threw some of it overboard in a couple of the more extreme parties, especially as we neared Cape Town.

We made some good friends on the ship and let's say that things became a bit risqué during the two week voyage but I don't want to bore the reader with too much of that stuff. Once in the Cape we stayed at my relative's horse-breeding ranch east of the city in the Hottentots Holland mountains, a very beautiful place indeed. We loved riding the horses there and it was a very special time for Jess and I but time went by and before we knew it we were on a Jumbo jet to Salisbury, Rhodesia. I remember the latter half of the flight being very bouncy. It was the tail end of the rainy season and we hit a massive storm, or skirted it rather, kicking and thumping the plane from side to side and up and down. At one point, in the loo, I could not stay standing long enough to pull my shorts up, that's how bad it was! This was Africa…wild!

I had often told Jess how nice and welcoming Rhodesians of all races were so I was mortified when we met a horrid immigration official who gave poor Jess a hard time, just like the Aussies did to me, but after some wrangling and a promise that she would find work within two weeks of arrival (we were due to apply for permanent residence but had not done so) we went through to meet my parents, which I knew in my heart of hearts, would be tough on Jess because if my mother did not like anyone their life would be horrid, not that she was rude or anything but everything would feel like walking in glue. I am sad to say that after a few days under my mother's roof she had formed an opinion of Jess and while not totally antagonistic her manner was not one of favour. She did not like the age difference (five years my senior) and thought Jess was a bit of a hippy, which she was in her own sweet way and that's what I loved about her.

It was routine in those days for immigration officials to notify the Ministry of defence when young Rhodesian males entered the country. Due to manpower shortages in the unfolding war, we were snapped up as soon as possible. I had noticed, in my drive from the airport, under heavily bruised skies and wet roads, just how many military vehicles were around and for the first time a glimmer of panic set in. Did I really want to fight? What the hell had I brought Jess here for? I had been having a ball for two years and the thought of slugging it out in the bush was too much too soon. Maybe I could marry Jess and get a green card and go live in the USA? But no matter how I felt, nothing changed my position and within two weeks a plain brown envelope was popped into the mail box by the postman. I had to report for duty next month, to the army. My brother had done his National Service in the police so I asked for a transfer to them but the army's reply (which I still have today) was that I had leadership potential (how the heck they knew that I do not know) and the army needed men like me.

Jess was absolutely mortified and I really pitied the position she was in, a new country, nowhere of her own to live, no job (and a threatened deportation if she did not find a job) and me about to be carted off to the army where I would hardly see her for a year, which was eventually extended to eighteen months. We both felt hopeless and a few pillow cases were stained by tears from both of us. What the hell could we do. We toyed with getting married and going to the US Embassy in South Africa to get an entry permit for America but it never happened (a sliding door!). So we concentrated on finding Jess a job which we eventually did up at the University of Rhodesia in the library. She was also very fortunate to get staff accommodation which was a comfortable one-bedroom flat on the first floor of a block of flats on the university's premises.

We clung to each other as the days ticked by and then on the night of the thirteenth of April 1976 we hugged each other goodbye at Salisbury train station. Jess was in tears and I felt like screaming and running away with her but I just looked at her out the window of the train, as did many, many other young men, all waving goodbye to sweethearts, moms, dads, siblings and children. We waved until the track bent to the left and then she was gone, out of view.

The country was entering traumatic times, coming to terms with daily attacks on farmers, civilians and the military from both major ethnic tribes;

the Ndebele, an off-shoot of the Zulus in South Africa, which formed the Zapu party and the Mashona tribe which had formed Zanu. The former was led by Joshua Nkomo and the latter, eventually, by Robert Mugabe who would totally destroy the country under his corrupt and evil rule. But that was still four years away and the interim witnessed a terrible struggle to keep those swine at bay.

I have had some dreadful things said to me about being a Rhodesian and the war we fought, even this year (2020) I had a terrible Facebook discussion with an ignorant prick who said we were like Hitler's SS. I have trained myself to remain calm in most situations but that made me explode and I used, much to my shame, the most terrible language in our heated exchange. I pointed out to him that by far the biggest group of people being killed by the terrorists were their black countrymen and we white boys were drawn from comfortable civilian lives to go into the bush and kill the bastards responsible for some of the most reprehensible murders anyone had ever witnessed and at the same time protect the innocent black peasantry. How could we possibly be racist thugs under such conditions? Yes, we realised that majority rule of some type was inevitable but we wanted it to come gradually with local people trained to do the job. We could hardly expect success if we handed power over to a people that were throwing spears at us only ninety years before! And this is why all of Africa eventually failed. I also told him we did not press women and kids into huts and set them on fire, or cut off lips and ears before being forced to cook them and eat them. This was the barbarity we fought against and I will never, ever be ashamed of my role in trying to prevent this from happening. We were not racists out to keep slaves on farms and indeed many thousands of blacks fought alongside us, voluntarily at that. Indeed, the army had to turn many thousands of black volunteers away because of the cost of training them.

I made some friends on the train and the uncertainty of the morrow was eased by laughter and a few Lion Lager, a really good local beer but nothing could forestall gliding to a halt at Heany junction, twenty three kilometres outside Bulawayo, the second biggest city in the country where not so long ago I went to play school rugby and went fishing with my cousins. This was where we got off, exiting like maggots being squeezed from a wound, the steam engine hissing up ahead. A military policeman in a red, peaked cap bellowed at us to get under cover from the rain at a nearby siding, claiming quite wrongly that we were all 'mommy's boys!'; how would he know?

Like all things military it was hurry up and wait, which we did for two hours before some old, rickety Bedford troop trucks arrived. By the time we got on them we were shivering with cold and the drive to Llewellin barracks a few kilometres away was miserable indeed, whereupon we were insulted and called 'fresh-poes' (pronounced *puss*, a rather obvious and derogatory comparison with female genitalia) so I shouted back at the mockers 'old smelly poes!" which resulted in a coke bottle or two being thrown at us.

I very quickly learned to keep my trap shut and in no time we had dumped our civilian kit in a big hangar where we were divided up into platoons or such like. If I remember correctly there were no separate companies, even though there were six hundred of us. We all fell under the banner 'Depot Rhodesia Regiment', although I am sure some readers will remember otherwise.

Nonetheless we were herded into a big hangar and our medicals commenced, including coughing while a man held my balls, which nearly made me sick. We got three-in-one jabs that hurt like hell and some crazy stuff to test the longevity of our eyesight dropped into each eyeball. Like a crazed millipede, arms suffering tortuous pain and almost blind, we were shouted at and harangued into yet another huge place, where to our left things were being thrown everywhere. It was only when I got to this enormously long counter did I realise we were receiving our kit from high shelves and behind perhaps a dozen or so white guys stood ranks of African helpers.

'Neck size,' demanded a little twat the size of a nipple at the shirt counter, which was called 'combat shirt, long.'

'Seventeen,' I replied without certainty.

'Seventeen what!?' spat the little turd, jabbing tobacco-stained fingers at one barely recognisable stripe on his upper arm. I knew what the stripe meant but chose to call him 'sir' instead.

'I'm not a f*^*%*g sir!' he spat, I work for a living!'

'Corp,' I admitted

'Corporal to you, shark shit!'

'*Corporal*!' I conceded in my best foot-stomping manner. Next, combat trousers *long*, then boots, then a belt, then socks, a sleeping bag, webbing, a bayonet and so on until we looked like Amazonian ants carrying a dead frog back to their hideout. Staggering under a huge pile of stuff was a young Afrikaner guy and when he smiled at me he had no front teeth; it was all too much for me so I started cackling away, only to be admonished by someone who 'didn't work for a living' and I assumed the pip on his shoulder earned him that privilege.

The next day, before a very rushed breakfast, we went for a run and I liked the sound of our boots going thwump, thwump, thwump in unison.

To the east a pink smear warned the darkness to the west it was about to be obliterated. The air was fresh and cool and birds sang in the trees. It was actually very beautiful and I thought of Jess as I trudged along, hoping she was okay.

After breakfast we endured what all young men fear, a military haircut and as we filed through I was fascinated by all the multi-coloured locks of hair lying in heaps on the floor; men's faces varying between calm resignation, dread, anger and hate as the electric clippers mowed paths that widened until only white scalp peeked through a few millimetres of hair. But it was actually quite liberating and we dashed off for lunch, where the rule was get to the front of the queue as best as possible. I averaged between twenty and fifty men from the front on most occasions while behind me this squirming python of men looked ahead for their dishes to have pudding slopped over meat and so on but who cared, we were ravenously hungry.

'Reckon they put that blue shit in our tea to keep our peckers down?' the toothless Afrikaner enquired, looking into his mug.

'Shut up Dutchman, you dunno what a hard-on is you piece of navel lint,' said to much laughter and an even bigger toothless grin. The poor bugger was dead a year later and I often wonder if he ever got one of his little legs 'over' before his personalised Russian bullet exploded his head all over the ground.

The next day, all six hundred of us filed into a large auditorium that looked like a theatre. The murmur of six hundred voices filled the room, soon to be silenced by a Regimental Sergeant Major, before whom *all flesh* quivered, telling us to 'be quiet and sit down!' Obeying, the hall fell into silence and then the camp commander strode onto stage, whereupon the RSM brought us to attention.

The Colonel told us to sit and after the fidgeting of six hundred men had fallen into silence, he gave us a welcome speech, reminded us why we were fighting and then outlined what lay ahead. Immediately after the talk the lights went down and we saw a brief documentary about the order of battle in the Rhodesian army and finally a video about the consequences of venereal disease, which brought great merriment to the minds of young men in their prime.

'Got that from your mom,' a big guy said thumping the guy next to him as images of a grotesque penis flashed across the screen, slime dripping out the end of it; much laughter everywhere.

The next lot of slides did exactly what they were supposed to do and we watched in stunned disbelief as silent slide after silent slide showed what the terrorists had done to rural tribes' people, city dwellers, women and kids, of all colours. The deafening silence and contorted faces of the men in the audience said it all, we were aghast, horrified, saddened, angry and a little scared but mainly bloody angry and raring to go. I wondered who the little white girl was that looked like she was asleep on her back but the congealed blood from her nose to her ears explained the real reason for her pose. Tears welled in my eyes and there were a few damp ones that day. Cattle with hamstrings cut, people with lips and ears cut off, bits of charcoal with a scorched human head attached. It went on and on. I was forever changed in that hall, my innocence floated out my body like some spiritual disconnect and it never came back, ever again. And during the run that evening, we were all silent and I looked at the orange embers of the retreating sun, desiring to kill as many of those bastards as possible. Even supper was a silent affair.

The next morning we were heralded and ran to the hall once more. What now I asked myself? The Colonel strode onto the stage once again and cleared his throat.

'This is where we sort out who among you will become leaders,' he said. It had not occurred to me that some of us would get rank but the thought of it inspired me. 'I would like all men who have 'O' level and above to remain behind, all others may leave the hall. I estimated that perhaps two thirds of the men remained in their seats. When the hall became silent again, the Colonel instructed the remainder of us to meet in in a designated hangar in an hour's time and we filed out the building, chatting among ourselves.

We were all there on time, curiously watching what was going on around us and one by one we were called forward to get cloth number plates that we wore like a double-sided bib, fastening them at the back. We were then split up into our platoons and so commenced three to four days of tests to see who could think clearly, talk clearly, remember details, make plans and give clear instruction to other men. I vaguely remember being told it was the same test used in the British army, indeed a number of our instructors *were* British or regulars from our sole commando battalion, the Rhodesian Light Infantry.

To see if I was imaginative and could process thoughts I was asked to talk on toilet paper, *without* pause, for five minutes. Sounds easy but try it some time. I had to get an ammo box out of a roped enclosure with only a couple poles and ropes, with no feet touching the ground inside the enclosure, I had to plan an escape from a prisoner camp and all the time asked why? why? why? There were tests of logic and the more tired we got the quicker and more accurately we had to perform. I went to bed crushed with mental fatigue every night but by the fourth day there were only thirteen of us left out of perhaps four hundred men, let alone the two hundred that were disqualified due to a lack of formal education. That was no trivial accomplishment.

The next night we packed and off to the railway station we went, headed for Gwelo, the fourth biggest city in the country, on the road to Salisbury. It was there that we would enter the 'college of knowledge' or the 'School of Infantry', our local equivalent of Sandhurst.

We were greeted at the station the next morning by a screaming Colour Sergeant called Bartlett who threatened our livers for breakfast if we didn't get on the f^&*%*g truck instantly, our corporate call-sign becoming 'shark shit' or if we had done something bad, '*lower* than shark shit!'

And so began just under five months of hell. As National Servicemen we did a shortened, condensed version of the Regular Officer's course, which lasted about twelve to fourteen months, but it was so thorough and indeed tough, that if a National Service Officer wanted to transfer out to a regular unit he could do so without re-training, unless it was specialist training and he would be put on three months' probation to see how he coped. My good friend, Neil Jackson from school did that as well as one of my corporal's, Theo Nel, who turned out to be a superb soldier with a number of kills and the Bronze Cross of Rhodesia to his name. Our air force pilots generally rated us highly when, on many occasions, we were deployed by helicopter or operated as Fireforce personnel in lieu of regular soldiers. I recommend the reader, if interested in military matters, to read up on the Fireforce concept of vertically enveloping an enemy position by either helicopter or paratroopers or both, while a helicopter armed with paired machine guns or a 20mm cannon suppressed both enemy fire and movement until our encircling troops had closed in for the kill.

For the first six weeks the course was very, very physically demanding and exhausting, which imitated battle fatigue; an officer had to be able to think and lead in all circumstances, so long runs in the middle of the night followed by written exams and classroom lectures, where our course officer had plonked a bucket full of water at the front of the class so that if we dozed off in lectures we would have to put our heads in it to wake up. We did log runs, punishment PT, which made me vomit from exhaustion and long marches from over forty kilometres away, on the other side of Selukwe, in full battle fatigues, packs full of rocks and on some marches we had to drag car tyres behind us. When we eventually passed the course, we donated a plaque to the Officer's Mess, a small tyre mounted on varnished wood, a rope coiled across it, with the wording 'Ask of me anything except tyres' stencilled on it, which was a play on words, because we dragged those tyres so often and our course instructor, Theo Williams kept saying 'ask anything of me but time gentlemen, anything but time,' and so his saying and our tyres became a sort of anagram.

'The hill' at the camp was another horror story where we had to carry a 210 litre drum full of water to the summit, empty the drum, then run to a tap a long way below, where we filled two water bottles each, before running back uphill to empty the water into the drum. I think each bottle was less than a litre so this this took a long, long time and at least ten journeys each to that bloody tap, oh so far below us. The side of the hill consisted of loose stone and the odd thorn bush so plenty skin went missing that day. All the while we had to make our beds in traditional pack style, with blankets, mosquito nets, brushes, belts, boots etcetera all matching the bed next door, using string to line the beds up, down the row of them, putting fruit boxwood into our pillows to keep the edges of the pillows square. We never impressed the inspecting officer and went on many runs around the camp in our gleaming parade boots, which we called 'stick' boots. On one occasion the course instructor put some moths in a mosquito net and the resulting punishment was to dig one human-sized grave between two men, toss the 'moth-pets' into one of the graves while we had our backs turned and then we had to fill in the graves only to be asked if we had prayed over the 'coffin', which was a matchbox and the chorus of 'no sir!' resulted in us having to dig up all the graves, find the 'coffin', say prayers over it and then re-fill all the graves one more time. The soil was very stony and we had no skin left after all that. But that did not stop us stripping our weapons until we could do it blindfolded. And one night we chose, foolishly, to sleep on the floor rather than sleep in our beds, which had to be re-made in the pack fashion already described for morning inspection. In all honesty I barely remember the punishment for that, perhaps another long, long march where one of the guys, a South African called Charlie Pope, caught a taxi back to the camp thirty kays away, while I and all the others slugged it all the way back, him emerging from some tall grass outside the back of the camp, looking all fresh and yawning from a good night's sleep! The bastard! But clever really as we *were* being trained to think outside the box, not so?

By the time the six weeks ended there were only ten of the thirteen that had come with us from Llewellin and much to our great surprise we were due a full three days off, IF we passed our inspection! Well, I am sure the instructors wanted a break because we got the time off and headed out in

Charlie's car, called 'Miss Piggy', which was actually a VW beach buggy with a flat top welded onto the bodywork, designed to carry surf boards.

We left on a mid-Friday afternoon, stopping at a cafe to buy a coke and some cooked chips; the feeling of freedom was incredible and although only six weeks had passed it felt like a year. So much had been compacted and condensed into that period. A big gob of adrenalin shot into my system when I realised I would be seeing Jess in a few hours and worried inwardly as I had not written to her at all, I had just been too far gone most of the time. It was lovely to see the countryside of my homeland as we sped along and we soon came to Que Que and beyond that the big fertilizer factory where I would work in the coming year or two, but that was then. My mind turned back to Jess and I struggled to come to terms with the normality of life we had shared together and now we faced this scary separation and I didn't know what it meant for us and our relationship.

It was early evening when I knocked on the door to her flat. My heart was racing and my breath coming in shallow gasps even though I was superbly fit by that stage.

The door opened and Jess just stared at me in shock, her eyes going wide and then her hands went up to her mouth. I saw a tear form in the one eye as she turned her back on me.

'Come in,' she said thickly, as if I was delivering the shopping.

'How are you babe?' I asked

'As you can see,' followed by a pregnant silence. 'Want some coffee?'

'Please,' I said closing the door behind me, scanning the room as I followed her into the kitchenette. Jess had done well, the place looked good but my emotions were swirling as if I was meeting a stranger for the first time. She was my girl yet I was scared, who had listened to those records by the stereo with her? What had she been doing in her private time and who with? Thoughts and questions tumbled over each other to be the first to enter the analytical part of my brain, but they all arrived simultaneously. My previous life with her was gone, she was a stranger. Her shoulders were shaking faintly and a sniff pointed to the tears running down her cheeks. I came up behind her and held her tight, nestling my face in the crook of her neck, saying nothing. We held on for a long time.

'Six weeks and nothing…' she began. I turned her gently to face me, resting my hands on her shoulders.

'I'm sorry Jess, I've been through hell the whole time, I have barely had a minute to myself, there is only one public phone there and it's either in use or doesn't work and I just felt too tired to write letters, I'm really sorry.' She shrugged herself free of my grip and put the kettle on. 'Tell me about yourself, how have you coped, what you been up to, has my brother or parents been in contact?'

We went through to the lounge, putting an LP on the stereo and talked for a long time. I could sense her unwinding and we even shared a laugh or two. She smiled when I regaled her of all my experiences and I think she began to understand. Wine mellowed both of us. I suddenly felt very tired and decided to take a bath. I eased into the water and slid my head into its silent depths, listening to my heart beat and the muffled sound of the LP coming through. I sensed her before she touched me, she was standing naked next to the bath.

'You look gorgeous,' she breathed into my mouth, 'the army's done wonders….' Our kiss was deep, slow and passionate and the teasing caress of my inner thigh made my belly wobble, sending shockwaves from my feet to the top of my head. I did not realise how much passion I had suppressed and we were like two hungry, wild animals that had just found food for the first time in weeks. It went on until the early hours of the morning and then we fell into a drugged sleep, the best sleep ever, I could not tell if I was dead or alive.

We were short of food for breakfast so I walked to the shops at the Grange, looking at life and letting life look at me and enjoyed the freedom of the walk, looking at the nice houses, the sprinklers going tush-tush-tush, the kids playing on bikes, ladies gardening. I wonder if any one of them knew or cared that I may die to protect them one day and I couldn't help the thought that we could not sustain this lifestyle for too long, there were too many powerful forces working against us.

When I got to the shops I used a public phone and begged, pleaded and cajoled my brother to lend me his 1275GT mini, after all Jess and I had carried the bloody stainless steel exhaust pipe for it all the way from the UK; an exchange is not robbery. Amazingly he agreed! By the time I got back to the University the car was already there. Brian was doing a civil engineering degree at the university and after leaving the keys with Jess, he ambled back to the large concrete beams he was pressure-breaking for the practical part of his thesis and dad would collect him later. I felt so uplifted being allowed to use his car, floating backwards to the moon without a spacesuit on was easier than being allowed to drive that hallowed vehicle! And I loved its 'get up and go', enhanced by Brian's tweaks and additions to the engine.

By noon we headed out for Mazoe dam, a lovely drive through very prosperous farms and rocky hills. We paused at the kiosk where they sold bags of oranges and fresh juice from fruit picked at the massive estate below the dam wall, indeed the dam was built to supply water to the orange trees. Of course the best orange crush in the world, Mazoe Orange juice, was made there and it was so popular that when Rhodesians emigrated they asked for relatives 'back home' to bring the juice in plastic bottles when they came to visit them.

A large army convoy pulled in while we were there. Jess enjoyed the wolf-whistles but I felt a tug in my heart as I would be them soon, so I watched on with surging emotions. I wanted to cry actually. We packed a bag of oranges in the boot of the car and headed downhill, past the dam wall, over a bridge where the fever trees stood and hung a left to go and sit in the sun at the Mazoe club but as I looked left at the turn-off, my heart sank. The swimming pool where we used to swim as kids was full of weeds, the band enclosure had collapsed under the weight of Bougainvilleas growing wild over it and the lawn where we had suntanned and teased girls was now grass six foot high. I drove to the hotel bar where we had nagged and whined dad for a Hubbly Bubbly and chips but it was dark with only a few 'locals' loitering around the bar counter. We drove away in silence, my mood sinking really low, this was my first taste of Rhodesia's Uhuru and I did not like the feel of it one little bit. Jess did not have my attachment to the place so when she asked me why my face looked so long she may not have understood the answer.

'Well, black people have rights too,' she said.

'Their rights being expressed have put bat shit and weeds in the pool back there,' I snapped rather abruptly and then apologised. My mood only softened when we had found a place to park overlooking the dam at the Mozoe rowing club. I expressed all my fears of change in the country and even questioned why I was bothering to fight. I certainly thought of going AWOL but it was my home, my folks lived here, my friends and other kin lived here, could I just abandon them? Not likely, no, indeed the answer was a resounding 'no' in my heart but Jess and a life of freedom, marriage and kids was lurking in my heart too. I was so torn, but talking did help. We splashed a bit of vodka in the orange crush we'd bought and before long I couldn't see the dam anymore, her hair was in the way as she faced me, sitting on my lap, kissing deeply. Everything 'out there' fled away and I didn't care anymore, well, not right then anyway.

* * *

The guard lowered the boom to the front gate of the School of Infantry. My heart was somewhere in my boots and my gut was wobbling like a drunk in need of a fix. What the hell lay before us? And the memories of my time with Jess swirled around inside my head, pushing my mood lower and lower. It had been so good with her that I was pining already, I really hurt like hell and Jess had been sobbing when I left her. I think we both knew the stress we were under would break us up and that's just what happened sometime during the remaining twelve weeks of the course. To this day I do not know the technicalities of the break-up and even contacted Jess in Mexico to go over it again for the purposes of this book but forty four years is a long time to hold memories in any form of clarity. She seems to remember my second weekend off was a disaster. I had apparently arrived drunk and allowed the guys with me to make lewd comments towards her. I do not remember that and it's out of alignment with my character but maybe I can't remember because I was indeed drunk. Anyway, when it came to the graduation ceremony I felt Jess must be my date and she hitch-hiked down to be with me, staying with a couple from the Edinburgh Castle who lived in Gwelo. I don't recall seeing her during our final march-past, the weapons display or the mock camp attack and that night, dressed in a tuxedo and dickie-bow tie I was dragged into the fun and games being played by my course mates and simply do not remember doing anything with her, which is appalling after the effort she made to come and see me. I have often been a complete bastard to those I love. I just don't know why.

That night we played 'Bezant' whereby we had to put a short stick on our forehead, rest the other end on the ground and then run in circles around it. On standing erect we had to swipe at an empty Bezant Orange tin and whack it like a golf ball. The only problem is that your head spins so much you stagger off sideways, thrashing at the air, before falling over and laughing your socks off. This game was conducted by the pool and at least two guys landed up in its chilly water.

We also played tug of war among ourselves and any hangers-on. I had borrowed the tuxedo and it was too big for me around the waist so it had been pinned with a safety pin. Well, all the exertions pulled the pin out so when I stood up my trousers fell down, resulting in much mocking and merriment. I remember that! Earlier in the day we had handed over our wooden plaque to be hung alongside the plaques of many other courses, in the mess and even donated a 210 litre drum called Felix to the next training course, which was double our intake size. Felix would keep the drum we carried, Felicity, good company in all future 'hill exertions'. However, little did anyone know that someone went to Felicity in the night and punched it full of holes with a pick! Ha!

The weeks leading up to this night had been very interesting and all the bullshit slowed to a crawl from the seventh week onwards, although long runs and bastard assault-courses waited for us when we cocked up. I excelled in everything we did and loved learning tactics. The counter-insurgency training, COIN for short, was probably the best in the world at the time. I enjoyed going for helicopter rides to prepare for Fireforce duties, learning how to assault positions and commence a follow-up, which involved learning how to track. The third phase was all about Classical war and that too was fascinating, marching to a start line very early in the morning or near evening, helmet on, bayonets fixed, charging with a mighty roar when we got close to the enemy trenches; learning how to prepare sand models for an attack and how to leap-frog back in a withdrawal. Ant Marsh, the sword of honour recipient for best recruit, had twisted his ankle badly and was tasked to lead the troops we 'attacked', situated in a long trench. We had marched miles to the start line, arriving there before dawn and then put into our assault positions, lying face down on the hard, cold ground, helmets heavy on our necks; green start lights faced us, they could only be seen in one direction and that was us. Then we got up and walked slightly uphill to the defending troops, our calves making a snake-like slithering sound as they brushed through short grass. Then, as we approached the enemy trench we charged, yelling like crazy, bayonets forward, firing rapidly.

Ant said if it had been a real attack he would have crapped in his pants. Dawn and sunset are chosen for attacks because there is a transfer between the use of cones in the eye to the rods in the eye, which takes a few seconds; it's called the 'twinkling of an eye'. The quantity of men charging at you in a dawn or evening attack is thereby hard to determine, often looking double the number which adds fear to the hearts of the defenders. Enemy minds are also numb with sleep in the morning and relaxed in the evening.

We Suffered attacks in the middle of the night with real tracer arcing overhead, eating cold or no food as the trainee officers always ate last. I loved-hated it but I did well in the third phase, according to my course officer and I inwardly thanked all those toy soldiers I had played with as a sixteen year-old, instead of chasing girls; well, some of the time!

At the end of the evening I could not find Jess, so, finding out where she was staying, stole Phil Laing's motorbike and zoomed out the back of the School where the gate was all but a shadow of its former self. In fact there wasn't one, but it was a long circular ride to get to the house she was in. If I had been able to leave by the front gate it would have taken me five minutes to get there but I had to go to the end of a small ridge line, part of the 'hill', then come back on the other side to almost the gate once more, taking at least twenty minutes. I was tipsy and stupid and misinterpreted a bend to the right as a straight road, due to the street lighting and went somersaulting over the kerb and sidewalk until a pine hedge slowed my advance. I felt very little pain, which was more than could be said for the motorbike with its wobbly front wheel, twisted handlebars and a front headlight pointing at the moon. I feared what Phil would think, my dear, dear friend who was made to drink pool acid by Mugabe's thugs many years later but for now I had to get to Jess and wobble-limped the remaining few kilometres to her home.

Jess was wide awake when I got to her and she was sitting silently in deep thought under the soft glow of a table lamp, glass in hand when I knocked on the front door. Her eyes went wide like that time we had our first weekend together and after a cryptic comment about pine needles in my hair we came together and squeezed each other for a long time. A bloody great big invisible axe had crashed down between us and it was impossible to rekindle what we had. Even making love to her would have felt like bedding a stranger and so we sat and talked and reminisced about good times and what could have been. I had no idea then and only discovered forty years later when Jess contacted me out of the blue, that she had desired marriage and kids but it had never been mentioned to me, not once. Our time together ended when I opened the door and stepped into the bright sunlight of early morning, it was day one of the next chapter of my life. She was gone and it was all over, but our end has gutted and confused me to this day.

* * *

I went back to Salisbury for four days R&R. It was so painful knowing Jess was just a few miles away but I resisted going to see her. I carried home in my left breast pocket my deployment orders. Only three of us had come out of the 'college of knowledge' as Officers, three out of an intake of six hundred men. I felt very proud of myself and no matter what anyone thought of me in the coming years as an Officer, this was something that could not be taken away from me. In fact, our course had been deemed 'too tough' by the School's Commanding Officer. He was worried too many good men would be sent back to their units in the next intake of trainees, if the level of physical pain we endured, was continued. And I had survived that!

That Sunday afternoon Phil Laing, Pete Wells (a giant of a man) and myself headed off for our postings to 4 Independent Company, Rhodesia Regiment. The troopers were all National Servicemen while all the Company Commanders were from Regular battalions. It was an awesome and potent combination of experience and youth and in some cases the Independent companies performed as well as Regular outfits. Like I said earlier, our training was not to be sneezed at and we were all proficient soldiers in a small, but efficient and disciplined, army. I am very, very proud of having served with such an incredible body of motivated and intelligent men.

I had not been beyond Bulawayo but by the time we had finished with touring a few bars in Bulawayo it was dark and the car's headlamps cast a spear of light into the inky blackness ahead; eyes from animals reflected back at us. We arrived at 4 Indep's base camp in Wankie in the early morning. It was a coal mining town, sitting atop one of the biggest coal reserves in the world. The village wallowed in a basin, hot and steamy whereas our base was up on a hill where the breeze blew. Phil parked the car outside a building with a sign that said 'Officers Quarters' and before long we were walking down a corridor on a superbly polished parquet floor to our private rooms. Rank has its privilege, no bunking down for me!

We ate a superb breakfast and then it was time to meet our troops at 09:00 hours. I made the rookie error of walking bareheaded up the tar road to the parade square whereupon I was admonished to go and get my beret on top of my 'bloody head, now!' What a way to begin my command and by the time I got back one hundred and ten men stood at attention, facing Pete Wells and Major Pearce, RAR. The latter commanded 'at ease' and when the odd bit of shuffling died down the Major gave us a welcome speech and briefly outlined which area of the country we would be protecting, which was vast and easily big enough to lose an entire Division of fifteen thousand men in. He also explained where our individual platoons would be based. I commanded 4 Platoon; a list of names was passed to me and I was told to prepare my men to take them to Victoria Falls, one of the world's seven wonders, that's how staggering it is. My heart leapt at the thought of it. Pete Wells commanded 5th Platoon if my memory is right, also to Victoria Falls while Dino Quinn, who got three stripes at the 'college of knowledge' was allocated 6 Platoon, based in Wankie. I could see him mouth 'shit' followed by a small shake of his head. It would be a terribly hot place to patrol, dry and full of Baobab trees and bugger all else. He would also provide troopers for Fireforce duties. It wasn't all bad because we did rotate between the two bases but for some reason my Platoon only had one tour of duty in Wankie.

My time at Vic Falls would transform my life like never before; what would the outcome have been if I had been allocated Wankie? Another sliding door question!

Once we had been dismissed we were sent to the Quartermaster who allocated weapons, magazines, ammunition (including hand grenades, smoke canisters and white Phosphorous), micro flare pistols, bivvies (small single-sheet tents to sleep under). I got six A76 medium range radios, big boxy crappy things, six Belgian .762 (long) machine guns, sleeping bags and so on, all of which I got my sergeant, Torode to sign for. Let him swing if anything got lost; it was his job to sign anyway.

I then went down and inspected the two × seven ton Mercedez Benz troop trucks, mine proofed with layers of conveyor belting, sandbags and steel over wheel arches. Large roll bars would protect the troops strapped in, facing outwards towards the enemy, in the event of a roll from a landmine taking a wheel off, or any other misadventure. The sides of the truck could fold in half lengthwise and that's where the men would rest their feet and propel themselves off the vehicle in an ambush. They were bloody good vehicles and could go anywhere if put into 'diff-lock' mode.

* * *

It was lunch time by the time we headed for Vic Falls one hundred kilometres to the north west and the climb out of the steaming 'giant's potty' was most welcome, to feel the cool, fresh breeze at the top of the nearby escarpment and as we trundled along the countryside became greener, the trees taller and all in all it looked just beautiful country. I was sad we were at war with our countrymen and I despised the big players out there that were using us as a pawn in their big power games. Negotiations swayed back and forth but all the while the amazing lifestyle we had come to expect as normal was being eroded, with farmers leaving the land, holiday resorts here and there shut down or threatened daily of an attack by pretty cruel, rabid, unruly men sold a lie that they would get a farm and a car and job when the white man was gone. But our volunteer black soldiers, truly fine men that fought with distinction in World War two did not swallow the red pill and fought shoulder to shoulder alongside us. The drain on our manpower resulted in six weeks in and six weeks out of the army through the whole war, so emigration started to accelerate and there just weren't the crowds at sports events and we had to buy coupons for fuel and so on but we pressed on anyway.

My first glimpse of the mighty Victoria Falls was the spray towering up into the air, visible from near the airport about twenty kilometres away. We glided down the main street, houses draped in Bougainvilleas to our left, followed by shops and on the right the police station and national parks offices. We slowed and entered the gate to the police camp. It was a warm day with sun and tourists in shorts and slops and a fair degree of road traffic.

The 'cop shop' was a modern building, its plaster painted pale grey, the same as all police Land rovers and the walls were topped with a few courses of concrete breeze blocks, painted white. A very tall aerial poked up into the sky with various antennae aimed this way and that. I dismounted, climbed four steps and entered a long passage with a shiny floor and fans swishing overhead. I asked a passing policeman where the army ops room was and headed in the direction of the man's outstretched arm.

Captain Von Stranz, a man about thirty five with sandy blond hair, looked up from a desk he was leaning over when I walked through the door. Two radio operators with earphones on were casually reading magazines and the wall off to the left was one large map of the area, a few coloured pins pegged here and there.

'You must be Ballinger,' he said offering his hand, 'Sean Von Stranz.'

'Yes sir, correct'.

We spent an hour or so together while he outlined what had happened in the area, where our neighbouring troops were and what natural markers, like rivers, separated us. I was horrified by the size of land we had to cover, from Kazungula in the west, which borders on Botswana, south east to Pandamantenga, then east to Wankie, north to the Zambezi river and then back along the Zambezi river all the way to Kazungula, which is thousands of square kilometres and *we were it*, one hundred and ten men! The chance of intercepting terrorists was akin to pinning the proverbial tail on the donkey in a huge football stadium. But we were good soldiers and the enemy, rather lacking in ingenuity, often used the same points of crossing the Zambezi river, thanks to their unimaginative Russian handlers and the very rugged terrain we operated in. I was not very happy when Sean told us we were going out on patrol that night. What was the hurry if nothing had happened so far? I thought it madness, this whole area was totally unfamiliar to us, we were green recruits and had not even set up camp yet.

Maps were handed to me and I went outside to brief my guys and to ensure they were getting sorted out for the patrol, their eyes wide in disbelief that we would be operational so quickly. I told them where to dig their shell-scrapes, in an arc backing off the police building and once everything that would remain behind was buttoned up, we ate a light meal and headed off on patrol, all blackened up, full combat kit weighing us down. Our trucks turned left out the main gate, back up the incline we had coasted along to the police station earlier, then right towards Kazungula, then first right onto a dirt track that ran straight down to the Zambezi river, at the bottom of a long, gently sloping escarpment. It was almost dark by then but we could not go further than a hundred metres from the tar road for fear of detonating landmines and de-bussing, we formed up into a long snake of twenty four men, primed to react instantly to an ambush. Although fit were soon panting a bit and sweating due to the incredibly soft sand underfoot which felt like walking on the upper part of a dry beach.

It was dark by the time we reached the valley floor and I must admit the unknown unnerved me a bit and I got a hell of a fright when I neared some Elephant grass, which stands three metres in height and this wall, swaying in the breeze in front of my straining eyes, looked like an alien of sorts, until my vision cleared and I saw what it was. The smells there were unique, of dust mixed with the vinegary smell of urine and dung, not at all offensive to the nostrils as it was from wild game and not from a pig or cow. In fact it was pleasant enough to occasionally set alight to keep the incredibly annoying Mopani flies at bay during the day. Crickets screeched and in the distance some animal or other cried out an alarm. I surveyed the area around me and settled on a flat patch of ground to my right, just up the sloping ground. I put the men in a circle facing outwards, set the guard and lay back on my sleeping bag, sweat drying slowly, muscles twitching as they relaxed. I put my hands behind my head and marvelled at the magnificent crystalline display of stars winking at each other, set like tears against the darkest of velvet, so close I could scoop up a handful. My mind drifted, recalling all my adventures overseas and of course Jess. I still felt the empty ache and confusion of it all and it was late into the night before I found the nothingness of deep sleep.

Two weeks later, after patrolling the river front in groups of four, separated by small tributaries on the map, we were collected by our trucks and taken back to camp for twenty four hours R&R. The countryside was magnificent, tall trees had vines draping off them like an old man's braces, sparse leaves scattering the sunlight, spreading dappled shadows all about, very little or no grass. Vervet monkeys in their hundreds darted here and there, their little eyebrows bobbing up and down as they stared at us in wide-eyed wonder and confusion. A big male Baboon strutted his stuff nearby, his pink bum a pallet of delight for the admiring harem that gibbered around him, swatting miscreant babies away lest he kill one in a pique of anger. The land unfolded like a rugged, undulating movie as we headed the fifteen or so kays east to base, passing the massive, thatched A'Zambezi hotel slap bang on the water's edge to our left and then up ahead, looming out of the background of trees flicking by, like a towering massif, was the roof of the Elephant Hills Hotel made of greyish, faded straw, atop whitewashed walls. The Crocodile farm flicked by on the right. I was fascinated by the sudden contrast of the rich green fairways of the Gary Player designed golf course, divided by the road we were driving on, rising to the 1st and 18th hole set just under the towering hotel itself. Golfers hacked away at little white balls, dressed sassily in shorts, T-shirts and white golf shoes, some fending off ever-aggressive Warthogs that were kneeling on their front legs, doing a 'communion' on the sweet grass, munching it as quickly as it grew; constant pests to the poor groundskeeper.

But what struck me most was the difference between the golfers and my men, still blackened up, stinking to high heaven, shirt sleeves removed and trouser crotches split open for aeration and those pansies with fawning women in frilly skirts tittering behind painted fingernails and big sunglasses. They didn't even look at us as we drove by, they did not even notice us, wave or whatever. Nothing, no nothing at all happened. I felt riled to say the least.

* * *

It felt like Heaven showering and dressing into clean clothes, shaving and having a crap in a toilet bowl. The men were, sadly for them, barred from the two casinos, which were restricted to sergeants and above but good for us with rank as competition getting to know the lovely croupiers was vastly reduced.

Torode and I headed for the opulent Elephant Hills Casino Hotel which was a real eye-opener with its padded carpets, flowing curtains, tastefully decorated walls and up-market furniture covered in the best pig skin one could buy. We bought a drink and sat at one of the roulette tables, shrinking in embarrassment as we knew not what to do amid commands like change, splits, orphans and so on. I handed over ten dollars, placed a few bets and lost it in seconds, as did my second, third and fourth bank note; simply swallowed up. That was a lot of money in the 1970s, indeed a quarter of my salary but it was the superior smirk on the croupier's face that did it for me.

'I'm out there protecting you!' I screamed in my head 'and you don't care!' and then to Torode, 'let's get the hell out of here!'

We went to the magnificent Victoria Falls hotel next for a beer and a superb Rhodesian steak, served on the patio beneath towering hardwood trees, illumined by green lamps. A very good band played music of the day like 'rock your baby' by George McCrae and I swallowed involuntarily when my eyes zeroed in on a few girls turning slowly on the dance floor. The sight of their firm bodies and womanliness made my breathing become a little shallower but I didn't have the guts to ask anyone to dance, even though they more often than not glanced in our direction as we sat there in full-length uniform, rifles lying on the floor.

'I'm off to the other casino,' I said at length, but Torode opted to stay where he was. I walked the few hundred metres to the Casino Hotel and immediately noted it was a bit more run down and threadbare than the other hotels but, as I got to know later, the place was owned by a single man, Don Goldin whereas both other hotels were part of big hotel chains. I trotted up the staircase and entered the casino where five or six tables occupied quite a large, square room with a high ceiling. There were about thirty punters at the Roulette tables. Donna Summer's 'Winter Melody' washed over the room. A big man who looked like a Mexican strolled over to me and introduced himself as the Casino Manager, inviting me to take a seat at one of the Roulette tables.

Marilyn came over to serve, with one or two new people joining me. She was the spitting image of a young Gloria Estafan. I couldn't help looking at her green, flashing eyes but, like at the other hotel, she used them to look down her nose at me. This was no love at first sight thing but it would turn into a heady relationship that would rip the guts out of both of us and more.

I left dejected and quite broke at about two in the morning and found it hard to sleep in my smelly sleeping bag in my slit trench by the cop station. The next morning I put on some shorts, a shirt and my trusty car-tyre slops, enjoying the downhill walk to the Casino Hotel where most of us went to swim. I was in peak physical condition, brown and young so I enjoyed the dipping of the odd pair of sunglasses of the ladies as well as the odd head swivelling to look at me. Why not? Who wouldn't?

I suntanned until late in the afternoon, whereupon I slid into the cool waters, going under to listen to the silence, surfacing with a blow of bubbles, floating on my back and looking up at the clouds. I bumped someone's head and turning to see who it was, found the green eyes staring at me. My heart leapt and I felt even more buoyed when she smiled.

'You need to watch where you're going,' she quipped in her typical mercurial way that I soon came to know, love and hate. It was part of her character, she brooked no fools that's for sure.

'Didn't know you'd been given the right of way,' I tossed back. She smiled again.

'I have to get ready for work soon, fancy a drink up there in the meantime,' she said, hooking her thumb behind her head. I looked up at the parapet walls of the Summit Bar, the pointy top of a folded beach umbrella just visible at this angle.

'Sure, you're paying for colliding with my head,' I smiled.

We met twenty minutes later, the silence of the lift giving way to the swish of doors opening. She was already there, dressed in a red trouser suit, so popular in the 70s and 80s, big auburn hair, make-up on, high heels with a dainty gold chain around her right ankle. She looked amazing and I swallowed nervously. I could see she was a bit older than me but I liked that. I asked what she wanted and ordered a Ginger Square at her recommendation. It was a fruity drink made of Ginger Ale, Ginger Brandy, bitters, lime, fresh mint and cherries, with frosted sugar around the lip of the glass. It was like a Manta ray with a big sting in its tail. We chinked glasses and I sat facing her. The golden embers from the dying sun caught the green of her eyes, emphasizing how lovely they were. To my left the spray from the thundering waterfall towered upwards, a gateway to the Heavenlies, boiling within from the glow of the sun, long streamers of spray floating to earth among the small stretch of jungle still surrounding the falls.

It was relaxing talking with her and we laughed easily. The tail of the Ginger Square was doing its magic and I felt a thrill and attraction like I had never felt before. We teased out our time for as long as possible, in fact right up to the casino opening at 8 pm and then she left me sitting there. I was tired and the temptation to go and see her in the casino was tempered by the fact that I had to deploy the following day so in the end I went to bed.

* * *

The dense Mopani trees gave way to scrubland as we moved east into the African tribal trust lands just shy of the airport, spreading inland for about forty kilometres. We were headed for an Internal Affairs outpost in the furthest part of the inhabited area, a square sand-walled structure approximately sixty metres by sixty metres with a pill-box at each corner. I met the Internal Affairs guys then instructed each stick leader to mount a machine gun in each corner of the keep, with spare boxes of ammo, grenades, flares and radios. I also met Ian, the leader of a police Blackboot company and his second in command, ideally nicknamed 'nipple' due to his size. It was a first for me, shaking hands with the forward part of a tit.

We began patrolling in the area the next day, ambushing at night and this went on for weeks at a time. It was hard to stay concealed because the goats belonging to the peasants had eaten everything and I mean everything, flat! And it was continuous hot work that never seemed to end, those darn Mopani flies (actually very small bees that produced superb honey) aimed for any moisture which meant eyes, nose, mouth and even one's ears. We would gather dry dung and light it, the flames giving way to smoke which drove the pests away, they were so irritating that you could go mad, quite literally. As soon as their day shift ended the mosquitoes started the night shift, with maybe an hour's grace between the two, although this entire area had few mozzies. Not like Mozambique on the 'Russian front' which literally heaved with the little bastards, their screeching whine loud enough to keep you awake.

It wasn't long before we killed a few curfew breakers which naturally upset the local population and to this day I regret my part in the shooting of a young man that was only seventy metres from home, having delayed his departure from a beer drink. The sounds of his wailing mother will stay with me until I die.

After some weeks of this, the enemy decided to hit back. They had no choice in the matter because if they didn't have a go at us their prestige among the local population would falter. And they went overboard with the assault on our keep, numbering fifty or more men, with mortars in support. I had been out deploying men when I saw a flare rise into the far off night sky. Faint rumblings echoed down the valley and tracer criss-crossed the inky blackness. My heart sank. I raced back to take charge of the situation but by the time I got there the attack was coming to an end or quite possibly came to an end because the enemy might have thought the vehicles were reinforcements. Whatever the reason, when I approached the main gate, the air was thick with the smell of cordite, stinging my throat. No-one was brave enough to come and open the gate until a skinny little guy slid down the earth embankment, undoing the lock quicker than a professional safecracker. It was a long night calming nerves with a few beers. Two Intaf guards had been wounded. I was very impressed with those African men, they had remained atop the earthen walls without any overhead protection during the two hour bombardment, their dated .303 bolt action rifles at the ready. That took guts let me tell you!

We did a sweep the next morning and found over fifty mortar shell tailfins, several inside our keep. The remainder of the shells landed within twenty metres of the earthen walls, which is pretty good shooting from over a kilometre away at night! One small crater was laid bare just behind my command bunker and I often wonder what would have happened to me if I had been in the keep at the start of the attack (a sliding door event for sure).

A few nights later I was deploying men when the lead vehicle I was driving hit a landmine. It is not common or even acceptable for an officer to drive a truck but call it a premonition or whatever, I told the driver to get on the back of the vehicle. It had just finished raining an hour beforehand so I was most surprised to see footprints in the soft sand. I was thinking there must be a curfew breaker out and about but the thought was never completed. A bright red flash, instantly followed by a massive explosion, blew the left, front wheel off the truck. In that split instant I saw the windscreen wobble, in slow motion, fold in on itself and disappear in a cloud of dust. All went dark and through a numbed haze I saw tracer racing away from us at a mad lick. It was the guys on the back clearing any potential ambushers away. I looked for my weapon but it was wedged tight between the back of my seat and the cab wall. It had been tossed out of its clips by the bang. I got out of my seatbelt and scrambled up through the cupola in the roof of the truck; thick, sandy dust was settling on us, the moisture in it instantly vaporised

'Stop firing!' I shouted, 'de-bus off the rear of the truck and walk back fifty metres in the tyre tracks and form an all-round defence.'

I ducked down and this time I managed to retrieve my rifle. The cab was full of glass cubes which crunched under my feet when I finally exited it for the last time. The next morning, after a sweep for anti-personnel mines had been conducted, I went back to have a look and get a few snaps taken. It shocked me no end that some armour plating had come up from the foot well on the passenger's side of the cab and pegged into its steel casing roughly where my head would have been. The 'big guy' was looking after me!

It was with great relief when another platoon took over from us and we headed back to town. We spent the next two days moving camp to old, disused national park quarters, cutting grass, painting the walls of the buildings, getting the plumbing and electricity working. The first night off I had a lovely hot shower and walked down to see Marilyn. Her eyes lit up when she saw me and a big smile revealed white, even teeth. My heart fluttered and I knew, just knew we would become lovers, which we did that very night. She lived in the casino's staff quarters literally one block away from the new army camp and a quick three minute sprint would get me there. I virtually, but not quite, moved in with her. On my days off I would go to the Croc farm with her and have English tea and scones on the green grass, laughing when a big Croc bit the snout of another at feeding time, pulled one-armed bandit machines at Elephant Hills, walked in the rain forest, getting soaked to the skin and dreaming our lives away on the very romantic evening 'booze cruise' on the majestic and mighty Zambezi river. It was the booze cruises I loved, with the afternoon sun caressing our tanned skin and Mally would cuddle into me, her back to my chest and we would sit in silence, looking at the beauty of Africa around us, the big Elephant coming down to drink, as well as Sables, Kudu and infinite numbers of bobbing and diving Springbok, leaping as high as any athlete. The Captain of the boat always paused before turning for home to allow tourists to photograph the sun balancing on the surface of the golden water like some huge alien orb and Hippos would deny each other with their loud 'Uh, Uh Uhs', Fish Eagle's would scream their lovely cry, throwing their heads back in flight to let the sound echo far and wide. I simply adore Africa, there is no place like it on Earth. And we joked that the second bang was the door shutting behind us when we got back to her place, the first bang being us of course as we were so intensely into each other. We loved lying on our big double bed listening to the massive rain storms outside, water lashing the roof, sounding like a million toy soldiers hammering their feet on the galvanized iron. Our sweat cooled, accelerated by the air coming from a rattling old air conditioner the sound of which echoes in my mind nearly forty five years later.

It was soon time to be deployed once more and my task this time was to 'show the flag' along the Botswana border. An old ferret armoured car was attached to my small fleet of vehicles, as well as an Eland armoured car which packed a big punch with its 90mm gun. In addition we were given a two inch mortar tube with two cases of shells, twelve in each. We drove west along the lovely tar road to Kazungula, the latter fifteen kays being a very good dirt road and after spending a day in the area we would head south east to Pandamatenga before returning via the same route, just to let the locals know we were still around and looking out for trouble-makers.

We met the armoured cars at the police camp just east of the border with Botswana. The camp commander was a bit wild, like me and one night we went out in his speedboat and shot up the plate glass windows of the Zambian army's officers' quarters, clearly visible from the Zambezi river, the ride there on water so calm it looked like a carpet of stars was below *and* above us. But that was for later. After chatting to the sergeant who commanded the Eland, we drove to the border post with Botswana where we got as close to their troops on the other side of the border as possible, just to make them a bit pissed off. I noted with joy that a few put their helmets on.

Steve at the police camp had recommended we turn north at the customs and immigration post and, running parallel with the border on our left, we could reach some bunkers overlooking the Zambezi river. This we did, passing through flat, waterlogged land with big monitor lizards scurrying off the nice, warm sand of the track we were driving on. The first bunker was full of hornets and rather run down so we went on to a second, smaller bunker right on the river's edge. The ferry from Botswana to Zambia was only two hundred metres to our left and across the Zambezi river was a white building with a red roof, this being the customs and immigration offices for Zambia. A large concrete ramp led into the water to allow cars driving off the ferry to enter Zambia at this point.

We settled in and watched the opposite bank for a while. We very quickly established the presence of a large Zambian army bunker just to the left of centre as we looked across the river, with possibly a smaller one between the big bunker and the immigration post. Not long after our arrival Zambian troops climbed on to the roof of their bunker and started insulting both ourselves and Ian Smith in perfect English, well Zambia, like us had once been British territory. We swore back at them telling them Kaunda was a shit and so on but their jibes about good old Smithy, our Prime Minister, started to wear thin on me. Maybe calling Kaunda a little girl in a skirt annoyed them but before long and a little more provocation to boot, we had started a war with each other.

We dived into our bunker and I ordered the men to return fire. I would have been disobeying strict instructions not to fire on Zambia first but could return fire at will, if attacked. They fired first so we let rip with machine guns, the ferret scout car and the 90mm main gun of the Eland. The latter was a precious weapon and I was fascinated to see the water ripple rapidly as the big round sped over it to its targets in Zambia. We demolished their bunker in a huge cloud of dust but we didn't have it all our own way because a 12.7 mm heavy machine gun opened up from just downstream a bit, so well camouflaged that I had not seen it. The gun's white tracer flashed past the ferret, causing the gunner to duck inside the steel hull for protection but in all honesty if their aim had been a bit lower the ferret would have been Swiss cheese. The next thing there was a loud whooshing sound from near the 12.7's trench and suddenly branches from a tree just above the ferret, came crashing down on its cupola. I told the driver to withdraw which he did with great alacrity, pulling back several hundred yards to the immigration post. The Eland had been hammering away with its main gun and the coaxial machine gun but he too was now very vulnerable. The noise was intense as the barrel of the Eland's long gun was lined up with our eardrums and we had to duck and cover our ears every time it fired.

Deciding to help squash the enemy, I ran out to the nearest truck and retrieved the mortar tube and both cases of ammo. Luckily for us the army unit previously based there had built a mortar pit just behind the bunker and into this piled three of us. The seriousness of the moment was eased by Abbott asking if there was 'room for one more' which was a line from a local soap advert, where the narrator explains there is always 'room for one more' if you used their brand of soap. I laughed nervously.

I had had rudimentary training on the 2 inch mortar at the 'college of knowledge' but to be honest it is such a simple weapon to use the training did not need to be very intensive or long. I set the charges to the base of the shell to the best of my ability, aimed and pulled the firing trigger at the base of the tube. The dear little round left the barrel at a luxurious pace so I was able to watch it go high into the air before arcing back to land at the target, which in this instance was the 12.7 mm gun and the RPG 7 operator somewhere in that area. I was very pleasantly surprised to see the first round explode just where I wanted it to and while I adjusted the angle of the tube ever so slightly to compensate for it having bedded in a bit, one of my men set the charges. I fired maybe a dozen more shells at the base of a big tree where the 12.7 mm gun was and thankfully no more rounds or RPGs (rocket propelled grenades) came from that direction. However, we were still in a bit of crap from some other unseen weapon so I dropped all of the remaining shells into likely targets and among some enemy trucks parked under a tree. One of the rounds I dropped on the 12.7mm machine gun nest had set the grass on fire and by the time the sun was setting, huge, swirling flames were reaching into the sky, the burning arms doing a reflective dance off the now dark waters of the river. An easterly wind blew, pushing the flames towards the big bunker in front of us and the vehicle park a bit further back. By the time it was fully dark the opposite bank was a glowing mass of embers. I'm amazed the immigration post survived.

I instructed my guys to walk out the back of the fence that enclosed us and wait for me a couple hundred yards back. I then got some empty cardboard ammo boxes and wedged them over the brake lights of the troop vehicle, the other vehicle having been left at the immigration post earlier in the day. Having commanded the protesting driver to go back with the other men I started the engine up and eased quietly out of the bunker compound, keeping the revs low and making sure I used the handbrake and not the brake pedal lest I light up a glowing, red brake light. Even though I had put cardboard over them one may have fallen off and even chinks of light in that darkness could be seen easily.

We literally cheered when we got back to the safety of the police camp a few kays east. Steve invited all of us in to buy a beer in the amazing pub they had there and the laughter and release of tension was awesome. But at about eleven o'clock that night huge rumbles and explosions from the west stilled our cheer. Steve grabbed me by the elbow and said 'follow me' which I did at a fast pace. We went out the pub, ran back towards the gate and then, slightly ahead of me, Steve started to climb a very large communications tower, his bum disappearing into the darkness above. I clambered after him and thankfully the night removed any fear of heights because I couldn't see how far up we were but we were indeed high up and had an excellent view of the vicinity of our bunker being blown to bits by some heavy ordnance. It was obvious our silent withdrawal had them thinking we were still there and they wasted a lot of ammo blowing up sand. It was the next night that we scurried up the river in Steve's boat, with pay-back in mind and I emptied a couple of machine gun belts into the Zambian army camp with great delight.

* * *

I had no idea where to go or what to do when my National Service ended. I dreaded leaving the Falls but what work could I get here? Well, Mally solved that problem. She offered to put me up and I got a job with her as a croupier in the casino. It was a wild ride. The village was attacked incessantly and on two occasions the mortaring was so bad all our hotel guests and staff had to be shoved into the basement while shells cracked and flashed outside. Light from the exploding rounds came through the upper basement windows in typical camera-popping style, lighting up the frozen expressions of scared people in an instant, searing the images into my mind. Like the night I was lying in bed at Mally's house, on R&R just before my NS ended and Elephant Hills Hotel was attacked by gooks using a portable B-10 anti-tank gun. Then too, the flashing lights of explosions had awakened me and I agreed with the neighbour to go to the police station and offer my services to the village defence system (I was no longer based at Victoria Falls then and was only there on leave).

We went to the police station where I was attached to three other guys. Our task was to get into a very powerful push-pull boat that could zoom upstream in a flash and intercept any terrorists rowing back to Zambia from whence they had come to kill, maim and destroy. We initially went downstream and got the inlet to the engine so clogged with weed that we almost floated, powerless, over the falls, only narrowly missing such a nasty death when the engine kicked back to life. We soared upstream and where we came to a narrow in the river and at this point the Zambian army ambushed us. I thought fish were jumping in the water ahead and around us but quickly established, to my horror, that those splashes were from incoming bullets! We about-turned very sharply so that the Browning .303 machine gun I was behind could come to bear, letting off long ripples of ammo into the smudge of darkness just above the water line. Their green tracer eased a bit then competed fully with my gun's red tracer, like an alien sword fight had come to Earth.

We eventually headed upstream and parked the boat on the Rhodesian shore, to the left of a big tree. I had radioed the army base to come and collect us as it was dark and we were about ten kilometres from base at that point. In hindsight no vehicles should have been despatched to recover us but while we waited for them we bumped into the gooks coming back from the raid on Elephant Hills. It was a quick, sharp fight and I can still remember the sound of their legs running through the grass to get away. I swore at them and they swore back but they were egged on their way by the sound of engines coming from the relief column. I sighed with relief but no sooner had my joy become manifest than a massive, red-fringed explosion rumbled and echoed down the valley like a gigantic set of drums being pummelled above our heads. We instinctively dived for cover and after making contact with the column commander, moved forward with caution to meet the troops sent to relieve us. As I got closer I saw a Ferret armoured car with a wheel off, compliments of a landmine and then we were on the high, German, Unimog vehicles heading for camp. The driver of the Ferret was wounded and his bandaged head swayed back and forth next to me as we drove along.

I felt, more than heard, a crushing explosion to my left and in the split second it took for me to turn my head, I just caught sight of that bandaged figure flying up into space, to land with a thud and grunt in some thorn bushes nearby. An invisible hand had hit me full across the side of my head and face, my ear hissed and shrieked. We de-bussed into the tyre tracks at the back of the vehicle to ensure we were not standing on any unseen anti-personnel mines, sitting there like dazed rabbits, feeling this oily-smelling mist rain down on us. (We used to fill our truck tyres with water which greatly reduced damage to the axle and nearby chassis. Shrapnel was halted by conveyor belting bolted to half inch steel over the wheel arch. The sand too, was fortunately very soft or else more power from the explosion would have come our way.

No sooner had I jumped off the vehicle than the Zambian army started mortaring us from across the Zambezi River and their fire was darn accurate. I did not realise it then but I had lost my eardrum and so my balance was affected, making me look like a drunk as I staggered along behind the men disappearing into the gloom ahead. Guys with ears intact could hear the shells leaving the enemy tubes by the familiar 'ka-thoooo' sound a departing shell made. We counted twenty seconds and then fell flat on the ground. The bush would flash-pop into stark relief before darkness enveloped us again and this went on and on for at least twenty five more shells.

Although I was injured, a mate of mine from school, then an officer in the SAS who had come out on the relief column, tapped me on the shoulder and said 'let's run back to the A'Zambezi to get help,' for by now there were two other injured men among us. I didn't want to sound weak regarding my eardrum nor the fact that running isn't my scene so I took off in a lop-sided gait after him, telling the guys to get in all-round defence and wait for us to come back. Well, it was about seven kilometres to the nearest hotel but because my system was awash with adrenalin I had no problem keeping up with him and in next to no time we had phoned the police station to liaise with our army camp for yet another relief column to be sent out.

Something has stuck in my mind for forty five years about that night. It simply amazed me that tourists were still lolling about the swimming pool, lit by fairy lights, waiters going to and fro as if nothing in the world had just happened a few kilometres away. Had they thought it was a fireworks display at another hotel or the army acting out an exercise, could they have ever thought it was the real thing? Certainly not judging by their dress and demeanour but the receptionist at the hotel knew it was very real, his eyes opening wide in horror at the sight of the two of us, camouflaged to the gills, appearing at the counter in front of him like a mirage from hell.

I didn't go back to the bush with the relief column as I was injured and technically on leave, the men I was with were policemen anyway. I caught a lift when they came back and went straight to the army camp with them to see a doctor, but the nearest doctor was in Wankie so an Islander was despatched to fly the four of us down there. Poor Mally was expecting to come home to me after work but I was one hundred kays away, fast asleep in a hospital bed.

Christmas Eve and New Year's Eve 1977 were both wild rides with the village getting badly stonked and yet again when the gooks attacked Peters Motel with a B-10 antitank gun. The Army Corps of Engineers came up from Bulawayo and erected a high fence more than five kilometres from the suburbs, in a big circle around the whole village, thus putting it out of mortar range on all sides except the front facing Zambia. We all felt more secure especially those civilians whose houses faced the bush to the west where there was nothing but animals and bloody ticks all the way to the Atlantic Ocean.

Mally and I would lie awake for hours talking about the situation, wondering what the future held. Things seemed to close in on us when various animals like Baboons and birds landed on the ploughshare trip wires in the minefield around us, thumping us awake after a long night shift. This constant, unexpected noise really put a lot of us on edge and the chemist soon ran out of calming pills and other medication. I think the school closed around about this time and we slowly but surely shrank in numbers and became more and more an army camp with less and less long-legged ladies from afar, dressed in clothes we could only dream of in our sanctions-hit country. It used to burn many of us up that we fought in large numbers for the British Empire in the first and second world wars and in Malaya against the communists but here we were being sanctioned by the very country we had fought so valiantly for. It was an awkward time, we just seemed to be waiting for a political or military axe to fall on us, from the West, our supposed friends. We could accept Russia and China defeating us but defeat from the West was unpalatable to say the least. It was a horrible feeling.

Every year Don Goldin, the owner of our hotel, would send us to Bulawayo to the agricultural trade fair to win big and help raise our dwindling hotel coffers; things were tight and the décor alone was looking threadbare enough to keep people at bay. Well, we won big in 1978 but the bonuses we all expected and depended upon, were cut in half to help keep the hotel afloat. While we understood the need to keep our doors open the loss of all that money was too much for Mally and I. We both resigned in protest, as did several other staff members including, I believe, dear Old Fred who managed the place, such a lovely man. It was a terrible tear-jerker leaving Vic Falls and we cried buckets when we did a final tour of the village before catching a plane to Bulawayo and from there a train to Que Que, the next part of my story. (There is a danger at this juncture that the "snapshots of my life in Rhodesia" will become a novel so if you want to know more about my *incredible* experiences at Victoria Falls you can buy my other book called 'A walk against the stream' which fully covers the two years I spent at the falls, my relationship with Marilyn and the war that swept over us. Many readers, even international ones, have told me 'A walk against the stream' is in the top ten of all books written on the Rhodesian struggle, a comment I find very humbling. Its aura is a mixture of 'Gone with the wind' and 'Blood diamonds' but is true in every detail. There are two versions of the book, one I published myself and the other done by a professional publisher, so please select the one showing a soldier standing in front of the Victoria Falls waterfall if you choose to buy a copy – see photo).

* * *

Que Que (pronounced Kwe Kwe) is a sleepy little town in the middle of the country. We went there because that's where Mally's parents lived. I felt unsettled moving in with an elderly step-father and a mother that I am quite sure did not like me (she treated me a bit like my mother did with all my girlfriends) and certainly disapproved of us sleeping in the same room. Mally got a job as a barmaid at the local hotel and I got a job at the large fertilizer plant, Sable Chemicals, about twenty five kilometres from town. I hated the job as it involved twelve hours on and twelve hours off, rotating from day to night shifts. It was exhausting and left little time for pleasure or other activities. I could not get used to sleeping in the day time and the slightest noise would wake me. I became a bit grumpy.

It was also a dangerous job as I sat next to one hundred tons of liquid oxygen, a by-product of the massive electrolysis plant that split water into Oxygen and Hydrogen, using one quarter of Kariba's electricity output. My own Air Separation Plant split air into Nitrogen and very high grade Oxygen using enormous, two-storey high Sulzer compressors that somehow, miraculously separated the atoms. The Oxygen would be put through heat exchangers and dropped to -297 degrees Fahrenheit, liquefying it and then tankers from hospitals and industry would collect it in bulk.

That was not the only danger, the Nitrogen from my plant was sent to the 'loop' where it was forced to join the Hydrogen from the electrolysis plant, to form Ammonia. Any explosives expert will tell you that explosives are made from Ammonium Nitrate, so yes I was helping to produce a highly dangerous compound that once liquefied would be stored in a gigantic sphere holding over one thousand tons of it. What a spectacular target for any terrorist with an RPG7. A comment went around that if indeed the sphere exploded, Que Que would be damaged, certainly all the windows in the shops and houses would be shattered.

I found my shift work numbing, even the drive to the factory was scary as the war was in full swing and our coach full of unarmed operators was a plum target, but never attacked for some reason. I had been given a .32mm hand gun by Marilyn and it went wherever I did, out there in the darkness. But, as one guy joked, the bullet would bounce off their thick skulls at the distance they would be ambushing us from but at least if someone came to finish me off I would give him a 'third eye!'

There was tension mounting between Marilyn and I so it was with relief and gratitude that we moved into our own apartment, with two bedrooms and a bathroom upstairs, a lounge, dining room and kitchen downstairs. It was such a relief to be out of that house and as much as I came to like Mally's mom it was good to be free of her too. We felt normal and whole again.

However, the army was about to put paid to the bliss. I had already done one call-up with A Company, 2nd Battalion, Rhodesia Regiment, out in Mozambique with its hellish mosquitoes and bugs and gooks and now an envelope arrived instructing me to go to Bulawayo for another six weeks in the bush. My heart sank and so did Mally's, it just came at the wrong point in our relationship. I felt scared for the first time as it was no longer cops and robbers out there, terrorists were moving in groups up to thirty or more and we had now started operating in half or full platoon strength to combat their increased firepower.

One night, a week later, Mally dropped me off at Que Que's railway station. We hugged and held on to each other, in silence, for a long time and then she walked away into the mist, her shoes clack-clacking on the concrete. I pulled the collar of my combat jacket up against the cold, burying my hands in its deep pockets. My beret kept my head warm but a chill swept over my face; I was not sure if it was fear or the cold of the night. Mist blew past at a gentle gait, shrouding the platform lights in a halo of orange. A whistle blew in the distance and slowly but surely a train emerged from the gloom like some Neanderthal creature, hissing and puffing, its steel arms dancing over wheels. (This reminds me of the airport scene in the movie Casablanca, it's so similar).

It was a dreadful call-up. I was sent from Bulawayo to Chiredzi by plane, as my company had already departed for some reason and waited at the airfield to be collected. My Company Commander and I did not see eye to eye which made an already tense situation even worse and my sagging morale dropped even lower when he told me that we would be based in

Matibi 2 tribal trust land, a place some said, had already been liberated by the gooks. And that's what I discovered while there, base camps with parade squares, wells dug through sandstone to provide water to large numbers of people in a very dry area. Camps that had strips of beef hanging in trees, coiled and fly-blasted, filled with maggots, grass bashas erected for accommodation and lecture halls. It was simply frightening and I knew then we had lost the war. It felt futile carrying on but, like the Germans in 1945, with the allies at the outskirts of Berlin, we pushed on in hope.

A large 'high density operation' or HDF was put into effect there, with two full battalions of RAR, paratroopers and foot soldiers alike, scouring the area for terrorists. I counted seventeen contacts all around me and our guys hit gooks and base camps all over. It was like invading another country. I had a contact too which was electrifying but the overall effect was my nerves becoming stretched to the point where I had blisters develop on my hands. I watched parachute drop after parachute drop during vertical envelopment operations where gooks were boxed in while 20mm gunships turned them into mincemeat.

When Mally collected me six weeks later she met a brown, gaunt man who was just that little bit fidgety around sudden noises but she also met a man who was silent and introverted for the first time in his life. Lovemaking was strained and working at the factory was a nightmare. Our shift patterns ensured we saw little of each other and slowly but surely I suspected Mally had interests in someone else. She was a bit late coming home one evening and because I was banned from the pub for kicking a hole through a toilet door in a fit of alcohol-fuelled anger, I was unable to sit at the bar with her until closing time. So I walked the six hundred metres to the hotel to see what was going on. I ducked behind a wall when I saw Mally exit the hotel with a guy, getting into a car immediately in front of the entrance. They appeared animated in conversation and then their heads came together and they kissed, for a long time. My heart was thumping away as I watched this and I felt the nerves in my hands start prickling away. After about twenty minutes Mally got out the car and walked towards her own little green Renault R4. I turned and ran like the clappers back to our apartment and only just managed to get home first because I took a short cut a car could not engage.

I didn't say anything to her as I had decided that if she could do that to me I could do it to her and set about to deliberately bed someone else, which did not take long to achieve. Mally found out about it and we split up, she going back to her mother's place and me staying in the flat. But I hated myself and hated being apart from her so I went around one afternoon to make our peace but when I walked into the lounge at her mom's place they guy from the car was sitting next to Mally on the couch, her parents off to my left. As I explained I always carried my hand gun and for the first time in my life I physically saw red and without knowing what I was doing really, pulled the handgun out of its holster and aimed it at 'couch-man's' head. He went as white as a sheet. Mally's eyes grew like saucers and Gordie (her stepfather) darted out the room to my left. Mom's mouth opened and closed like a Guppy in a fish tank.

I swung my arm to my right and put three rounds into the TV they had been watching, laughing at something on it like they had no care in the world, then swung the weapon and aimed at a big glass crystal cabinet immediately behind 'couch-man' where I emptied most of the magazine. The shots brought me down to reality and it was at this stage I sensed someone behind me. It was Gordie trying to make a run for the front door. I kicked the glass-panelled door as hard as I could to prevent him escaping, shredding the arch of my bare foot in the process. The pain and the enormity of what was transpiring made me start to shake. I walked outside onto the lawn, gun hanging down. A shadowy figure appeared to my right and when I had focused it was the next door neighbour with a military-grade FN rifle pointing straight at my head. I was tempted to shoot him but he said firmly,

'Try it and you die, Tony!'

So I dropped the gun and started to shake uncontrollably. There were tears and much agitation going on in the house but after drinking a glass of whisky I started to come down. Mally bandaged my foot, big, salty tears splashing on the bandage as she worked. I soon fell into an exhausted sleep only to be woken a few hours later by my parents who had dropped everything and raced down to us from Salisbury. The neighbour was still there and may have been a policeman as he insisted we go to the police station to report the incident. None of them wanted to press charges as they knew I had had a nervous break-down and so I paid a $100 fine for 'discharging a weapon in a built up area' thus becoming the first criminal in my family… I still have the admission of guilt form to this day.

Mally told me she cried her eyes out as we drove away in my dad's pale green Datsun. She was very broken and taken overseas later on by 'couch man' to get over what had happened and she told me many years later she cried so much in Europe that they went their separate ways in Switzerland, enabled by her winning £1500 pounds in a casino there. Well, she was a darned good croupier after all!

* * *

I sighed audibly when I dumped my suitcase on my bed at my mom and dad's house. My suitcase and its contents was all that I possessed, all the furniture in the flat was hers anyway. I lay on my back, looking up at the toy model planes and ships that my brother and I had constructed together as kids. The gently billowing window netting could not hide the Avocado tree from sight, its branches sagging under the weight of its fruit. Memories of selling it to the Greengrocer up the road depressed me. I was twenty three and had nothing, absolutely nothing to show for my life, much to my mother's caustic glee, remonstrating 'that you'll never come to anything', which she occasionally hung around my neck like an award in failure. My mood sunk even lower when I realised Jess was still in Salisbury and I knew where she was to boot. The next day I borrowed my dad's minivan and went to see her.

Her eyes opened wide when she saw me hobble towards her but her manner was awkward because her boyfriend was due home soon. I didn't even get invited inside for a cup of tea. But it was good to see her and after a few cursory words of 'how are you?' and 'what are you up to?' we parted ways. I simply could not believe people could drift so far apart so quickly, it made me even more melancholy.

I had a lot of spare time so I went into town. Things had changed. There were less white people around, less males and quite a lot of military vehicles. The shops pretended to be full of goods, angling the same product in different windows to fill the space where imported goods once stood. Our local factories had done wonders to fill the gaps sanctions had created and all sorts of locally manufactured items like stereos, garden equipment, ploughs and so on were on display. But after seeing the same WRS stereo in four different colours it became a bit tedious. Sweet shops lacked the Cadburys chocolate we all loved. Instead we had an ersatz version made from who knows what? A storm was created when the local car assembly lines got some hard currency and for a while the display windows were filled with Datsun 'Sunnys', Renault R4s and Peugeots, all models in the same four colours...sigh. A few young eggheads that still had long hair zoomed around in Datsun 120Y hatch-backs thinking they were driving a Ford Mustang. Yeah, so cool being in a car that struggled to do a hundred kays an hour! I guess the drive-ins would get a few more customers now.

I went back to underwater hockey for a while but almost all the guys I knew were on call-up and none of the girls from before were there so that was a bit of a dead loss although I revelled in the caressing waters and sunbathing which helped me unwind a lot. I realised I had really snapped, for real, not like some TV star that cried over her cold coffee, demanding instant attention.

Night clubs like Bretts, Le Matelot, Le Coq d'Or, Samantha's, Barneys, Beverly rocks, Club tomorrow, Coco's, Galapagos, Inner Circle, Kamfinsa, Oasis and so on were still full however, full of young men with short hair and brown tans, young women with simple mini-skirts or tight trousers, high heels on, big hair, lips painted as the 1970s demanded. All ready for a fight, male and female alike. The Rhodesian Light Infantry adopted the Coq d'Or where fights abounded, the 'smiler' throwing many a pissed soldier down the stairs. If they got banned there they joined the SAS at Oasis where they probably got banned again. The tall Monomatapa hotel was curved in design and looked just like a military claymore and so it became known as the 'Claymore Hotel' or just 'the Claymore'. Many guys booked in with girls and didn't come out again until their R&R was completed. I was starting to drink too much again.

I can't remember if I met Rose in one of those places but we obviously met somewhere. We became lovers quite quickly and I enjoyed going to her flat for a meal or coffee or out to the pictures. I really liked her and felt something could grow between us. Not that the army would let anything happen! While I was working at Sable Chemicals I was exempt from call-ups as I was classed as a Nationally Essential Employee, my expertise contributed to making fertilizer, which our agriculturally-dominated economy depended on for hard currency, exporting its fine, international quality products all over the world. (I remember when I was involved in the HDF at Matibi 2 tribal-trust land that the management of Hippo Valley was so grateful to have us in the area that they sent a five ton tipper full of tinned fruit and dumped it at our base. The fruit, grown and tinned locally, had a foreign country's name stamped on the tin as the point of origin, I think Israel or South Africa, I can't remember but that was how we got our goods past the sanction watchdogs (yes, *British warships* off the coast of Mozambique ensuring we couldn't export our goods).

Now that I had left Sable Chemicals, I was no longer exempt from military duty and our ever-efficient manpower department grabbed me as soon as they could. It was compulsory to notify them of a change of circumstances or address. I received a little Brown envelope instructing me to report to Victoria Falls in two days and to wait at 4 Independent Company's base. Included in the envelope was a one-way air ticket. The fact that it wasn't a return ticket was rather ominous! But Victoria Falls, what were the chances of that?

I spent the last evening making love with Rose at her flat and the next day I was dropped off at the airport. I really struggled to reconcile being in uniform again, this civvy-army life was so disruptive and soul-destroying. I was tubbier so my mom had to let out the seams of my army denims a bit and although fit enough for underwater hockey I was really unfit up on terra firma. I fretted about what was ahead but the fact it was old stomping grounds I was going to actually excited me as well.

I whiled away time in the domestic departure lounge. A few tourists in shorts and T-shirts and colourful skirts strolled around looking at this and that. The plane taxied to its loading bay. It was a four-engine Viscount identical to the two that had been shot down by terrorists using Sam-7 Strela missiles earlier in the year, which made me as nervous as heck. The Rhodesians had, however, applied paint to the plane that made it hard for the missile to lock onto as well as extending the exhaust pipes downwards to help confuse the source of heat. Cartoons of the day showed the planes fifty feet in the air with trailing exhaust pipes just leaving the ground. Necessary humour to deflect something so terrible.

We went via Kariba dam, straddling the mighty Zambezi river. The landing there was 'hairy' to say the least. The drop was very steep and quick to frustrate a would-be plane killer from locking on to us and the take-off was peculiar too. We climbed to cruising altitude, out of Sam range, by doing very tight circles over the airport; that being a patch of territory patrolled and protected by the army to thwart any such action.

The Sam-7's were a big problem in the country. One bright Saturday morning, when Marilyn and I were visiting the deputy casino manager's house in Victoria Falls, to collect a kitten he had offered us, there was a mighty bang that echoed down the valley. Mally came running back to the car where I was listening to the radio.

'Come see, come see!' she shrieked. Rather unnerved I got out the car and stormed after her. Ivor, his wife and the cook were standing next to Mally looking at the scene a few hundred feet below them when I arrived. Ivor's wife had her hands clasped over her open mouth. The majestic, beautiful, magnificent Elephant Hills hotel was on fire. Evil fire-devils swirled and licked upwards as the flames got higher and higher and more aggressive. People were dashing hither and tither out the front door, to turn around and look at the hotel in despair. We could hear their cries and the loud crackle of burning thatch upon splintering wooden beams. The roof billowed into a towering inferno. Some brave soul managed to move a small tourist van away from the smouldering portico before it collapsed in a shower of sparks.

'What the heck!?' Mally gasped.

'Missile,' I said simply and I was proved correct. The Zambian army or terrorists based just across the river in Zambia had fired at a RUAC tourist plane doing a flight over the falls but the missile either went crazy or got attracted to the massive heat source the hotel roof emitted but whatever happened that beautiful, luxurious hotel went up in smoke in about forty minutes, or even quicker. The irony was that the sprinkler system had been checked only the day before but the manager had gone off duty and no-one knew where the keys were when the fire started. What a waste! We had spent so many hours pulling one-armed bandits there it was like a second home to us and was yet another reason for us to leave the village.

* * *

There was no significant difference in the outward appearance of Vic Falls but definitely less tourists than before and the camping grounds had been taken over by our armoured car regiment, the long barrels of Elands (South African Panhard AMLs made under license) poking out from behind trees and cute British-made reconnaissance ferrets covered over with netting.

I had been instructed to report to the CO at 4 Indep's base camp, the one we had helped build. He frowned when I walked through the door, saluting.

'Lieutenant Ballinger you say?' and then 'oh yes, the new mortar team boss-man….good to have you aboard.' I shook his hand. I had not been happy in Infantry and had applied for and received a transfer to mortars and anti-tank guns which I felt was more my cup of tea. I could not have been more excited as it was an independent command reporting to the JOC commander. I would be my own boss, my own decision-maker and I could not believe I was here at Vic Falls again. The Major suggested I get some tea and a sandwich from the cook and wait outside for my mortar and anti-tank platoon to arrive. I did that, sitting on a chair on the grass we had planted, under a large hardwood tree, looking at the ruins of the Elephant Hills hotel in the middle distance, perched on its lonely terrace like a crushed and blackened sentinel. I had so many thoughts rushing through my head, so many, many things to mull over and remember. I figured that if my unit had left Bulawayo at the earliest ten o'clock this morning they would not be here before four or five pm. It was now three pm. I told the Major that I was popping out the back gate for a while and then headed off to see the bungalow-style house that Mally and I had shared. It didn't take long to walk there and suddenly I was leaning on closed gates at the head of the driveway. The pink Bougainvillea at the front door was a bit unruly but the flowers we had so painstakingly planted were erect and smiling at the sky, bees buzzing around them. I caught sight of a butterfly, reminding me that Tookie, our kitten, loved chasing them, bouncing along on ungainly paws but never quite succeeding in catching one. I looked for a long time, remembering, before big salty tears welled in my eyes, and I cried.

It was exhilarating watching my platoon drive into camp, they looked a tough lot and very experienced. I believe they had a lot of hairy times at Villa Salazaar on the 'Russian front' where they exchanged shrapnel with Mozambican soldiers, Frelimo. I seem to remember the sergeant being an Afrikaner called Johan but it's so long ago I can't really remember. I think we had 2 × 81mm mortars, 2 × 60mm mortars and 2 × 106mm recoilless rifles mounted on the back of 2 × 'two-five' German Unimogs. The latter weapons were used with great effect in the Israeli – Arab wars where Arab tank crews would abandon their tanks as soon as they heard the 12.7mm zeroing round hit the hulls of their tanks!

The European guys in my unit numbered about fifteen or so and the Africans about ten or twelve. The Major of 4 Indep said we were to be based at the rear of the Elephant Hills ruins. I hopped in next to Johan and showed him how to get to our new camp. We turned left out of 4 Indep onto the narrow tar road that led to the A'Zambezi hotel and beyond that lay virgin bush where the vehicle I was in had been blown up by the landmine so many months before. My ear still buzzed at the thought of it. We turned left again at the entrance to the hotel, climbing steeply up the western side. The odour from the fire was still there, the smell of ash and burnt wood and it saddened me to look up at the blackened walls above me. The ground flattened out at the back and after driving about eighty metres into the bush we pulled up. I told Johan this was our new base where we camped for the night. The next morning I watched Johan go to work. In a few hours all the men's sleeping positions, basically set in a big circle, had been allocated, crates of ammo broken out, stacked next to two separate ammo pits already being dug by four men.

Johan established a command tent, a kitchen/ dining area tent and a tent for me. A generator was started and batteries for the TR48 long range radio connected. The vehicles were spread out to reduce the chance of retaliatory fire taking out all trucks in one go. Eight men slaved away at digging four circular pits, each lined with sandbags on the rim. By the time it was too dark to see it was all done. I was very impressed indeed. I instructed Johan to set the guard and flipped some playing cards to see who could go into town on a liberty run, the winners whooping their heads off. I showered at the squash courts of the Elephant Hills hotel as the showers and toilets still functioned, so too the squash courts. One of the lower bars still operated and before long golfers were back, having a few downers at sunset. I showed Johan the ruins and we agreed it was a good spot to put a forward fire controller because the view over the river and into Zambia was spectacular. The Zambezi looked like a silver serpent under a full moon, the eyes of the head being the small town of Livingstone glowing over in Zambia. It was a very romantic spot. It also occurred to me that the roof of the Casino Hotel, where I first met Mally at the Summit Bar, would also be a good forward-fire control position and so Johan and I alternated between the base camp and the Summit Bar as duty officers, rotating with Sergeant Accorsi for a night off every third night. It was an idyllic posting, I simply could not believe I was here again. It was from this very hotel that I had borrowed the manager's Land Rover and raced over to the Victoria Falls Hotel next door, during a massive mortar attack. I will never forget the fear I felt as I drove there with bright flashes and crushing bangs going off everywhere. I had feared a gook would step out the bush and kill me.

When I had reached the hotel foyer, the lights to the whole area had been switched off but in the dull glow of a light or two further down the hall I could see many people, mostly tourists, hugging the carpet in long passages that fed off the reception area. The noise, the bangs and the lights popping never stopped and I feared for their and Mally's life. Terrorists had killed white people in the Congo in similar circumstances, I think in a church or hotel, gunning them down.

'Marilym!' I screamed several times before getting an answer. We stepped/half fell over legs getting to each other and then she was running behind me to the vehicle and then back to the Casino Hotel. She was terrified to go out into the night, who could blame her? But I pulled her along, got in the vehicle and zoomed back the six hundred metres to the Casino Hotel. When we got there I went upstairs and collected the hotel manager's hunting rifle, a beast of a weapon and two bandoliers of ammo, which I draped over the jacket of my evening suit. I looked like James Bond all trussed up with a bow tie and rifle slung. We ran along the corridor to the bedroom wing of the hotel and then down into the basement. This was New Year's eve, 1977/78 and it was the second major attack in a row, the first being Christmas Eve the week before. Fred had put a fridge down there and a roaring trade for beers and shorts was being conducted by Ivor the Assistant Manager and older guests were singing 'roll out the barrel' and 'it's a long way to Tipperary' and so on.

I stayed with Mally for about ten minutes and then making sure a guard of armed men was posted at the door I slid upstairs in the silent lift, to emerge at the summit bar where mortar and artillery controllers were directing fire back into Zambia, whence the attack came.

And here I was, over thirteen months later as one of the very fire-controllers that prosecuted the war back then. I lay on my stretcher looking up at the glittering stars, my two-way radio hissing silently next to me. The spray from the falls mimicked a ladder reaching far into the sky and the irony of the whole thing made me sigh deeply as sadness washed over me.

The next day our Support Company commander arrived to see if I was settling in and I was so pleased that he was easy to get along with and as he was only one Pip higher than me in rank, it was okay to call him by his first name, Roy. We chatted away most of the day and early evening by the swimming pool, well who would choose an alternative venue with so many bikini-clad ladies lolling around? It tempered talk of politics, the war and so on. We both agreed things were rising to a climax in the country. Big airborne raids were being conducted inside Mozambique which encountered simply frightening numbers of terrorists while our own manpower was shrinking due to emigration. I think we both realised the writing was on the wall but even so our morale was very high and we dared not contemplate any change from what we had, we simply could not envision defeat, even then.

Roy flew back to Bulawayo the following day and at lunch time I was summoned to my first Joint Operations Command (JOC) meeting, which was held at the A'Zambezi hotel. I arrived there with Johan and after passing an armed guard who saluted us, we entered a rondavel with French doors to the left, set ajar. Seated around the edges of a three-sided tent outside were radio operators listening to three or four different radios, their faces set in typical radio-operator boredom. The centre of the room was taken up by a massive oval teak table with name cards neatly placed in front of chairs, orange juice and biscuits in the centre of the table. I found my name card and sat down with perhaps eight other officers. Johan and other second in command personnel sat on chairs a few paces back from their respective officer's. We stood to attention when a Brigadier of all people walked into the room, sitting when instructed to do so. This was most unusual, to have a Brigadier at a sub-JOC meeting where the senior rank was normally a Major or at the most a Colonel. I knew something was brewing, the arrival of so many troops in the village spoke for itself. Locals had sniffed the wind and the odd car with a trailer attached could be seen heading south east for Bulawayo. What he said still shattered me though. It went something like this, 'Gents, the time for all out Classical War has come,' he paused for effect, 'at this moment there are over twenty thousand Regular and Armoured troops ready to invade Rhodesia, from here at Vic Falls to Kariba dam. However, our assessment is that Victoria Falls is the greater of the two threats, possibly because Kariba is a defender's dream.' He looked at us over horn-rimmed glasses before continuing, 'to this effect, we are going to prepare a nice welcoming committee. We have, as you know, two squadrons (twenty four) Elands parked in the Municipal camping grounds, a company of Greys Scouts, a Company from 9 RR, 4 Indep Company and a platoon of mortars and anti-tank weapons; about a Battalion in strength. You may consider this a low number compared with our opposition but quite frankly the bridge sits on a very narrow piece of land making their larger numbers moot. We must contain them there or risk losing the war. We will have support from the South African air force if things get iffy. The terrs' plan is to put about two thousand of their most seasoned fighters in a train and shunt them across the bridge, scattering thereafter to overcome all opposition in the village, thus paving the way for big columns of men and materiel to enter the country.'

I looked at the concerned faces around the table, swivelling to look at Johan who was nonchalantly digging dirt out from under a fingernail. His calmness made me smile, but this was serious stuff and I knew many women would be raped if they succeeded in their aims. The Brigadier then set about explaining our dispositions. Looking from above the spit of land looked like a Lizard's neck and head. The railway line entered the bridge at the tip of the 'mouth'. Roughly where the base of the 'neck' was, stood a building and a shed in a siding. The building would house the operators of a remote-controlled bridge demolition system and a TV camera mounted to face the line over the bridge, plus a couple machine gun nests. Then, over to where the right 'ear' would have been, were erected two big bunkers. The walls were 44-gallon drums, two deep, filled with sand and a lot of machine guns and ammo were stored in them. Directly in front of the remote TV room two bunker defences had been built to insert our 106mm anti-tank weapons into and another for a couple of Elands and more machine guns. The engineers quickly erected a fence down the south side of the rails (there was one on the left or northern side already) and covered it in nasty things that would go bang if touched and Claymores that would be detonated from the bunkers to the right. A B-10 antitank gun was positioned near the right 'eye' to fire into the train. (This gun had been captured that night we came ashore after being attacked on the river, the gooks leaving it behind near that big tree. We had disembarked on one side of the tree, its branches hanging in the water, and they had parked their dinghies on the other side of the tree! Follow-up teams found the dinghies the next morning after our contact). The final link would be our mortars that would be zeroed in on the bridge, as well as artillery up on the escarpment above the village.

There was a lot of chatter after the meeting ended, pausing to sip orange juice and eat the biscuits on offer. I decided to immediately practice getting our anti-tank guns into position as we were not allowed to keep them on site due to prying eyes and spies among the locals going over to Zambia to shop for essentials. I also got Johan to give me a crash course giving orders to our mortar crews and how to operate the range/charge tables as well as setting the direction the tubes would face, or deflection, to bring rounds down on the enemy. After a few days of this I was getting to grips with things. We did drills and dummy runs several times of the day and in darkness to ensure all was in order. Some of the guys would go on the booze cruise dressed as civilians, two-way radios hidden in civilian backpacks, to act as forward fire controllers in the event the tour boat was attacked. Then we sat back and waited.

I found the casino a bit boring as all the staff were new and I could not get to grips with them so I spent most of my off time at the lovely Victoria Falls Hotel, its colonial elegance and charming atmosphere very appealing. I danced and felt young and alive there, even though at the back of my mind I was waiting for the proverbial shit to hit the fan. It's where I met and made friends with a female tour operator. It wasn't long until we were attracted to each other and the attack came when I had just climbed into bed with her for the first time. The irony is that in the room next door was my course officer from the 'college of knowledge' which I found that quite a hoot actually! What irony!

We both shuttled down the same staircase to our respective vehicles, sniggering our heads off at the weirdness of it all, trying to button shirts and put on boots as we ran. The sound of ripping paper rent the air. White tracer from a heavy machine gun came in from Zambia, plus the distinctive sound of our machine guns returning fire.

Theo's vehicle went straight on into the darkness where his troops were billeted near the A'Zambezi hotel. I almost collided when Sergeant Accorsi and his teams raced down the Elephant Hills' access route to the bridge; we had agreed travelling with lights off made it harder for the enemy to guess our movements and once at the T-junction, turn the lights on again for the remainder of the journey to the bridge.

The camp was a hive of activity when I drove into base. I checked that all protection troops were in their positions before going to see Johan who sat at a table with plotting boards and a map in front of him (before GPS was invented). Ammo had been taken out of their cardboard tubes and waited the priming order, to see how many surplus rings of propellant were needed for the desired range. I checked communications with the Summit Bar and Accorsi and all was in order. The whole of the village was now an activated and fully armed camp. There was an intense exchange of fire down below us on the river and it puzzled me why it was so intense, what was going on and why no firing at the bridge, *that* was the target! I could only see the odd tracer shooting up at an oblique angle from where I was sitting so I grabbed hold of a spare radio and went forward to see what was what. We had not, for some reason, put a forward fire-controller into the hotel ruins this night. Selecting our internal channel I tested the radio as I ran forward. Johan received me strength five (the maximum strength of reception).

'Make sure you are in comms with 'Zero' (the sub-JOC commander) on your other radio and tell him we are standing by for orders!'

'Copied,' Johan responded. I broke through a few saplings and then, sitting on the lip of the escarpment the hotel was built on, looked at the wild, panoramic view beneath me. The moon was as bright as anything, like a silver dollar floating on top of a vat of engine oil, the river shimmering under it with a deep, dark wedge of bush outside the glow of the moon, which had turned everything to grey in its immediate arena. There on the river I saw boats crossing, big boats, with as many as sixteen men in each boat, their heads bobbing up and down as they bent into the water with their oars.

White tracer was coming over their heads at one heck of a rate, landing in one position only and judging by the returning red tracer, it was one of our river ambushes that was being hit. The rattle of an armoured car's coaxial machine gun tripped along at a rate similar to the Russian 12.7mm support weapon but ours just did nothing to impress me. The red darts it and other weapons emitted were focusing on the dinghies and the massively panicking occupants, who were getting pushed by the swift river into the Eland's killing field, were starting to dissolve like lumps of sugar in hot tea and all of a sudden some boats became devoid of their men and simply floated downstream. I could not begin to imagine the horror those men experienced. Very few Africans can swim and falling into a croc infested body of inky black water at night must have been sheer terror. I admired them for their guts. But we were losing and the rafts marched on. This was obviously a diversionary attack or designed to come in behind our men at the bridge and attack them from a quarter they did not expect, which is precisely what they were doing as we discovered the next day. I asked Johan to contact Zero to join in the fun but got now answer.

Suddenly, the hills behind me flickered like a far-off lightning storm approaching. Artillery shells came screaming in, *just like the movies* with whistles increasing in pitch just before impact. I am prepared to say that air burst rounds were being employed as black puffs appeared above the boats which were now in very serious trouble, while high explosives were used in other rounds, pushing up columns of spray high into the sky; diamond-glitter water droplets smudging out the scene on the water. Our firing went on and on, not only at the boats but onto the spit of land where the 12.7mm supporting weapon was firing from and then more east to where the dinghies had been slid into the water. The rounds fell and fell in big red flashes, the thumps and thuds and explosions rolling down the valley like a tormented drummer was at work. I was so mesmerized by it all that I forgot we had weapons that could reach the enemy's starting point and like a complete dummy I just sat and watched the fireworks. The 12.7mm gun fell silent, smoke wafted over the Zambian bush and then it was all quiet. Just like that, it had started very quickly and ended equally quickly. I had missed my chance to see action with my crews and I have kicked myself for forty five years that I did not open fire on the enemy! I could see the annoyance in Johan's face as well as the other guys but it was too late to bitch now. I stood the guys down at midnight as nothing seemed to be happening at the bridge and after a few beers which we had left chilling in our deepfreeze we settled into a restless night. What an experience!

The next morning I was summoned to the sub-JOC Commander and he asked me to go west with our two 81mm tubes and protect clearance teams operating along the river front. We went about a kilometre past the A'Zambezi hotel before turning hard left up a steep bush track. Our German Unimog trucks were amazing machines that could climb 51 degree slopes with a 38 degree tip angle and with its powerful Mercedez Benz engine pulling us up and over rocks with ease, was a sheer pleasure. I stopped the vehicles at a level patch of grassy soil we reached and in two minutes both tubes were set up and ready to fire with a direct view of the area being patrolled below us, ammo cases cracked open and waiting. We contacted the follow-up troops and told them they had a big brother looking out for them and then I sat, knees drawn up, looking through powerful binoculars at the scene below me. It was an eye-piercing blue sky up above and the grass looked green this close to the river, little flecks of white skidding over rocks and in Zambia, not too far away, thick bush and no movement. I could see our guys in sweep formation and looked ahead of them to see if anything moved or if anyone took off as they approached.

The sound of rustling in the grass to the left of me and a horse whinnying attracted my attention. I put the binoculars down and looked up, mildly startled by a dozen or more Greys Scouts moving towards me in extended file, the odd horse's head bucking up and down against the strain of the reigns. I was impressed as these rugged looking men covered in weapons and ammo sauntered past us, faces blackened. It was a surreal moment I will never forget as they drifted past us one at a time, horse tails swishing, with not a single word spoken between anyone. They looked at us and we looked at them and that was that.

The next morning I went with Johan to the tourist booze-cruise jetty as word had come through that quite a few captures had been made lower down on the river. The double-decked boat hove into view. On the top deck there were about twenty Rhodesian soldiers dripping in weapons, machine guns draped over the railings while down below there were maybe ten more of our men and perhaps fifteen or twenty of the enemy.

They looked cold, wide-eyed from fear and dejected. They were young but tough looking and all of them were dressed in dark brown with black boots on. These guys were from a Regular unit, which sent a shiver up my spine, there were 20 000 of them still to come. I watched them hobble forward, some had been hit by bullets or shrapnel and they eyed us with a mixture of fear, contempt and relief that they were still alive. I stood in silence as they filed by, smelling the putrid aroma of bodies washed in fear and the sweet, cloying pong of blood. I was glad it was them and not me. From the jetty we went to the police station where the enemy dead were laid out in rows. It was hard to see why some were dead, there was no sign of injury, while others had heads, arms and bowels missing. Brains spilled out of skulls that had taken direct hits with big black flies licking at the congealing, dark blood.

It took me over forty years to learn, from Theo Williams, my ex course officer, who was actually 'Zero' during the battle, that hundreds of the enemy died and Livingstone, the nearby town in Zambia, was 'awash' with enemy bodies. I know several cadavers floated in the river line for a few days and one poor tourist pointed at what she thought was a Hippo waddling in the shallows until she realised it was a man, his head small compared with his massively puffed up body. The crocs had taken a bite out of his leg but didn't seem to like either of them for some reason. The poor lady became quite faint and after being escorted to a chair was given a stiff whisky to calm her nerves. Another terrorist went over the falls, head missing, and did a curious circular 'break-dance' on top of small waves in the cauldron at the bottom of the waterfall, every bone in his body must have been broken. The army tried shooting at him but 'floating Fred' as we called him refused to dissolve and entertained the troops and tourists for a week or more until he suddenly disappeared one day.

* * *

Just before the end of my call-up, the A'Zambezi hotel held a closing-down ceremony in a large rondavel, near the swimming pool, that housed the main pub of the hotel. It was quite a wild night with lots of young men and women in attendance and we dared each other to drink various combinations of alcohol. One was called the 'Landmine' and was mid green in colour. I had no idea what was in it but after two I felt as if my head had been taken off by dynamite. There was loud music and I asked one of the girls at the bar to dance with me. She had thick, black hair with a dog collar necklace around her neck and a tight dress that ended just above her knees, around about where her boots stopped. The chemistry was mutual and we held each other during the mellow records, turning slowly and looking into each-others blurry eyes. We left the party early and went back to her place, where I made love to my first wife.

* * *

It was surreal moving into my mother's house again with yet another female! She pursed her lips when she saw Dianne, shrugging her shoulders when we made eye contact. Like all the women I took there they had to learn to love my mom who, in fact, was quite a sweetie, rather like a Rottweiler that was still a pup inside; all teeth, all bark but no bite. But you had to work for her loyalty and love.

My life was going in circles and like one commentator said about my other book, my life was a bit like waiting for the same bus on different routes. I had no job but Dianne quickly got a secretarial job at Founders Building Society in Manica road. It paid just enough for us to rent a house in 91st Street off Hallingbury road in Mabelreign a, very comfortable bungalow-style house on a quarter acre of land with a fish pond and palm trees. We bought a VW station wagon, the curved bonnet of which made a perfect place to make love when the urgency moved us, which it often did. She was a bit wild with a quick temper to boot but we always made up.

Dianne caught a lift to work with our neighbour while I attempted to write my other book but her approval soon turned to niggles; I wasn't looking after the house well enough (we couldn't afford help at that stage), which became serious shouting matches and threats to move out. I couldn't focus under the circumstances and ended up shelving my book. 'A walk against the stream' had to wait until 2007! Ironically as I write this book my current wife keeps pointing out all the cobwebs getting thicker and thicker in our house but my philosophy is everything has its time and place and dusting is not for now.

So, I went to PGHQ (Police General Headquarters) to ask if they had a job for me, being ex-army and all. I was not disappointed, they snapped me up, gave me a Section Officer's rank, which I was unhappy about as it was not a commissioned rank, perhaps equal to a sergeant in the army and attached me to PATU, the Police Anti-Terrorist Unit which was a quasi-military outfit where citizens on call-up performed the same role as Territorial soldiers. As many were farmers, they knew the bush well and for the same reason had some of the best shots in the military. I was stationed at Morris Depot, literally five hundred metres from the swimming pool I used to play underwater hockey in and chase girls and perhaps the same distance from the golf water trap where Friday and I played as kids. It was at this very base that my mom used to go shopping and I would sit in the car eating chips or sucking white Sherbert out of its packet while men did drills on the parade square. It really fascinated me watching them and started my interest in all things military. The precise marching, the weapons glinting in the sun, the discipline of it all – lovely!

The Camp Commander was a red-faced guy called Shewell, a bit of a softie and not cut out for military stuff really. He was over the moon having an ex- army officer join him. He always felt he never knew how to integrate with army call signs in operational areas, especially with the different voice procedure on the radio. It was my job to head up training new recruits and taking guys on refresher courses before being deployed and I loved the job. Ian from Jambezi (Nipple's mate) worked full time there and as he was very physical and loved explosives I let him do all the cross-country training exercises, map reading and explosives displays. It was great that I only had to work from eight a.m. to five p.m. Ian would do barrack inspections and fitness training. My job was tactics, fire and movement training, voice procedure and many other aspects of training a soldier. After a few times out with the guys, I got permission to throw away the police training programme. I got my School of Infantry notes and diagrams copied, giving one to each man, as well as chief Inspector Shewell. I then worked out a training programme so that every man knew exactly what was needed of him and we stuck to its rigid timetable. I forget how long the new recruit's course was but it lasted maybe four weeks. It was an intense introduction to military life. It was not designed to make a man a soldier but to make a civilian an armed policeman, but they did bloody well in the war. I prepared my lectures based on what I had learned at the 'college of knowledge'. There was no time for the parade square, it was lectures, lectures, lectures the first ten days followed by practical examples of what they had learned on the blackboard, how to travel in a convoy, how to counter an ambush, how to assault a position, how to withdraw from a tight spot, how to talk on a radio, using both police and military jargon, like 'shelldrake' for artillery and 'ironsides' for armour, all words they would need if working in tandem with a military unit.

We did day exercises in the bush and farmland beyond Wingate country club. Stapleford, near lake McIlwaine, was reserved for overnight map-reading. Night exercises using flares, trip wires and tracer were done at the police firing range opposite Chikurubi prisons near Donnybrook. Our stay-over camps were at Mazoe dam, the place I had stopped to buy oranges with Jess so long ago. There we taught ambushes with real Claymores, how to fire old American 3.5 inch rocket launchers and anything to do with explosives, mortars and so on. We also did jungle lane exercises there for new recruits and refresher courses where we taught them how to fire with both eyes open over sites; 'double-tapping' enemy dummies stuffed with straw or even tin cans representing just a glimpse of the enemy. The guys got so good they could almost always put two quickly spaced bullets into the dummy and tin can up to twenty five metres away, the approximate range of most contacts. (I see today that US servicemen look through a scope when advancing to contact. I am not qualified to comment on the merits of holding a weapon up like that but to me it blocks out small areas of one's vision in which the enemy may lurk. We used both eyes and had 85% horizontal vision at all times. After many days of practice we could put bullets on target in a split second). It was a heck of a condensed course but I feel proud that the guys went on operational duties with a degree of expertise to keep them alive.

Ian had a wicked sense of humour and would set up tripwires in the jungle lanes that triggered a section of Cordtex nearby, giving the advancing trooper a hell of a fright. One guy spun in circles saying 'shit, shit, shit' in increasing volume before falling over an errant root. He came at us full volume with spittle exiting his slit mouth at 'Mach' one.

'You scared the living shit out of me!' he screamed, advancing. Ian put his hands under the man's chest webbing, lifting him six inches off the ground and shouted,

'At least you're bloody alive! If it was real you'd be looking for your balls, now piss off!'

We laughed the one time when we showed the guys how to fire an RPG7 rocket. We had maybe a hundred men attending weapons training that day. A flat piece of land with a deep gulley the one side was our chosen venue. The target was an old, rickety car about one hundred metres away. Ian slid the rocket into its launcher, unscrewed the cap, pulled the pin and after aiming for a few seconds, pulled the trigger. All that happened is that the propellant fizzed a bit with a loud hiss, letting off sheet of flame and smoke. Ian looked down at it at arm's length, his eyes as wide as anything and simply dropped it on the ground, whereby it swivelled on a stone under the pistol grip, facing the hundred men looking on! Never in my life have I seen so many men disappear so quickly and in some places the gully was so steep guys ended up dangling off the branches of overhanging trees! All of us laughed like a drain, slapping each other on the back. There was no sign of Ian for about ten minutes!!

* * *

Things were hotting up politically. Militarily we were being swamped by terrorists, we simply had insufficient manpower to win the war and anyway not many of our politicians had the stomach for it and were looking at ways of protecting their nest eggs which would surely come under new governance in the near future. There was restlessness in the black population, their even temperament changed to fear or anger towards us, depending what happened to them that day. We were losing maybe a thousand whites a month to emigration, which was a lot considering our white population never exceeded three hundred thousand and at this stage stood at about two hundred thousand. It amounted to a company and a half of white infantry leaving every thirty days.

A general malaise or seediness was creeping into the city, the kerb stones weren't freshly painted anymore, leaves swept less frequently and our fuel ration cut to about five litres a day. (I was thankful we got extra coupons in the police). There were more and more black refugees sleeping where they could, like at one end of the railway station. People were worried. Work was drying up for some and the festive nature of the lovely little city of Salisbury was becoming barren, out on the streets anyway but the nightclubs and booze flowed like never before. Fights broke out when shell-shocked troopers tried to hide exploding faces in the furthest recesses of their minds. Bombs went off. We were now living in a horrible caricature called Zimbabwe Rhodesia and our Prime Minister was no longer good old Smithy but Abel Muzorewa, a Bishop! We were already fighting for a black-run country and no-one could figure it out anymore. But we still carried on, clinging to the hope that we would be given a fair deal under the new regime.

On the 21st December 1979 a ceasefire had come into effect and as part of the peace initiative the Nationalist armies were allowed into Rhodesia and collected in 'Assembly points' although most of us knew they were kids with rifles and the real hard core were still in Mozambique or Zambia. Eight hundred Pommie soldiers and policemen (wearing traditional 'Custodian' helmets!) arrived to monitor the assembly points, resulting in some very hairy and frightening experiences for those Lilly-white gentlemen!

Dianne and I, though, were having a ball, going out to nightclubs, getting tipsy and then looking for a place to park our car! We befriended Phil and Paula Heritage and had great times as a foursome, eating meals at restaurants, dancing the night away and just enjoying life to the full. We often ate at the 'Claymore' or Tiffany's at the Jameson or at a nice steak house called The Sandawana, downstairs in the same hotel. But Dianne was English and was worried about the future of the country as was I and being in the police I could sense better than others which way the wind was blowing. I think by that stage we had no new recruit courses and the number of men turning up for refresher courses had dwindled to very little indeed. Our manpower roster, written up on a big blackboard in Shewell's office had fewer and fewer men's names on it. I was worried about the terrs going 'ape' after the forthcoming election and rape, kill and steal.

Then on the 18th April 1980, elections were held to determine the future of the country. Right from the start it was not free and fair. Ian Smith was not allowed to stand as a candidate and I am quite sure if he had been allowed to stand he would have led a large opposition party. Instead, whites had been promised twenty fixed seats for ten years in the new Zimbabwe which we all knew would wield no power although in fairness they did manage to influence the government on some occasions.

As for me, I had been selected, of all people, to be Mrs Indira Ghandi's Rhodesian-appointed bodyguard and liaison officer while she attended the Independence celebrations. I was put on an intensive small-arms course and given a very nice 9mm handgun and shoulder holster at the end of it, which I would wear under a jacket I was not allowed to remove at any time lest it be seen, despite April being quite hot on occasions!

There was much activity over the three days I was with her. Someone had donated a luxury car for her personal use and I drove a Peugeot with her other armed guards, set immediately behind her. We visited Indian schools, checking for explosives in advance of her appearance, we even tasted food to make sure it wasn't poisoned and I often wondered why I tried to keep a woman alive that had offered her country's wealth and facilities to the prosecution of our war. But I did not dislike her for any reason whatsoever. She was very polite and kind for the head of the Indian State and gave me a stunning silk cravat and breast pocket handkerchief which I kept until we lost it moving to the UK in 2003. In fact the other Rhodesian guards and liaison officers did far better than me. Many black African leaders offered full time jobs to our lads and others got wads of cash. Many Heads of State climbed aboard planes with bicycles and sewing machines and radios, it was incredible really. The main hotel for residence and gathering of all officials was the five Star Meikles and I rubbed shoulders with Mugabe, Lord Carrington and many others. I could easily have shot all of them, especially when I stood at the airport waiting for Mrs Ghandi to arrive, Mugabe was less than ten feet from me and surprisingly lightly protected at that. He even caught my eye and smiled at me!

On the night of the 18th April 1980 we took Mrs Ghandi to Rufaro stadium, a football facility in the black suburb of Mbare, which my brother had fun policing when he did his National Service as a cop. There were throngs of revellers lining the roads, a little too enthusiastic for my liking when they slapped our car roof with open hands, blowing whistles and ululating. We entered the stadium and parked near where she was allocated to sit, which if memory serves me was just behind the podium that Prince Charles stood upon to make a speech. The stadium was packed to the Gills and Jimi Hendrix had just been gassed out by teargas because some idiots got too unruly. A contingent of Rhodesian RAR marched in under the floodlights and they got booed in the loudest and ugliest fashion imaginable, with less boos for the Zipra contingent, the military unit Joshua Nkomo headed and then a riotous applause when Mugabe's Zanla men marched in, who were a lot more slovenly than the immaculate RAR I might add. I watched the goings on with a very, very heavy heart and my only upbeat moment was when Prince Charles refused the hand of Joshua Nkomo over the shooting down of the two civilian Viscounts eighteen months earlier. I hold him in higher esteem than I normally would have had he not done that.

Midnight approached and when the last speech had been read, at the stroke of midnight, the UK's Union 'Jack' (not the Rhodesian flag) was lowered and then the Zimbabwe flag unfurled in the breeze. The noise was catatonic and screaming, dancing and ululating rose to a crescendo only to end in jittery nerves, ducking and diving, hiding and running when the old British twenty five pounders let loose, twenty one times, a deafening, echoing and vibrating gun salute. The scampering in fear increased when several aircraft from the Rhodesian air force flew over. In the split second that they did so I wondered about the point of flying planes at night when they couldn't be seen, wondering if this was the greatest 'goodbye' of all time, when a few pilots killed most of the enemy's leaders all in one go! I got quite a fright! Maybe someone should have done that, it would have been lovely payback with the traitorous Brits, terrorist leaders and world leaders that funded the terrorism, all dead in one heap. I would have willingly accepted death if that had happened.

This is what I wrote in my book 'A Walk against the stream', about that night:

"I eyed the seething mass with barely disguised hatred and my mind began to float and wobble as if I was imprisoned in a horrible nightmare and as Prince Charles's speech dragged on, so my eyes latched onto the Union Jack and I realised that 90 years of white rule had begun with the raising of that flag and was now ending with the lowering of it. Fifteen years of rule under the green and white flag of Rhodesia was forgotten already and as I stared at the flag with floodlit, phosphorescent grass blocking out most of my teary vision, so images of people formed in my mind. They were images of dead people, people like Dave Kruger, Roy Orchard and Tom Shipley,* spirits of people who were now only memories or names on a gravestone. And as their faces formed before me like a developing photograph, so the tears ran freely down my cheeks to mingle with the dust that held their bones and I knew the country I loved was no more.

I didn't really hear the roar of the people or the rush of jets or the explosions of the cannons as the hour of midnight heralded in Zimbabwe. I could

---

*　These three guys were from my platoon. All three were killed by the same landmine, which broke my heart. I was on sick leave in Salisbury at the time they died, recovering from injuries I sustained from my own landmine incident.

only feel a breeze and see a bright horizon of swaying fields of corn, their heads proud in the bright sunshine. I couldn't hear the noise, for the sound of half-forgotten voices and laughter echoed and rolled down the halls of my mind and as I stood there, seeing but not seeing the perpetrators of Rhodesia's downfall, so I knew that it was time to go, that we would have to seek another land as beautiful as her – if indeed that was possible."

* * *

I can't remember when I left the Police, it may have been a couple months after majority rule. The writing was clearly on the wall for us and if I remember correctly no-one even turned out for training anymore, we just sat in the office all day drinking tea and gossiping. A sign of things to come happened when a couple of coach loads of Zanu fellas pitched up one lunch time. I had no idea if the uniforms they wore were Russian or Chinese but they had high-peaked caps on with red bands around them. The camouflage was definitely communist. One of our typists, an elderly woman with grey hair, left work at about the same time they arrived, as she worked mornings only.

From where I was sitting I could see the anxiety on her face as she headed for her cream coloured VW Beetle parked where they were milling around. She got to the car, white as a sheet by this stage, while a small group detached themselves from the crowd to commence harassing her. One or two sat on the bonnet while others bounced its springs. The poor dear was sitting rigid, her knuckles coming through her skin as her hands clutched the steering wheel. I jumped up, ran through to the armoury and got hold of a machine gun, clipping a long belt of ammo into it when I reached an old timber counter, training it on the crowd. I called one of the guys to man it and then went back into the armoury, quickly exiting with half a dozen pick handles.

Maybe six of us walked around to face them down, without exaggeration, there were forty or more of them. They quickly cottoned on to us approaching them and rather than form a defensive line that faced us they backed away. My heart was hammering away in my temples, adrenalin shooting into my system like a fire hydrant had been opened. We headed straight for the old lady's car and created a barrier around her. I tapped on the window and told her to take off, which she did with much gratitude. I was so wound up with nerves and boiling anger that I shouted at them, telling them what a bunch of bloody cowards they were for intimidating an old lady, what powerful men (sic) they were and then I overstepped the remark by shouting, 'Remember Nyadzonga Pungwe!!'* which caused quite a stir and for the first time I felt a bit of fear when their faces darkened. A couple of them started to move forward but we turned away and headed back to the office where the machine gun pointing at them was in clear evidence. That put paid to that.

A sense of lawlessness had washed over the land and stuck, like some big stink-bug had wafted in from high. It was unnerving. Dianne was in hospital getting a hysterectomy, which just gutted me as I wanted children and I remember walking down the long corridor in my uniform, totally unarmed at this stage and I could not help feeling people's eyes on me with questions like 'why?' on their lips. The death of Rhodesia and my wife being unable to conceive for the rest of her life went hand in hand with each other, the irony smacked me between the eyes.

I had an interesting incident happen to me before I hung up my uniform for the last time. I had popped into town for lunch with Dianne and was in Manica road to collect her when I heard screaming and the patter of running feet across the road. I turned to see what was happening and there in front of me was the new 'freedom' of Zimbabwe. A young man pleaded for help while a group of perhaps thirty men beat the crap out of him. I shouted to Dianne, who had just exited the Building Society, to call the police and then ran across the road shouting at the top of my lungs, 'hey, hey......*hey!*' so that they could hear me. I reached the man, pulled a smelly sod off him and lifted the victim up, pressing him against a wall behind my back, facing the angry crowd. It appeared my camouflaged uniform still warranted some respect or maybe they thought I was armed (*I bloody well was not!*) so they backed off for a metre or two. A UPITN cameraman, the massive lens of his camera stuck almost into my face, was recording the goings on. I turned to the camera and shouted something like,

'Is this your new Independence, is this the new laws of Zimbabwe?' A cretin wearing sunglasses shouted,

'He's Zapu!'** Several others screamed a few wholesome take-home-to-your-mommy platitudes that ended in 'death' or suchlike.

'Everyone has freedom now, he can choose who he likes,' I shouted half-heartedly, not believing a word I said. I was suddenly too tired to die for this bastard, so turning to him I told him quietly to run like crazy, which he did

---

*   This is a place in Mozambique where Regular forces penned terrorists up against the bend of a river and massacred many hundreds of them.

**   ZAPU means the Zimbabwe African People's Union, the political head of ZIPRA, Zimbabwe People's Revolutionary Army, headed by Joshua Nkomo.

at breakneck speed. Some of the crowd tried to wheel past me but I put my hand in my combat jacket as if I was reaching for a gun, holding out my free arm, palm open facing them, demonstrating stop! This caused them to hesitate for maybe three seconds and then they were off in a wild mob, poles, clubs and fists raised above their heads. Oh well I thought, at least he had a five second start!! A Year later, in Johannesburg, I had the TV on in my lounge while reading a magazine and I was just about to ask Dianne to turn the sound down when I heard my voice shouting the very words described above. I looked up and there I was, spitting mad, turning to stare straight into the camera! (I have looked for forty five years to find that clip to keep it as a memento, so if any reader ever comes across it, please let me know on my Facebook page!).

Things just did not sit comfortably with us at all. To hear the Minister of this and the Minister of that addressed as 'comrade' on our one and only TV station was a bridge too far. The queues forming outside various embassies to obtain entry visas to new lands stretched around the block, especially at the South African embassy. The police were nearly all black guys now and you could bet your bottom dollar they were shoving babies into burning huts less than a year ago. I do not expect a non-Rhodesian to understand how gutted we felt, how betrayed, how sad and anxious we were. Can an American feel empathy? What would they feel if China defeated them in battle and they now had little men with red stars on their caps all over their cities? It was just pure shocking.

I handed my notice in at the depot. Poor old Paul Shewell was down to next to no men and he looked down dejectedly when I handed in my letter of resignation.

'Another one bites the dust,' is all he said, shaking my hand. A door slid closed and I stepped into the next chapter of my life.

Chapter Five

Leaving Rhodesia to returning to Zimbabwe

We joined the 'chicken run' and emigrated to Johannesburg, South Africa towards the end of 1980. Dianne got a good job yet again while I sold Life Assurance for the AA and actually did pretty well. I had the cheek to go to the High Court there and convince the chief administrator that many men left their ex-wives high and dry with no pension or financial security for the future so, being a lady herself, not only took out a plan with me but gave me spreadsheets of names and addresses as leads on a regular basis. I shudder to think of my chances of doing that in 2020 as I write this book. Impossible! I also visited large typing pools and gave a chat to the ladies in their tea breaks or in the privacy of their homes after hours. I focused entirely on female clientele and I'm not exaggerating when I say I had more offers of a meal or a drink or even a bed than you can shake your fist at but I stayed faithful to Dianne although I sometimes regret not being single at that stage in my life for what she did to me later.

I soon got tired of having a job where I had no basic income and lived off commission only so I applied for a job as a Sales Rep with Marley South Africa, a company that essentially sold concrete roof tiles, all types of plastic plumbing and flooring. I will never forget the first Christmas dinner we had with them at a posh hotel where literally Crayfish, Oysters and Caviar flowed as richly as the Champagne and hard drinks. It was phenomenal, I could not believe it. We bought a Mazda RX3 for cash and rented a lovely house in the Southern suburbs of Kenilworth, got two cats and adopted two more and started to live like kings. We went all over South Africa together and loved Sun City and what it had to offer. It was a prosperous and happy time for us and we had a great bunch of friends who we used to party or go out to meals with. We would cuddle up against the chill and watch the musical lights at Wemmer pan and find just about every place to make love we could think of. But eventually we found the pace in Johannesburg a bit much and so I applied for a transfer to the Pietermaritzburg branch which was accepted. Our visit there to meet the manager confirmed we must make the move, he was a Rhodesian like me and I thought things would go swimmingly. It was the worst decision of my life up to that point for he turned out to be a bastard of a manager who gave all the plum jobs to the female reps, one of whom he was sleeping with. I ended up selling plastic kitchen goods, similar to Tuppaware. The senior executive in Johannesburg had this pet idea that we could swallow up that market. It was a crap product and all I could ever sell was packs of clear plastic cups like you would use on a plane for your whisky and ice. Naturally my returns did not justify keeping me and I experienced the first of many horrors in life by being sacked. Now what?

Dianne and I were living on the Zimmerman's farm out at Cato ridge, a good thirty kays away and the isolation started to get us down and we began bickering. Our sex life dried up. I managed to get a job in the warehouse of a company that sold every nut and bolt and fastener under the sun but I was bored out of my wits and the endless stock-taking drove me to despair. In the end I suggested we go back to Johannesburg as it was a good life there for us, so one day I set off to Johannesburg to find a job, which I got straight away as a Rep with USA brush, who sold every imaginable domestic product, made of plastic, you can imagine. The very company our executive at Marley wanted to overtake in sales! I found a place to stay in Parkhurst just west of Rosebank and told Dianne to join me. I waited a day before making a second phone call to her to see that the progress was with the removal van and so on but the call went unanswered. I tried many times a day and phoned all our friends but she had simply disappeared. I was in a right panic now, thinking she was sick or something worse, so early one morning I drove all the way back to Pietermaritzburg and on to Cato Ridge. I could see the house was empty even before I opened the front door. There was nothing, absolutely nothing in it at all. I rushed through to the garage where we had stored our deepfreeze, fridge, cooker and some other more valuable stuff like our stereo and so on but it was all gone. My heart palpitated like you cannot believe; tears stung my eyes. I went to every place that knew her but she had disappeared as cleanly as an alien abductee. I tried for a day or two more but eventually had to drive home with a heavy heart and tear-drenched eyes. Another one had bitten the dust as Shewell once said. What was it about me that drove women away? I considered myself kind and generous, even tempered and loving. What was the problem then?

It took about four months for her to phone me and ask for her overlock machine and some other items I had already moved to Jo'burg, plus some money as she was 'having a hard time!' I felt no bitterness by that stage so I sent her three hundred Rand and agreed to meet her at my aunt's house in Kensington. My heart pumped rapidly when she arrived in a pick-up with a guy with longish blond hair. Her face had hardened and there was no smile at all, indeed barely any recognition of me and what we had been together for five years. I had so much to ask and the most important question 'why?' got a shrug of the shoulders. And that was that, the sewing machine and a few other expensive items were loaded aboard and off she went. She did turn to look back though and there is no doubt in my mind she was suffering badly, her dark hair blowing in the wind, forming a halo around her big blue eyes. She mouthed a 'sorry' before moving out of visual range.

* * *

I had by then become a Christian, indeed it was Dianne that suggested, at the behest of her female boss in Johannesburg, that we go to an Assemblies of God church with them one evening. I had always been interested in the spiritual aspects of life and used to listen to Jehovas' preaching when they came around every month or so but even then I knew they were wide of the mark so I did not pursue their teachings. I had had an epiphany in the army when I was with John Bissett in Matibi 2 Tribal Trust Land. It was on the 3rd of August 1978 that I had been involved in a contact and that night, with the sounds of Hyena and Wild dogs yelping nearby, I lay on my sleeping bag and looked up at the carpet of stars above me and I talked with God for the first time, asking that if He existed would He please introduce Himself to me. I have learned after thirty nine years as a believer that nothing you say to God is ever wasted; you will get a reply in one form or another.

I went to the meeting that night with a degree of anticipation. I had become extremely burdened by the face of an African woman exploding from the entry of a full metal jacket round I had fired from my rifle. Her face remained whole but the back of her head detached itself, sucking the eyeballs with it, leaving a mask staring back at me, hanging on a branch like something you see at a Mardi Gras festival. The vision of it had been seared into my brain which played it over and over again like a looped video. I drank quite a lot after that.

But that night, the Lord of this Universe came down to meet me and I knew He forgave me when I asked for forgiveness. The tears that flowed from me that night, along with gut-wrenching sobs were so intense they had to take me to a rear room where they counselled me for over two hours. I could not stop crying and by the time I left there at about ten thirty that night I was physically taller than before, at least an inch or more, I noticed it. I also noticed that my conscience had been switched on and that some of the unsavoury things we did with our friends now offended me. That, more than anything was the wedge that drove itself between Dianne and I as I had taken off like a rocket as a new believer, devouring everything the Bible had to say and what teachers said about it. My belief was greatly boosted when I went to a healing meeting where people who had physical problems were prayed for in the Hope the Holy Spirit would heal them. Well, I had suffered intense back pain all my life as my right leg was shorter than my left, by well over an inch, which was verified by a doctor who prescribed built-up shoes for me. One can still see the curvature of my spine in photographs as evidence.

Well, I went in there expecting something to happen and indeed it did. I had a man say a very simple prayer over my leg before laying hands on it. A camera crew were filming from over his shoulder. I forget who cried out first but someone shouted 'look, it's growing!' and indeed it was, I could feel it and see it too. The room was in an uproar of excitement and later that evening when I walked out I felt totally out of balance on my feet. I was standing in the foyer talking to some folk when an invisible hand started to manipulate my back. My shoulders clicked straight, my ribs righted themselves and my spine became erect and strong. The relief to my system and my back was awesome. My father had on many occasions sat with me when I was in bed, until I had fallen asleep, that's how bad it was. I have suffered no pain to this day and additionally my legs were measured by a surgeon before my hip replacement in 2017 and they were absolutely equal in length.

God showed me the ugly, flip side of evil, too. While I was working in Pietermaritzburg with Dianne, one of Dianne's female staff came to work in tears. She explained to her that everything in her house was bursting into flames all the time and her and her husband were at their wits end. I spoke to my pastor and we collected the couple at café after church one Sunday. They showed us how to get to their house, being pre Satnav days and as we pulled up to the front door, it flipped open and a pair of burning shoes came flying out! My heartbeat rocketed skywards. The pastor said we should pray for protection before we went in and we did so.

Then, the four of us went into the house. The couple's maid was there, crying. It was she that had thrown the shoes out the door. I looked around in shock, every single thing that was flammable had been burned, chairs, curtains, pelmets, parquet flooring and so on, all with intense scorch marks in isolated patches. The pastor's eyes were open wide as no doubt mine were and I noticed the hair standing up on my forearms. I walked very slowly through the house and the story was the same, everything had been scorched, except in one room where a Hindu shrine was located. I called the pastor over and he agreed it was the Poltergeist's abode. I walked along the corridor to the kitchen. As I entered the kitchen I got a heck of a fright when a cupboard door was flung open followed by a tongue of flame a metre and a half long. I was paralysed to the spot until it eventually stopped. I moved forward cautiously and peered inside, it was empty! No wires, nothing inflammable stored in there. Only a small hand-held brush smouldered away. The small hairs on my neck were rigid. I backed away until the five of us stood in the passage just off the lounge. We explained to the occupants that only Christ could command this thing to leave, accompanied by much nodding of the maid's head who was a firm believer. The couple readily agreed and laying hands on them we brought them into God's Kingdom. I told them they must destroy the shrine, which they did with amazing alacrity, smashing it to bits out the back door. We then anointed them with oil and prayed over the house, casting out the wicked spirit in the name of Jesus Christ. It never came back and the couple flourished. I could not believe the look of peace in her face whenever I called into Dianne's office and she had gained a bit of weight too. She beamed at me every time she saw me.

I waited for months for Dianne to contact me again but nothing happened so I started proceedings to divorce her in absentia, which I eventually did at great expense to myself. I was now a statistic in the very records office that I used to get Insurance leads from. What irony! But it was a lonely and awful period as my job took me right up to the Botswana border and into the Northern Transvaal. I was away a week at a time, staying in lonely motels and crying a lot.

I eventually left that job because the factory in the Cape could not keep up with the orders I was handing in and as a result of that my commission, which formed the bulk of my salary, dropped every month. By coincidence or by the Grace of God (I choose the latter) one of the guys in my church offered me a job as a Sales Rep for his brick paving company so I handed in my notice with USA Brush, where I was actually being fast-tracked to management due to my selling skills. I had no fear of man back then and could sell Irish whisky to a Scotsman. The owner of Care Pave Ltd., was a laid back Natalian called Neil D****n. It took me about a week to learn how to lay paving and a week more to digest the names of all the finishes and brick types that were used as borders and accessories like flower beds and so on. Not that I laid the paving, we had a team of maybe a hundred men with two Bobcat skid-steer loaders to load, move and carry stuff, as well as plate compactors, Bomag rollers and three five and seven ton Mercedez-Benz tippers. My job was to sell the finished product to the client and pass the order over to admin who would arrange a start date and have bulk materials delivered to site. It actually was a great job as I was fairly independent of everyone and leads came straight to me from enquiries to the office. We also did commercial paving and some of our jobs were quite big; parking areas around big warehouses, done in concrete 'I' blocks about half the size of a laptop or more colourful and decorative ones around schools, new builds and offices. Our most popular style was forming concentric circles from broken bricks then washing a grout in-between to hold them in place.

In those days of course there was no Satnav and Johannesburg is a very big city, spread out over rolling hills and open veld and has now almost met Pretoria to the north, which means the two cities, which are essentially one city now, is about ninety kilometres from Pretoria North to Alberton in the south! So it was with great annoyance that I had to be with a customer at seven in the morning, before he left for work. I looked at the map and guessed it would take an hour and fifteen minutes to get there so I set off at five thirty a.m. to be sure but after stopping and starting a dozen times to read the map, I got there just after seven to be told by his wife, sipping coffee and smoking a fag that he had left for work already 'because you're late, my man!' (the last two words pronounced *may munn*). I was livid as I had to pay for my own petrol. All the while I had been talking with her, this little, white upholstered rat of a dog was yapping at me and making for my ankles, without any restraint from the owner. I told her what I thought of her husband for not even waiting four minutes for me at which time she spun on her heels and walked indoors. Well, 'socksies' was still yelling at me and as I neared the steps of the raised veranda we had been on, I slipped my foot under his belly and flicked him like a rag doll over the railing, landing with a satisfying whelp on the damp grass below. Little bastard!

Another time we did a big job, a long driveway leading up to a house and who walked out to discuss his needs with me other than Arnold Vosloo of 'The Mummy' fame. He was a gracious man that was quite welcoming and I enjoyed a nice chat and a glass of wine with him. He represented the upper crust of Johannesburg with its mansions in Sandton and Bryanston, the latter hosting the 'Bryanston bitches' so named because they were so vain they would not even talk to you; Ferraris and Porches spilling out of enormous garages, where everyone was called 'babe' or 'doll', little kisses on either cheek and tiny poodle-like dogs (Chinese takeaways) in their purses. It was while the Bob-cat ripped up an old driveway that I saw the other side of the coin in South Africa. I was idling away my time, eating a sandwich when all of a sudden the thirty or so men on site dropped their tools and took off in every direction imaginable, over fences where neighbouring dogs attacked them or hid in bushes or whatever.

'What the hell's going on,' I said to the white foreman.

'Police checking for passes,' he answered lazily as if it was no concern of his, well in a way he was correct, he was white and would not have his ID checked by the goons in the van that had just arrived at the entrance to the property. Behind the smaller van was a big truck painted SA Police yellow, a cage erected on the flatbed, made of supporting poles and mesh just big enough to let your fingers slip through. A lot of fingers were angled through the mesh so I sauntered up and looked at all these poor sods that did not have the correct ID for working in that area. It looked like a scene from the Planet of Apes with all the humans bundled into the back, being driven by Apes up front. I felt sick. And I saw the same thing when I visited Pam in Yeoville one evening, with black people running like crazy down the street to get away from a police sweep. I found it hard to reconcile the fact that I was a white immigrant, not even a citizen and I could go where I pleased. This was apartheid at its ugliest, but before liberals try to get all cosy with me, go and look at Johannesburg today and you will see why keeping out hundreds of thousands of underprivileged people was necessary to maintain the standards the white community had built up for themselves. Johannesburg, once a buzzing cosmopolitan city full of night life and strip joints is now a cesspit with no running water or electricity in many of its buildings. And as the whites moved out so did the jobs and so there is no winner there, just another cesspit in Africa that is once again darkening like it was at the beginning of time; where life is cheap and murder the national sport.

The writing was on the wall in 1985, with South Africa starting to experience its own death throes and I did not feel like experiencing MkII of African liberation. In addition to this, Neil, my boss, had allowed his accounts with brick suppliers to get so high they would no longer supply him and every job was touch and go as to whether we could find a brick supplier to meet our needs. The straw that broke the camel's back came when Neil bought his wife a fancy, brand new Renault but could not pay my wages. In desperation

I took a cheque from his desk drawer that he had signed in case there was an emergency when out of town and cashed it at the bank. He was furious but not as furious as me. I gave him my two weeks' notice and walked out the door.

By this time I had met Coral at church. At the time I was still seeking my divorce and was pretty messed up, not needing another relationship. But there was something about her that drew me in. She wasn't like the selfish women I had been dating or had been part of my life in the past. She was good looking, kind, sensitive, supportive, loving, slow to anger and had a lovely, lovely laugh which I have enjoyed for the last thirty four years. I had just met my second wife.

I could no longer afford my rented accommodation and anyway the landlady expected me to be her gardener as part of the lodgings so I left her and moved in illegally with Coral at her University of Witwatersrand lodgings where she was training to be an opera singer. She was gorgeous and I fell for her quickly once the dust with Dianne had died down.

It was about this time that my brother had resigned from the Rhodesian Ministry of Water Development as an Engineer and had started his own building business. One of his private jobs involved doing paving for the customer so he asked me to go north for a few weeks to help him out. One can imagine this caused me a great deal of angst as indeed poor Coral as she must have wondered if I was abandoning her, poor girl. So, very early on a cool summer's day I packed up my Toyota Corolla and headed north. It was a frightening departure because a car load of black guys, looking very suspicious in their massive American car, all slunk down low to hide their features, stopped next to us and asked the way to the motorway. I put up my open palm as if I wanted to chat to Coral and quietly told her to walk slowly but firmly for the front door of her block of flats and then to run like the clappers for the telephone in her flat, to call the police. I believe my guardian angel protected me that day because there I was with a car load of goods including a new television for my mom and dad, which they were all eyeing and no doubt armed to the teeth. I gave them directions to the motorway and the man doing the talking looked at me for the first time. He looked mildly alarmed for some reason and then he indicated to the driver to press on with their journey. No sooner had they disappeared around the corner than an unmarked police vehicle, not dissimilar to the 'thieves' car, pulled up with six plain clothes police in it. I walked up to the window when I was called over by the front passenger and just ogled at the array of weapons the men were carrying, from pump action shotguns to rotary riot shotguns and

Magnums big enough to make Dirty Harry weep with envy. I explained to them what had happened and where they had headed. The man's departing comment that I was 'bloody lucky' really unnerved me. After a final kiss goodbye with Coral I drove north to an unknown future.

* * *

I was amazed by my reception at the border post that straddles the Limpopo River, or sand bank as it was the day I arrived there. Apart from the process of gaining entry being a bit hit and miss I got a big smile and a 'welcome back to Zimbabwe' from a very happy looking young man. I was dumbfounded, expecting a rude or indifferent greeting.

It just felt so good to be back on familiar territory, the land looks different there. The trees are different from most parts of South Africa, which by and large is not that endowed with trees as vast tracts of the Transvaal, Orange Free State and the Cape only have grass about shin high and very little else to call vegetation. Only the Northern and Eastern Transvaal have anything close to Zimbabwe and of course Natal was very lush in places. And it was simple things like the road signs, donkeys standing dumbly on the side of the road with pot-bellied kids running after a bicycle wheel, stick in hand. Then there were the conical thatched huts (domed in South Africa), with chickens clucking, scratching at bugger all to see if it was edible. The cars were older and the people so friendly. I felt more elated in that run down little border town than the glitzy suburbs of Johannesburg. I bought a coke and Willards chips and headed out of town, where I had my first reality check. I had just passed the last houses and, seeing the national speed sign up ahead, put my foot down. I was just twenty yards from the sign that allowed me to drive legally at one hundred kilometres an hour when a policeman stepped out from behind a very convenient little bush, waving me over to the side of the road.

'Good afternoon sah,' he said with a flourish, pulling out a pad of tickets, 'you have been caught doing one hundred kilometres an hour in a sixty zone. There is a statutory fine of two hundred dollars for that,' and then, without showing any remorse or embarrassment, 'fifty dollars if you pay me cash now.'

'I would like to see your radar equipment,' I responded.

'It's now sixty dollars to let you pass,' he smiled narrowly. I could feel my blood pressure starting to rise and all the memories of all the frustrations from his kind sprang to the surface. But I knew it was a losing battle.

I noticed another man behind the shrub, which I could see at close range, had been planted there and held up by bricks and sticks, its leaves withering under the hot sun. What a perfect little scam!

'God is not happy with you my friend,' I said, handing over forty South African Rand which he seemed to prefer anyway. After a perfectly executed signal to move on, I accelerated away from him, determined to report him when I got to Harare, which I did try to do but found their phone dead all the time. Zimbabwe was rapidly pissing me off already!

After a meal at the Lion and Elephant Hotel I pressed on to Harare. I watched the land slowly but surely become lush with long grass and Msasa trees standing ever taller the further north I went. The leaves were pale green and in a very short while would turn blood red or dark orange before going dark green. The Msasa forests looked amazing when the tree was in its blood red and orange phase making the Rhodesian landscape totally unique North of the Limpopo, as far as the southern Congo. At last I reached the city and apart from it looking a little more rundown there were plenty of cars on the road and everyone looked happy. It was great seeing my brother again as he was waiting at my parent's house to meet me. We slapped each other's backs and laughed. We were both getting on now, both getting a bit thin on top, me with my terrible 70s porno moustache and him with big sideburns and longish hair. Mom and dad welcomed me in like manner and then a handshake from the new cook.

We had supper at about six p.m. and then Brian and dad tuned in the new TV for us to watch awhile. Well, that lasted three minutes as Zimbabwe still only had one TV station and it was boring crap spoken in Shona. I felt tired so I went to my room at about eight pm after putting a call through to Coral. It was so good hearing her voice and it reassured me no end. I lay on my bed and looked up at the models of ships and planes and wondered what the hell I was doing with my life.

Brian collected me bright and early the next day for work and it was a pleasure to be with him and wear shorts, veldskoens and a T-shirt. Not bad attire compared with all the 'suits' in their sweaty offices in town!

'What's on the list today?' I asked, thinking we were off to the paving job he had asked me to come to Zimbabwe for.

'We've got a carport to build for the manager at Barclays bank in Avondale.'

'I thought we were doing a paving job?'

'We are but it's not due to start for a week and I picked this job up in the meantime.'

'What the heck do we know about car ports?'

'You mean, what *don't* I know?' he said sarcastically, 'I am an Engineer you know,' followed by a little scoff. I shrugged my shoulders.

We only had his Renault station wagon as transport and had to collect asbestos roof sheets (two trips to site), steel poles, support timbers, bolts, primer and silver paint. He had two shovels and a couple of picks. Brian, being an Engineer is very fastidious and to this day remains the same, every 'i' dotted and every 't' crossed to perfection. I would have just measured the sheet lengths and dug six holes. I was nearing tearing my hair out when he gave the go-ahead to start digging and we, with our own hands, dug out the dirt for the support poles, positioned them as vertically as possible and poured the concrete around the feet of each pole, checking the vertical sides one more time. It was gone six p.m. when we got home and I felt strangely elated. Harare is much less sophisticated than Johannesburg and it felt lovely chugging down the avenues under the magnificent purple Jacaranda trees whose flowers went pop-pop-pop under the car tyres, as we went about our business. In the avenues the purple flowers gave way to the burnt oranges and yellows of Flamboyant trees and sweet smelling Frangipanis competed with Hyacinth and Lilacs to colour the air with scent. The Avenues were as lush as ever. With many more modern cars going by and with business all over the country accelerating I began to wonder why we had fought the war. Had the Leopard changed his spots, could there be genuine peace and prosperity for all here? I reserved judgement for a later day but for the first time in my life I had the feelings of coming home and not just physically either, mentally and spiritually too. I had a new hope lit in my belly.

The next day we bolted the roof's support timbers into place. Once done, we put pink wood-primer on the timber and when dry applied a coat or two of white gloss. Then we fitted the roof sheets and by the end of the third day we cleared up the site and stood back to look at our work. It was very good and very professionally erected. I could see now why my brother insisted on perfection and I am pleased to say this carport is still standing in 2020. The manager was over the moon and asked us if we could enclose the veranda off the lounge at his home to form a TV lounge for his kids. We said we would pop around in a day or two and give him a quote. The down side was that my brother had a mortgage and a family to feed so he got all the profit from our very first job. I had a few bucks left so that was okay.

In the meantime the paving job arrived. This required a lot more kit than putting up a car port so I was tickled pink and actually laughed when he collected me one morning with a couple of wheelbarrows shared between the roof rack and the back of his Renault station wagon, with picks and shovels stored next to a folded plate compactor. It was hardly Care Pave and I felt a bit embarrassed when we offloaded in front of the customer. Brian had told one of his men to find a few labourers, which was as easy as breathing in air and soon had twenty men at the gate, all eager to find work. We chose about six of them and I set to telling them what had to be done. A big fellow called Charles said he had experience with compactors so that became his job. We removed a hundred and fifty millimetres of top soil, turned over a pick-head's depth of soil and moulded which way water would run when it rained. Allowing water to pool against a house was a no-no. Much to our mutual embarrassment we didn't even have a spirit level at that point. The soil was then compacted by the plate compactor after being slightly dampened.

Then came the river sand, which was levelled out with a straight edge. I showed a couple of guys how to lay the broken bricks we had bought, in concentric circles. I started to relax as I watched it come together. It was a large area so by day three we got some cement on site and mixed it with white pit sand which was watered before being brushed into place using yard brooms; of course we didn't have any so Brian had to rush off to the hardware store one more time! We then did the edging strip with full bricks on top of a small bed of concrete, sloping mortar on the outside face. Once it was watered, compacted and cleaned with a bit of acid, it looked fantastic, as good as anything I had done in South Africa. We really felt proud of ourselves and the customer was over the moon. The second rub came when Brian told me he needed this cheque too and all I got was a hundred dollars or so, but the Rhodesian dollar went a long way and it took some of the sting out of it. At that stage we hadn't even registered as builders or informed the tax man so everything felt up in the air for me.

It was dawning on me that I had to move towards marrying Coral or get bogged down in Zimbabwe and marry someone else. As it was I dated my sister-in-law's sister and the time I spent with her had the capacity to possibly make me forget Coral which I did not want to do. But before I am judged too harshly I was not married to Coral and I was in two minds whether I wanted to marry again so soon after my experience with Dianne and I was lonely, there were ghosts of Jess and Marilyn and others all over the city and in my parent's house; I just felt mixed up. The time we had been apart started to fade my memories and thoughts of Coral but it was my dad who read me the riot act and said I must either drop Coral or marry her. I chose the latter so I went to Durban in South Africa in December 1985 to marry her, which I did on the 4th of January 1986 and brought her home. I was really broke by that stage and had to borrow a suit for my wedding. I bought a rather gaunt wedding ring from a widow but Coral's eyes lit up like Guy Fawkes when she saw me and in less than half an hour we were making love in her bedroom at her mother's place.

I was introduced to her vast family and fell in love with them and their crazy antics as well as Coral's twin sister Lasandra. That family could put the stories of Payton Place and Dallas to shame! I helped her dad set up the marquee and move all the chairs and tables into place for the reception at his lovely home in Kloof and then the happiest day of my life arrived, getting married to Coral. It was a lovely day even though it poured with rain, a sure sign of success in a marriage I am told. So much water poured off the tent the head table was seated in that we could barely see our guests ten metres away on the other side of the swimming pool. Real blessings would come from that for sure!

We left for Harare straight after the wedding in Coral's little pale yellow Datsun 1200, loaded to the gills. We had asked for cash instead of wedding presents and with that we had bought a big TV which I knew would sell for a small fortune in Zimbabwe, that type of product was still in short supply there. Our honeymoon night was spent at the Oyster Box, a lovely quaint hotel on the Natal coast, but we were so tired we just fell asleep in each other's arms, totally contented. It was probably the happiest night of my life because I knew I had a real gem in Coral and I would like to honour her by saying she has never changed, has always loved and supported me no matter what. She has been a superb mother, lover and friend and God smiled down on me the day I saw her at church in Johannesburg.

It was strange bringing Coral into my mother's home, hopefully fourth time lucky and I wondered, not for the first time how things would turn out. As I have said before, my mother was a lovely person really but she had an unfortunate knack of judging people and making comments that, well, riled you! I watched my amazing wife take flak from her, like a B29 bomber, deflecting every assault and undermining comment. She never got angry or raised her voice but we both knew living there would drive us mad. Coral got a job behind the counter of a bakery as she really had no qualifications to speak of but was a superb cook, so that talent came in handy there. I regret to this day that I did not get her a position at the College of Music where her real love and talent lay which was singing and teaching people how to sing.

Our company was growing from strength to strength. We designed and printed off some pamphlets which we distributed around the more prosperous parts of the city and the response was so encouraging. There were very few companies like ours in those days as people were still recovering from the shock of independence. Ex Rhodesians were coming back from South Africa and overseas and our farming community prospered greatly. New cars started to enter dealerships but it was, initially, only for those with access to hard currency. On the surface all seemed well but in hindsight it was probably the twenty white seats reserved in parliament that steadied the ship. It is also with hindsight that I see how patient Mugabe's government was to wait for their tenure to end before doing their own thing. And the fact that such a mineral- rich nation, which exported Gold, Chrome, tobacco (the best in the world) and later on, Platinum and diamonds was unable to let people buy hard currency when they needed it to import, export, go on holiday or whatever was very disturbing. It never occurred to me that billions of US dollars were being milked from our coffers and spirited away to Swiss Banks and Cayman Island accounts. But there was enough to give us a semblance of prosperity and happiness and we thought we had won the lottery when we could get a hard currency debit card with access to US$5000 per family, or was it per person? I can't really remember. Our contracts too had passed from erecting carports and closing in verandas to new houses, multiples of new houses, factories, warehouses, schools, housing complexes and so on, but that took time.

A really joyous event happened that warranted us moving out of my parent's house, which was no longer tenable, and that was the announcement that Coral was pregnant. It is one of the few times I have seen my mother cry from happiness and indeed I was over the moon. I got to know the owner of some duplex flats in Glen Lorne when we fitted new ceramic flooring in his kitchen and bathroom and discovered that one of the units there was to let. We signed on the dotted line even though our income was tenuous to say the least and moved in with borrowed furniture and packing cases as a dining room table. I was the happiest man in the world and simply loved it there, my own little family surrounded me, which it did when my gorgeous son, Rowan came on the scene. I cried so much watching him being born, I could not contain my joy and even the doctor delivering him was laughing with me. I could not stop staring at his little fingers and nose and lips and eyes and ears and toes and would rush home from work just to be with him and hold him. When he was two we put him in little dungarees and I used to carry him around by its straps, like a travel bag, much to the amusement of everyone, but he loved it. A friend I had made in Australia called him a Rugrat when she heard of Rowan's birth and so he became our little 'Ruggie' or 'Rowland Rat' and my love for him grew as indeed he did.

Seventeen months later our gorgeous, bright and talented daughter arrived. I missed her birth by half an hour because my sister-in-law who had been with Coral an hour earlier, said that Coral wasn't ready to give birth yet and that I could wait with my mom maybe another hour or two, which is what I did, only to miss Amanda almost flying off the end of the delivery table, literally, she simply flew out of Coral. The doctor barely caught her in time! And so entered my darling, lively, vivacious, good looking, independent little girl into the world. She ended up having several nicknames, when her teeth failed to materialize she became 'Gummy Bear' and when we bought a fish tank that contained Guppies her nickname became, well, 'Guppy!' followed by 'Guppy bubbles' But over time she simply became 'Bobby' for no rhyme or reason and it has stuck to this day. 'Bubbles' would be my second choice.

Our business was prospering and we now employed about one hundred and fifty men full time. I had watched Brian do quotations and after examining his technique I took on the responsibility of tendering on a new build in Greendale or thereabouts and we were chuffed when we won the tender. However, when we saw the comparative quotes I went pale. It was many thousands lower than the others, but we signed the contract anyway. When we went through my calculations I had completely forgotten to factor in the roof trusses and roof tiles!! I nearly died from embarrassment and my brother was not too kind in his comments at all which was unfair as it was my first attempt ever at building up rates and estimating a reasonable profit. We needed cash flow at that particular time so we went ahead with the work. We were simply shocked when, having told the client why our price was so low, that we were novices and so on, that he added back many thousands on the final payment 'for doing a very good job'. I could not believe it. I had learned a hard lesson and fine-tuned the next tender and the next and the next for sixteen years, where I consistently quoted on projects that came in lowest but by only a hair's breadth on many occasions. I had developed my own spreadsheet on the computer, which was no mean feat in those days where computers had so little memory and appalling speeds. All I had to do is input new supplier prices and press enter and every rate changed automatically and no-one taught me how to do that.

We still had the TV we bought in South Africa and Coral went and did something truly amazing off her own bat and that was to find the owner of a magnificent piece of land in Cutter Close, Glen Lorne that had a stunning view a score or more miles to the horizon. Not only did she do that but she offered them the TV plus $10 000 dollars (borrowed from my mother) and they accepted it! To this day I cannot believe she did that, it was amazing! We now had 1.7 acres of the best piece of land in the whole of Folyjohn Crescent, so named because the man who bought up the entire area for housing was told it was 'folly' to do so and because his name was John it became Folyjohn Crescent. Cutter close was just off that and number 135 was our stand! The house quickly took shape and apart from a small loan to put in the Aluminium sliding doors I paid cash for the whole project, later putting in a swimming pool, a separate office, a downstairs sewing room for Coral and the design already had a semi-detached cottage on the other side of a double lock-up garage. I bought Coral a Mercedez Benz and we went to the Cape for long holidays in our Mazda pick-up/trailer combination with the kids sleeping in the back under cover.

The reputation our company grew and grew as we did not cut corners and we had trained, pilfered and pinched some of the best artisans around, paying them a cut above the run of the mill guys. Architects gave us work as did Quantity Surveyors working in league with Architects and before long we were maintaining a lot of properties that belonged to the British High Commission. The Brits spoke to the Yanks and the Yanks to the French and before we knew it we had mountains of work, some of them paid in foreign currency too which enabled us to get a new pick-up for Brian. There was no white privilege here, we worked damn hard for what we had. Our kids went to private schools.

I soon realised that doing work for other people was a waste of time and that we should go into property development so we bought stands in Glen Lorne, Mt Pleasant and a commercial stand in Umtali, just past Sakubva. We built a thousand square metre warehouse at Sakubva and toyed with the idea of getting a rail siding into the yard, which would have opened up countless export opportunities. The railway line ran just the other side of our boundary. Then, in Glen Lorne we pegged out seven garden flats and commenced work on them, completing three reasonably quickly. Everything was sailing along nicely.

We loved our family social life too. Eating out at Nandos or being ridiculously diabetes-tempted by the sweet hut next door where we piled sweets and chocolate peanuts into a bag, to sit outside with others and munch. Or, watching movies in the cinema complex. That's where I saw Jurassic Park for the very first time and then Westgate shopping mall opened with much fanfare and shops like Woolworths came back from South Africa and there too I watched Armageddon for the first time.

Mandy loved ballet and soon we were taking her to and fro to her ballet lessons and slowly but surely she worked her way into leading roles at Reps Theatre. This was normal life and once again I asked myself why did we fight the war? Why did so many of our soldiers die? Life could not be better than this. Yes, admittedly services had declined; it was frustrating to apply for new power and water connections or get a phone linked, which I had to do all the time in my business but my right-hand man did all that anyway; being a black man he was more easily accepted by the authorities who showed some bias against us. It was still all okay, roads were being maintained and rubbish collected, what did we fight fifteen or more years for? But in the depths of my soul I knew frustrations lingered in the black population as they had been promised the Earth and had only received a rock so far. They still lived in crumbling accommodation and for sure they were better off under white rule. If anyone denies this they are fools. In fact when Louis Theron, a UK investigative journalist visited Soweto in about 2014 he asked the black people there if they were happy and what could be done to make their lives better? Their unanimous response? 'Put the whites back in power!' (A quick search on the internet will find this interview.

My son was a real daredevil from day one and I have loads of pictures of the ecstatic look on his face when he was going fast, fast, or even faster on anything with two wheels. It was only logical that he should enrol in the BMX club next to Old Georgians and at age, perhaps six or seven he was out there, helmet on, pumping away on the pedals. Mandy wanted in and soon her little pink bike and yellow helmet was whizzing around the track while we stuffed our faces with burgers and cheered from the side. It was there at Old Georgians that we experienced a funny event. It was Friday night and we were attending a big fireworks display. We had pumped our kids up all day about how exciting fireworks were and that they would love it.

The sun only truly fades at about eight p.m. or so in summer and we sat among several hundred parents in great anticipation of a wonderful evening. The display started off with a few sparklers and fuzzy little things and Catherine wheels which the kids adored. I loved looking at the wonder in their eyes, the colours of the night reflecting off them. I tried to remember seeing such vivid colours for the first time and oh yes, it was at nursery school. After about thirty minutes of increasing size and intensity the really big rockets were launched. They exploded in massive, multi-coloured fireballs, sending out their sparks far and wide. Boom, boom, ka…powww they went and I turned to look at my kids to see if they were enjoying it only to see them among a wall of screaming children running back to the club-house with dozens of moms and dads chasing after them. I laughed as I ran and soon caught them up into my arms. 'Guppie' was shivering in tears and 'Ruggie' looked as if he had seen a ghost. I kneeled down to their level and cuddled them, assuring them it was all okay and before long, in the comfort and security of my arms they settled down and watched the remainder of the display with glee. It was so sweet, just a little memory that sticks forever.

Every Wednesday I collected Amanda from school and took her on a 'daddy-daughter' afternoon, which lasted well into early senior school and that time was reserved for us. We would go to Golden stairs nursery for tea and scones where I would ask her about her day and then on to the shops at Chisipite where she could buy something for herself up to a certain value. Well, little miss social climber once asked me for a rather beautiful stuffed dog that was extremely expensive and after much ado and hesitation, I bought it for her. She still has it on her bed in London to this day.

Why I never had son-dad days I will never know. For some reason I felt that a father's relationship with his daughter is very special and that she needed reinforced knowledge of what a decent, loving man is and I believe it worked well in her life. In many ways my time spent with my son was not on a dedicated day but it was him I took shooting and dicing death on my motorbike or swimming in our pool together. Dad-son stuff was just as important for him, to pass similar values to his children one day. (We did join the rifle club near Donnybrook and I paid for him to get his Padi diving ticket which enabled him to dive at Sinoia caves and Mtorashanga, I guess he lived out my life by doing that!)

However, it was my darling wife that brought the most fundamental and uplifting changes to my life. It was her music and her superb soprano voice that changed who we met and what we did. I joined in when she did shows and was a cowboy in Oklahoma. We met and made friends with several people at Reps Theatre including Debbie Wratten, as she was then and we often went to parties at her house and had braais there while our kids ran around. Coral also linked up with Peter Cresswell who lived directly below us in a rambling thatched house, the lawns of which flowed down to a river threading its way through some trees. It was an idyllic spot for soirees and every month or so a select group of musicians and their guests would gather for a candle-lit dinner and then move into the lounge to hear artists perform solos from singing, to Cello, to violin and piano. They were very cultured evenings and we had to wear bow tie and suits for the gents and elegant dresses for the ladies. After the performances we would retire to a large patio off the lounge door, which was surrounded by warming briars, to chat among each other over a glass of Brandy or wine. Of course this was not free but we wouldn't have missed it for the world. I can still hear, in my mind, Coral and Peter note-bashing down below while I sat on our viewing platform watching the sun go down. I weep from sadness thinking of those days, I honestly do.

By far the most enjoyable times occurred when Coral was invited to sing at weddings out on farms and we encountered generosity and lavishness like never before, being treated like Royalty at farm homesteads and put up in luxurious rooms. It makes me feel physically ill to think those farms are gone now with some owners having been given an hour or two to vacate a life's work. The one property that stands out in my mind belonged to the Firks family. Coral sang at the son or daughter's wedding which was weird to say the least as the vows were totally New Age but the reception is something I will never forget. We arrived at the Firks' homestead towards late afternoon. I have never seen nor will I ever see a farm so picture-card perfect in my life, with fields superbly ploughed, ready for tobacco, fields divided by neatly dressed trees and barns off to one side with tractors neatly lined up; all buildings under fresh paint. The house was a huge and I mean huge double-storey thatch abode with a very big marquee to one side. There must easily have been four hundred people there and every car was a luxury vehicle, I have never seen so many Mercedez Benz's in my life. This was the crème de la crème of the farming community and if I remember correctly the Firks had won many awards for their superb tobacco quality and quantity. At the time Rhodesia produced the best tobacco in the world, without doubt.

We left the reception at about two a.m. and it was still going wild. I can honestly say I have never seen trays of food like that pour out of the kitchen all evening and such quality! There was lamb, prawns, chicken, beef, venison, caviar (!), fish cutlets, canapés, egg devils of unique design, vegetable wraps of the utmost delight and a thousand other items that landed softly on one's palate, all washed down with imported whiskies, spirits, champagne, wine and beer that literally never stopped all night, for four hundred people!!

At two a.m. we followed another farmer about ten kilometres to stay the night with them and the enquiry about what car to follow was curious and went something like this.

'Jim,' (addressing another farmer), 'what car have you got today?'

'My green Merc,' followed by 'jolly good' from the enquirer, then two other people were asked the same question and they both replied 'Merc'.

When he asked me what car I had, I saw four faces, eyes under bushy brows, set in reddened faces turn to look at me with enquiring looks, wives pensive lest I should say 'Renault' or 'Datsun'.

'Merc,' I said proudly and they all beamed an inclusive smile with the odd one sighing in relief. No peasants among them wot!!

The 'other' farmer's house was eloquent and well-furnished and we sat around with brandy and cigars (except me on the latter) until maybe three forty a.m, and then we hit the sack, to be wakened for a big breakfast at about nine a.m. This lifestyle went on for years and we visited so many farms I lost count of them and went to shows and eisteddfods in Bulawayo and Harare and more at Reps. It was a full life but I must admit the rehearsals that Coral had to go to became the bane of my life and many times when I wanted to do something spontaneous it was cut short by her getting singing lessons from Lorna Kelly or trying out something new for an upcoming soiree or Eisteddfod. But it was good.

We loved our holidays to Victoria Falls, which were very nostalgic for me and on one booze cruise I told Coral all about the times I spent in the army there and the fence of the minefield was still there with a 'danger, minefield' sign flapping in the wind, its skull and cross bones clearly visible. Dianne and Mally had been on this cruise so many times with me it felt odd being there with someone else. We stayed in the cottages in the National Park but sadly got terrible diarrhoea from the Kariba ferry so most of our days were spent sleeping in a hot rondavel. I never did see the casino or the lovely Vic Falls Hotel. A sad visit really.

Kariba was one of our favourite destinations and we normally stayed at the Christian Hotel right at the top of Kariba Heights where the view down the lake was just sensational and we drove up to the highest point where the cell tower was built by my brother. We went on many booze cruises as well as getting up close and in danger to Elephants along the power lines just outside the town. We took plane rides over the lake, finding it a bit scary but exciting nonetheless to land on water floats. Our fishing trips to Sanyati Gorge on the south side of the dam in the Matusadonas were very memorable. I cannot believe how stupid I was back then when I allowed my son to sit on the edge of the boat while fishing, a superb target for a wily Crocodile. Even thinking of it now makes we squirm. Once back on the north shore we would go to the Caribbea Bay Hotel, have a few drinks and let the kids go down the water slide near the lake shore. It was just superb fun.

Inyanga was a thrill for me as the memories of that place started from when I was a tiny boy and for just one night we slept in Rhodes's room so my children could smell the coal-fired oven light up and drink tea and eat scones on the veranda at three p.m. precisely. But we mainly stayed at the chalets just below the Hotel or Udu lodges. The hotel in the village of Inyanga became a firm favourite too as we had our own rooms off a long concrete passage and would wander down for our meals at leisure, playing snooker and darts with each other. It was while there at breakfast one day, that scouts from a Flemmish film crew came and asked us if they could borrow our kids for the day as they were shooting a film called 'The Congo' about thirty kays down the road at an abandoned farm homestead. I asked them rather sarcastically if they would let their kids go with strangers but soon realised it was a language barrier problem. So we accompanied them to the day's shoot where we got as much food and drink as we liked. Our children had to pretend to be at a kids' party, obviously in a home in the Congo and as the food and toys were real it wasn't too hard to persuade them to join in but they soon looked a bit sick after each scene was repeated about six times. Coral had to wear an old-fashioned brown dress with her hair pulled up in a severe bun, no make-up on and bulky flat-bottomed shoes an older head mistress would wear. I laughed myself stupid when I saw her and she chuckled back when she looked at my shorts, long socks, brown shoes, pipe and shorn hair as was the fashion in the 1950s, the shirt being some ugly thing with vertical stripes. Our role was to mumble and groan when an unruly black man approached the veranda the kid's parents stood on (there were about fifteen adults), point a finger, swear and cause general agitation, all in Belgian, which I daresay he had learned off by heart or was actually a black Belgian actor. The Director made us shoot the scene three or four times and then we were done. We changed back into our own clothes and were then guided to the paymaster's tent where we got several hundred dollars for a few hours effort! It was truly fascinating! Of course we stayed at Troutbeck which burst with memories and did the milkshake and ice cream run up to the dairy farm in the mountains. And while looking at the view near Connamara we almost got struck by lightning from a flash storm, just like when Carol stood there a long time ago. Good memories.

The journey to and from Harare always included a little ritualistic game of getting the kids to see the 'rock monsters' living among all the granite boulders beyond Rusape and I would point at imaginary rock monsters and say 'there, there, see him?' and the kids would crane forward and look for the monsters but never actually see them. Shame, they got quite frustrated at times but eventually cottoned on to dad being a tease. Or the big quarry on the side of the road somewhere near Rusape and I would regale them of the same story my parents said to me, that it was a giant's potty and that if we could hit it just right while passing by we would see him come along and do a poo. I would slow the car down to give the 'giant' a chance but once again they never saw him. But...

'Where's his toilet paper?' my ever-sharp daughter (with three degrees to her name in 2020) asked of me in a suspicious voice.

'Well, he has to bring it with him, lest it blows away in the wind,' I replied unconvincingly to her. The deep frown and puckered lips told me what she really thought of me. Bless my lovely son though, a soft-natured, quiet lad who believed everything I said. I know for sure I was his hero at that tender age so if dad said there was a giant and a potty there *was* a giant and a potty!

I loved reading the Bible to my kids and we said prayers together every night but the one story they absolutely delighted in was the Rabbit and the Hare. They loved it so much and wanted to hear it every evening. It was lovely for them but exhausting for me and often when I came home I was tired and just wanted a drink and have a chat with Coral, so I cheated, to my shame! I tape-recorded the story one night and when our prayers were finished I switched on the tape deck and you know what, they were none the wiser and after a few minutes their eyes were shut. I could go and unwind then and have a drink or watch something on my newly installed digital TV system.

* * *

It went bad when the politics of the land started to heat up and our accountant suddenly announced we had a $400 000 tax bill to pay, which caught us by the short and curlies to say the least. We asked him why we weren't forewarned of this or why some type of plan could not have been implemented to avoid the tax, or have paid the taxes in tranches but he gave us some cock and bull story that to this day irks the hell out of me. Like fools we took that so called accountant's (more like bookkeeper) word as law and set about selling off chunks of our property, the value of which was starting to fall due to political tensions in the land and paid off the mouth-watering debt. I can still see that check in my mind's eye and feel the dejection of having to send it to the coffers of a government becoming so corrupt it beggared belief. We sold off two completed and four incomplete flats to some character we know not who.

Around about this time the World Bank was squeezing Zimbabwe for repayment of loans but due to the fact that most of our hard currency was being stolen by the top echelon in government, there was little to offer them. This resulted in all sorts of problems and suddenly our US$5000 debit cards were removed and the availability of imported goods slowed. The Chinese were in the land undertaking massive works like dams and the football stadium so almost all of the cement our two cement factories produced was sent to them. You can imagine, cement is like flour to a baker and it became a nightmare to conduct business. Completion dates slipped. We were, as an industry, allowed to import South African cement but that pushed the cost of our work up quite a lot, resulting in a few jobs not going ahead.

The eighth summit of the non-aligned movement was held in Harare in 1986 and despite Zimbabwe's international debt increasing by fifty percent from the year before, the government spent millions to impress countries like Cuba, Iraq, Angola and so on, the latter being bankrupt but still managed to send thirty tons of seafood to the big parties that went on all over the place, while their own populace starved. My brother and I were nearly shot by Samora Machel's bodyguards when we went up on a garage roof to give a quotation to a client without realising that Machel was in the house next door. Looking down at weapons being cocked and pointed at us was not funny I can assure you! We knew the guy who owned that house, we had completed a very big work around his swimming pool a few months earlier and he told us later on that they cooked a goat in his lounge and hammered a hole in the right front wing of his Mercedez Benz he had loaned them, so the pendant pole could fly the Mozambican flag on official outings!

Slowly but surely things started to slow down as the local populace were not getting their share of the pie and were aware of the lavish mansions owned by Mugabe, his terrible wife and ministers. Riots started. Petrol queues came and went and there was a general change in the attitude of locals who appeared ever more desperate to find work. By roughly 1995 we did not have enough work to support both of us and I think my brother had grown tired of being in construction anyway, reputed to be the third most stressful profession in the world. He had decided to open up a garden irrigation business, which actually did very well indeed as people were prepared to improve their homes but not necessarily invest in new buildings. So, one sunny day, with my heart in my boots, we met on the side of Manica road near the old market and basically agreed to part ways. We had just lost one tender that may have saved the day and that was that. I was left with a half dead 'baby' in my arms, the company!

It was around about this time, 1997 or so that the 'war veterans' (many of whom were too young to have fought as 'liberators') started claiming their share of the pie as a lump sum as they were dissatisfied with their monthly handouts. They agitated enough to scare the government into paying them fifty thousand dollars each, which caused an upward run on inflation like never before. I am quite sure that had not billions of US dollars been stolen by the big boys in government, the country could have afforded it. Instead, schemes like the National Social Security Authority (NSSA) were hung around the necks of every employer, who had to pay social security donations to the fund for every one of his employees, but this was misused and piped into the ever-demanding guerrillas hands. All ex Guerrillas (I choke on that word, they were terrorists plain and simple) not included in the National Army got two years pay in 1980 and disabled veterans were paid large sums on top of free medical care. The economy was coming apart at the seams; all the cake on the shelves had been gobbled up by the locusts! There was only one cake left, a massive cake indeed and that was the land that the four thousand white farmers owned, many of the farms having been bought through willing seller willing buyer deals with the government.

The World Bank, a Marxist entity if there ever was one, started fiddling more and more with the economy from about 1988 and introduced some pretty punitive regulations upon the country's finances; by the late nineties they had just about strangled and blackmailed Zimbabwe under its Economic Structural Adjustment Programme (ESAP). Mugabe and his henchmen were getting fearful. Their wars in the Congo and Mozambique were feeding diamonds to the elite but draining our coffers. Teachers and other government staff began enjoying hit and miss pay episodes. The ship was sinking and the rats were scurrying for cover. In approximately 2000 Mugabe proposed a constitutional change that would have consolidated presidential powers and allowed the government to confiscate white-owned land for redistribution to black farmers without compensation. By a miracle he was defeated by 697 000 votes versus 578 000. In view of the fact that the white population was only about 100 000 at that point made it even more of a miracle; it meant blacks were voting against Mugabe taking farms away from whites and giving them to blacks. This was incredible! On the outside Mugabe accepted this but immediately swung his plan to get rid of white farmers into action. He needed lots of farms to offer the cronies in his party, to maintain their allegiance and to take some of the pressure off from blacks demanding arable land for themselves.

I recovered from the dread of my brother dissolving our partnership by being awarded a sensationally big house to be built for Patrick Nicholls out on his enormous farm somewhere near Raffingora. I will never forget the house we built the family, nearly seven hundred square metres in size with hardwood sash windows made by Timberland in Bulawayo, stunning 'broekie-lace' wrought iron supports for the veranda which went around the whole house, a huge walk-in fridge for game and meat and vegetables. Imported Italian tiles for the bathrooms and kitchen as well as the endless passages, all overlooking a stunning view of a farm that had several Manager's houses, its own grain silos and so many centre-pivot sprinklers that they were given one for free. The Nicholls family group produced a quarter of the country's wheat and covered vast expanses of land. Patrick was given *four hours* to vacate this land by Mugabe's infant war thugs when Mugabe's plan of retribution went into full swing. Four hours to end a life's tireless work! Thousands of loyal staff instantly unemployed!

My staffing levels had fallen from about four hundred and fifty personnel in our heyday to about fifty now. I had closed my office and warehouse just down the road from the Coca Cola factory and built a lovely office off my bedroom wing at home, where I went into overdrive to keep my business afloat and I did indeed do very well for five years on my own despite the slide all around us. But by 1999 I found myself with very little work despite having been awarded some monstrous houses in Borrowdale Brooke. When they were completed I had nothing to do, but I had seen a lot of notice boards belonging to a land developer in Borrowdale Brooke, so I approached them and asked if I could become one of their nominated contractors, which after some haggling they agreed to. One of the haggles was that all work I was to undertake for them was at a fixed price. Several other companies, wiser than me, had turned them down but I was so desperate for work that I agreed. My plan was to add an extra ten percent to the project and up until that point increased costs in the industry had been manageable or variations could be charged to the client. So, to my mind, ten percent was fair and would protect me.

I was about four houses into the dozen or so I had lined up when a secondary Black Friday came along (the first being in 1997) and the currency plummeted by about twenty five to thirty percent. Now, I am not a mathematician but raw materials do not form one hundred percent of a manufactured product but in the simplified minds of black and white manufacturers alike, they put the cost of all their finished products up by the same percentage! I was horrified and mortally crippled financially. Window frames that cost four hundred dollars each were now five hundred or more and I could not pass the increase on to anyone. Staff wages went up by government diktat which cut into my cash flow even more.

On a personal level my sex urge dried up and I started to eat to compensate for the horror I was experiencing all day long. Suddenly my luxurious home with its satellite TV, smart cars and a swimming pool looked jaded. My house staff looked nervously at me every Friday wondering if they would get paid, no doubt they had listened to Coral and I arguing. We took our children out of private schools and sent them to ACE home schools where their classrooms became someone's garage. I cannot even begin to understand what my children were going through; I was lost in my own despair. It must have been horrible for them. I used to sit and look at the view from my sun deck in the evenings but I did not see the beautiful golds and yellows of sunset, I was drowning in fear. Legal, company protection of my home could not be guaranteed as Africa has its own way of dealing with its issues. I was locked into a contract that paid me about thirty percent less than I was earning. Things got so bad that all the developer would do is pay my staff's wages to keep things going and paying my home staff or fuel bills was a nightmare. Jut the odd tiny job or retention being released kept the wolf away, for now.

The straw that broke the camel's back happened one Friday mid 2001 when I was greeted by an irate customer claiming that $100 000 of imported goods had been stolen from the secure area he had established in the house I was building for him. I told him I had never agreed to protect his goods and that it was his bad luck but the argument broke me. I also had no cash to pay the workmen as money from the developer had been withheld until the dispute over the imported fittings had been resolved. I pleaded with them to no avail. I can still feel the agony in me when I drove to site and told the foreman I was closing the business and to lock the storage sheds. The look on his face was one of horror and despair. The sheds were locked. I paid the men half what they were due and I drove away crying my eyes out. The palms of my hands had become full of nerve blisters and I scratched and ate myself stupid.

Later that afternoon, as I was sitting at home, stunned, I got a call from my foreman Onard, a fine man whom I still send money to, to this day (his wife was our maid and I financed a part of their daughter's education) warning me my men were running en-masse to my house to demand the balance of their pay. I shouted at Coral to pack one or two items of clothing and get the hell out which she did in record time. I then phoned a friend and asked him to call the police for me. There was nothing else to do so I stood at my gate and waited for them with Onard at my side. I was too mentally lost to even pray but I have no doubt God was in control of the situation.

I could hear them singing in unison as they ran for my house, their beautiful, deep African tones rising and falling as they negotiated the hills and troughs of the area we lived in. It was a hellishly beautiful sound with feet stomping in unison. A calmness and serenity fell upon me.

At last about eighty men turned the corner and headed for me. Even at this distance I could see rocks in their hands. I greeted them and silence fell upon the scene. I was partly relieved to see a police van turn the corner and pull off the road, its passengers sitting silently looking at us. I say I was only partly relieved as it was unknown if they would allow me to be beaten but not killed or beaten and killed, as had happened to one or two farmers already. Remember, many of these guys were terrorists once upon a time; they had no love for me. The coin in the slot machine could go either way.

One of the more lecherous and nasty characters in my company addressed me in a quasi-aggressive tone, waxing lyrical about this and that. I'm not sure what I was being accused of but in sixteen years of working with these men they had never missed their wages, they got bonuses at Christmas and I paid many above the minimum wage as much for me as for them. But loyalty was the white man's vanity. Many a white had been killed by the most 'loyal' of their staff. Onard, to my immense relief, talked to the men, explaining why they had not been paid but all they could see was a luxurious home with a water spider sprinkling water on the grass, they could not see the swimming pool that had gone green because I could no longer afford the expensive chemicals. They could not see the basic seediness that was creeping into the place.

Thankfully I had thirty thousand dollars of my own money in the safe and spread it equally among them. It seemed to do the trick and smiles broke out here and there, the atmosphere became far more relaxed. Some of the men started to drift away while others paid debts back to fellow employees. The police van coughed out black smoke and slowly turned back the way it had come. I thanked Onard very much and to this day owe that man my life. I will and have, done so much for him and his wife over the years and we are still in contact. It took guts to stand in defence of a white man.

That afternoon I cried so much. I went down to the pool and dived into green water that was beginning to smell and leaning against the edge of the shallow end of the pool, looked up at the house towering above me, the house I had spent eleven years developing. I could see my braai (BBQ) unit, we had spent countless happy times around it, cooking massive steaks with good friends, laughing, quaffing beers or gathering there for tea and another braai for all the folk that stayed after our church service, which was now held here every Sunday. To my right, the neighbours thatched roof that almost caught on fire when one of my Guy Fawkes rockets went astray. There directly above me are the large aluminium lounge doors behind which Rowan had a big party for his friends, removing all furniture so the kids could dance. To my left, Corals sewing room under the viewing platform and further to the left my new office. By the time I left that pool I knew I had to sell the house to pay off all my debt. I could have just gone bankrupt and in any civilized country it would only be the assets of my company that would be sold off or stripped away, but this was Africa and Machetes reach further than a warrant. The Zimbabwe dollar by then was crumbling at an alarming rate and the fourteen million dollars I got for my beautiful home translated into sixteen thousand pounds. I believe now in 2020, even with Zimbabwe as rough as it is, the house is worth about four hundred and fifty thousand US dollars. When the day came to sign the papers over to a new, black owner, my pen hovered over the signature bar for so long the lawyer actually became impatient. I scribbled it rapidly and that was that. Another door had shut on my life. Another sliding door.

When the last load had gone from the house, Coral and I did a last lap around it, trailing our hands over the ropes that suspended the kids' horse swing, leaning against the railing with that stunning view out there. Thunder rumbled in the distance and the clouds became a dark smudge on the horizon. For a split second I knew the rain would make the pool go green but as I dropped my eyes down to it, it was already green, the waterfall that fed it silent and filled with dust.

Like a darn fool I had bought a stunning plot of land in Carrick Creagh road for four million five hundred thousand, from the sale of my house and set about building a cottage six months before we left the main house. The new owner of our house had been kind enough to let us live in the house rent free for a year or until we found alternative accommodation, whichever came first. He definitely had compassion towards us for some reason. I got a job as the manager of D*****a Pvt Ltd., a company that painted huge commercial properties like the New International airport, a massive office complex along Samora Machel road, the International School and a housing complex at Borrowdale Brooke. Coral got a job as a singing teacher at the College of Music and for a sniff in time life appeared almost normal again. It was odd beyond belief moving into a building thirteen metres by ten, so small we had no idea where to put all our furniture or clothing or whatever. Our poor Onard and his wife had to move into a shed that hummed with mosquitoes and our dogs ripped each other to shreds in the big cage we put them into. All the while I was at a loss about the future of us and the country, things were going bad everywhere. The poor farmers were being kicked off their land at a moment's notice; several were killed while others walked into their dams and committed suicide. It was simply horrible and nothing was normal at that stage. A lot of my employees felt they had been diddled and wanted compensation and even started pressing for money. The 'War Veterans Office' called me to say I should present myself at their offices in town at 9 am on such and such a date. I was in panic mode as I had heard of other whites being beaten to shreds when they reported there. This was Africa reclaiming its darkness. I never went.

My job was unsavoury as the owner brushed shoulders with thugs from Zanu PF who more than once arrived at meetings with AK47s in their car boots. He shared my office and would chain smoke all day. I could not get to grips with his quotation style, never winning a single local or regional contract, which was the main reason I was employed. He undermined my ideas about opening paint retail outlets and before long I simply could not take it any longer.

Chapter Six

Leaving Zimbabwe to live in England

I emigrated from Zimbabwe, six months ahead of Coral and the kids, in September 2002, arriving in England with £300 pounds in my pocket. Coral stayed with the children in our cottage which scared the hell out of me. I had lived and worked in England in 1973 and found life quite easy then but at the age of forty seven, overweight, balding and still sporting my 1970s porno moustache (which was *grossly* out of favour in the UK) I set about looking for work in Salisbury, Wiltshire. How ironic I thought to myself, born in Salisbury, now emigrating to Salisbury! The ride in on the train filled me with a sense of false belonging, looking at the rural surroundings with rolls of wheat stalks lying about in shorn fields. I stayed with the parents of my daughter's best friend who had moved to the UK a couple years earlier. They had no room for me in the house so I was put in a shed out the back. It was cold now and it got dark at four o'clock. There was no central heating, no toilet, no bathroom. I bought myself bread for 19p from Tescos and thumped the roads looking for work until I had worn holes in my shoes, literally. The application forms I had filled in, the indifferent looks I got at interviews were soul-destroying. And all the while I had no money to send my family or even contact them. I seriously contemplated suicide one night as I looked at the blackness outside the curtain-less window of my 'room'. I had no cell phone and had no idea how Coral and the kids were doing. I was so dejected, so miserable, so defeated, anxious, half-dead, frightened and alone that when a young female I met outside a pub showed me some friendship, I grabbed it with both hands. She was drunk and had fallen into the flower bed near the pub door. I picked her up and escorted her to the front door of her house about forty metres away. Once inside I made her a cup of coffee and said I would wait until it took effect before leaving, the steep stairs nearby being a genuine concern of mine. After the coffee had sobered her up a bit she thanked me and said good night, heading for the stairs. I was picking up my coat when I heard something like a table crash to the floor above me so I went upstairs to investigate. She had, indeed, fallen over a table so I carried her through to her bedroom, removed her shoes and covered her up. I sat on the corner of her bed to make sure she drifted off but she asked me why I was so caring towards a stranger. I shared my faith with her, I genuinely did that, I felt she had become my mission. But inside I was boiling and churning with so many emotions and fears and desires that I almost exploded. All resistance collapsed when she rested her hand on my forearm and we became lovers.

I have not, and probably never will, forgive myself for that act of stupidity. I was far gone mentally, which is no excuse but it's a simple fact. I was undergoing the second mental break-down of my life. I had moved into a make-believe world where nothing mattered and Africa was just a bad dream, it was literally like that. I had no concept of right or wrong, only survival mattered. My experiences with Charlotte messed me up so much. I did not want the life of horror, worry and fear that accompanied my family like a leper, like a corpse that just hung there, through no fault of their own. I wanted happiness and fun. I felt I deserved rest and peace after several years of hell, nearly losing my family in the process.

I had found a job (at last!) with Wiltshire Council in their building department, which became a lonely and intimidating experience. Even the building terminology I used in meetings was laughed at, like when I said hot water 'geyser' instead of 'immersion tank' or 'photostat' instead of 'photocopy' or attic instead of 'loft'. And I had no familiar bearings when I drove to various sites, map-reading all the way. It was cold and nasty, steam blew out my mouth in bed at night. I remember standing in Wiltshire Road, Harnham on a frosty November afternoon. My family was six thousand miles away and here I was doing surveys for properties that needed new kitchens and bathrooms. There was total silence, no people about anywhere. Smoke drifted out of chimneys and as I stood shivering I wondered what the hell I was doing there. I could not tell if it was a dream or reality, I mean that literally. Maybe a mental health worker will understand this divorced reality syndrome? I worked two other jobs as well, cleaning at night and driving cars on the weekend. I quickly got enough money to pay for my family's visas and plane tickets and it was amazing, breath-taking to see them again. I cried for ages on the way to the airport, hugging them when I saw them, my tears dripping on their hair as I pulled them to my breast.

It took a long time to adjust. For the first ten years in a new country you feel as if you are on a long, long holiday; nothing is familiar. I could tell you where my brother skinned his shin in Rhodesia, where we crashed our carts as kids going down a nearby hill, but here there was nothing familiar, not the jokes, not the accent, not the countryside, not the cold that leeched the sun from our bones. Mandy recoiled from the language the kids used at school, Coral sweated as a Carer in an old age home and life changed radically. Rowan cried in his room one night and when I asked him what was wrong; between sobs he said 'I want it to be like it was back home' and it made me slide to the floor and weep huge sobbing tears all over him, my daughter joining in. They had lost all their friends at such a developmental stage of their lives.

However, the 'sliding door' slid open in our favour and we stepped in to the light. My son is a heating engineer and he got married yesterday. He has a stunning daughter called Izabella, like my mother and my daughter is a Manager in the NHS. Coral cares for a few select patients and will be training to help disabled people in swimming pools in the New Year. She still sings. I am semi-retired and deliver new cars to customers when needed.

But it's all okay and I smiled knowingly, with so much warmth, when I saw Izzy cuddle into her mom's skirt the other day, looking shyly at the kids of her new nursery school, just like I did sixty three years ago and I knew then it was all good. It's all good and the ghosts have been banished at last.

www.ingramcontent.com/pod-product-compliance
Lightning Source LLC
Chambersburg PA
CBHW052021070526
44584CB00016B/1845